THE POETICS OF REVELATION

Is it Ulysses that approaches from the east,
The interminable adventurer? The trees are mended,
That winter is washed away. Someone is moving

On the horizon and lifting himself up above it.
A form of fire approaches the cretonnes of Penelope,
Whose mere savage presence awakens the world in which she dwells.

She has composed so long, a self with which to welcome him,
Companion to his self for her, which she imagined,
Two in a deep-founded sheltering, friend and dear friend.

The trees had been mended, as an essential exercise
In an inhuman meditation, larger than her own.
No winds like dogs watched over her at night.

She wanted nothing he could not bring her by coming alone.
She wanted no fetchings. His arms would be her necklace
And her belt the final fortune of their desire.

But was it Ulysses? Or was it only the warmth of the sun
On her pillow? The thought kept beating in her like her heart.
The two kept beating together. It was only day.

It was Ulysses and it was not. Yet they had met,
Friend and dear friend and a planet's encouragement.
The barbarous strength within her would never fail.

She would talk a little to herself as she combed her hair,
Repeating his name with its patient syllables,
Never forgetting him that kept coming constantly so near.

—Wallace Stevens, ''The World as Meditation''
(From *The Palm at the End of the Mind*
[New York: Random House, Vintage Books, 1972])

Studies in American Biblical Hermeneutics 4

THE POETICS OF REVELATION

Recognition
and the Narrative
Tradition

by
DIANA CULBERTSON

MERCER

ISBN 0-86554-310-0

The paper used in this publication meets
the minimum requirements of American National Standard
for Information Sciences—Permanence of Paper
for Printed Library Materials, ANSI Z39.48-1984.

Library of Congress Cataloging-in-Publication Data
Culbertson, Diana.
    The poetics of revelation: recognition and the narrative tradition
    by Diana Culbertson.
xii + 189 pages   15 x 23cm.—(Studies in American biblical hermeneutics: 4)
    Includes index.
    ISBN 0-86554-310-0 (alk. paper)
    1. Bible. N.T. Gospels—Criticism, interpretation, etc.
2. Bible and literature.   3. Recognition in literature.
4. Narration in the Bible.   5. Narration (Rhetoric)   I. Title.
II. Series.
BS2555.2.C85   1989   88-37662
226'.066—dc19   CIP

•CONTENTS•

For my parents

I give thanks to my God
every time I think of you
(Philippians 1:3)

·EDITOR'S PREFACE·

In *Reimagining America*—the initial volume of the Studies in American Biblical Hermeneutics series—I argue that the rethinking of the American mythos our contemporary experience calls for ought to be established on the basis of a new understanding of time and space. I suggest that only by thinking in a radically new way about our theological and cultural heritage might we have a glimmer of a hope in aggressively meeting the convulsions of an age that has witnessed the change from a fear that God might destroy the world to the nightmare that man will. That volume was intended to be suggestive, not exhaustive, in the way that the called-for *re*thinking might be carried out. It appealed to some provocative manifestations of the American literary heritage that might be utilized in such an imaginative endeavor. It suggested some nontraditional ways this body of texts might be brought to bear upon our theological traditions. Like nearly all of our work in the modern and postmodern era, the writing of this book was dogged by a sense of inadequacy and incompleteness. Hence the recognition of a need for a collective body of scholars to work on the problem, and the willingness of Mercer University Press to aid in this intellectual quest by undertaking the present series of hermeneutical studies. In the present volume, Diana Culbertson has taken a quantum step forward in one central aspect of this work of theological reimagining, specifically in the exposition of the literary category of narrative transformation she terms *recognition*.

As Culbertson clearly shows, if we are to rethink America from a theological vantage point that is able to penetrate the cultural walls of resistance, we can be aided greatly in this process by a fuller understanding of the way that both secular and sacred literature have addressed the issue of *change*. She necessarily discusses this issue as a part of the conversation between secular and sacred literature that has traditionally characterized the Western (including American) experience. If the American experience is to count for anything theologically, then such a conversation between secular and sacred interpretations of reality must be brought into play in as self-conscious a way as possible. In light of the general acceptance of Robert Bellah's civil-religion proposal during the past two decades, almost everyone would accept the notion that America is both a "civil" and "religious" phenomenon. So much is this the case that I believe that the primary task for North American theologians is now to clarify in no uncertain terms how much of the commonly acknowledged and pervasive American religiosity we can afford and still remain faithful to the contours of our biblical heritage. By centering her discussion on the theme of recognition, or self-understanding, in the narrative tradition of Western textuality, Culbertson advances the discussion of American biblical hermeneutics by demonstrating how the Bible might serve as a vehicle of transformation. Surely it is our hope and promise that the Bible will continue to do so for us as it has for others during propitious moments of Western intellectual history.

Since the theme of recognition in Culbertson's work is tied to individuals as the bearers of change in formative Western and New Testament narrative traditions, we enter cultural issues at their most finite level in this work. In these narratives we are not concerned primarily with individuals as individuals, but individuals as exemplars of cultural values and aspirations. We see ourselves in the narratives that Culbertson analyzes, in the sense of who we have been, who we are, and who we might become. The "American" is represented here in two broad senses: (1) the dominant European cultural heritage, and (2) the dynamic of change itself, which has accompanied the American experiment in the mythological guise of the New Adam in the New World. To be American is to make something new out of the European past, to be changed from one mode of existence to another. To be American is to experience chronological disjunction in one's cultural remembrances, if not in one's individual life. That is precisely why America itself bespeaks a religious experience.

At its most universal level, this book's genius lies in the way that it addresses the interaction between two enduring poles of the Studies in American Biblical Hermeneutics series: content and method. It has become axiomatic in the philosophy of art that these two realities ought to be distinguished from one another but never separated. Certainly, the act of reimagining is an artistic gesture or, in Culbertson's terms, a poetics. While it is the contention of the series that the methodological preoccupation of our day ultimately works counter to the liberating poetics of the

Bible, one ignores method altogether at great peril. The goal of the series is to bring method into dialogue with the content of our cultural experience. In these terms, while the theme of recognition serves as the focus of the content of Culbertson's study, the model of literary criticism that it embodies serves as its methodological axis. Perhaps nowhere else than America is the recognition that the Bible is through and through a *text* taken with more seriousness. (Cf. Calvin Mercer's study of New Criticism's impact on Norman Perrin in the second volume of the series.)

And, where there is text, there is literary criticism. To be fair, the historical critics have taught us for generations that the Bible was not created in a societal vacuum, but rather came into being in the context of historical realities and processes. Yet, the discovery of the inextricable role of the interpreter in the analysis of historical data, the subjective side of our knowledge, has forced us to look ever deeper into the nature of our interpretation of the world of the past. In a broad sense, the past is only known to us in terms of texts. It is a fact, in other words, that the audience is always at work in the interpretive act, whether in the guise of the real or implied reader of the text, or the text set in dialogue with its contemporary audience. Culbertson's book does not shy away from such complexities; it begins with them and moves us toward the new theological insights that they mask.

The title of this work—*The Poetics of Revelation*—is programmatic for the Studies in American Biblical Hermeneutics series as a whole. It implies that there is no revelation in a religious sense without poetic embodiment in a human sense. Culbertson explores the epistemology of this insight within a literary context; the series as a whole does so in a hermeneutical one. A recovery of the poetics of revelation implies a recovery of its aesthetic and mimetic character. The Bible does not contain the very words of God, but it imitates or represents them as a monument of art embodied in the slippery world of language. This language is bidirectional, moving back and forth between that which it signifies and the one to whom it becomes significant. What we hold in our hands, what shapes us as communities of faith and culture, is neither God nor the transcendent. It is, in the final analysis, "simply" text. But Culbertson is among those who understand the power of discovery that great texts offer. Revelation, to be revelation in any meaningful sense, must draw upon the general transformational aspect of all "poetry." Aristotle's distinction between history and poetry captures something of this: "One [history] tells what happened and the other [poetry] what might happen." He goes on to say that poetry is more "philosophic" and "serious" than history, "because poetry tends to give general truths while history gives particular facts'' (*Poetics* 9.2-3). In Aristotle's terms, the Studies in American Biblical Hermeneutics series is a labor of poetics with the goal of reimagining the past and the present so that we might have a measure of control over the oppressive forces looming in our future. Culbertson's poetics of revelation directs us toward the interiority of human transformation in a way that only the narrative tradition can do. It explores the transformative power of the Gospels against the backdrop of the theme of recognition in our Western literary heritage. As such, her text helps us imagine more fully what American time and space might become, set in the context of the general truths of human existence.

Christian thought requires that we understand specifically what the Bible as text means against the backdrop of traditional categories of theology. If we fail to bring the new literary criticism—which holds so much interest for our generation of biblical scholars—into dialogue with theology, then the importance of the contemporary "renaissance of the text" in affecting our self-understanding will be left within the small circle of literary technicians. Culbertson advances her argument on the basis of formative texts within the Western tradition rather than concerning herself with the current state of the scholarly paradigm. For this reason, this book will not go out of date as a result of the next gathering of biblical scholars: it will endure as long as we are theologically interested in the human side of revelation.

—*Charles Mabee*
Marshall University

• A C K N O W L E D G M E N T S •

Scholarly work cannot be sustained or brought to completion alone, and Dominican colleagues have been my particular support in this effort. My gratefulness for encouragement and assistance must be expressed here to Thomas Brodie, O.P., Stan Drongowski, O.P., Donald Goergen, O.P., Mary Catherine Hilkert, O.P., Elizabeth Schaefer, O.P., and Benedict Viviano, O.P. For careful reading of chapter 2, I acknowledge the assistance of Rick Newton of the Classics Department of Kent State University. To Robert Bamberg of the Department of English and to the College of Arts and Sciences of Kent State University, I acknowledge with gratitude the two years I was allowed away from teaching responsibilities to begin research on this project. To Mary Karaffa, my faithful and devoted typist, I offer thanks again. To Sister Mary Fath, who has shared life in Dominican community with me for so long, no word of thanks can ever be enough.

·INTRODUCTION·

Literary criticism is becoming increasingly important as a way of understanding both Hebrew and Christian Scripture. It does not replace historical-biblical criticism, but presumes it and draws from its resources and conclusions. It is distinguishable from historical-critical exegesis by its emphasis on the internal relationship of the elements of the text to one another, rather than upon their possible historical referents.

This book examines one component of plotted narrative—recognition—and traces the epistemology of recognition in selected literary texts that are especially representative of major literary periods. It concludes with an examination of this same literary device in two Gospels as a heuristic for examining the theology of revelation implicit in the Christian texts and, especially, how that theology is related to what we now call audience response. Recognition is the focus of this study because it can be considered as a model of the subjective apprehension of revelation. Understanding how it is used in literature helps us to comprehend how scriptural narrative can function as a revelatory event and why narrative is such a fundamental genre for the grounding of Christian revelation. New Testament story is unlike Western imaginative literature in its claims, and constitutes, for that reason, a distinct literary genre. Like all narratives, however, the Gospels depend on literary strategies, and those strategies need to be understood if Scripture study is to get beyond some of the limitations of exclusively historical-critical exegesis.

Part I, chapter 1 of this book considers the nature of religious experience and how recognition is related to that experience. It considers further how the recognition scene in literature functions as a model for the apprehension of revelation. The recognition scene raises for the author particular technical problems: how is the character to know what is yet to be disclosed and what will be the effect of that knowing? And how is the audience to know?

The strategy of literary recognition in different kinds of texts corresponds to epistemological problems: (1) the understanding of time that recognition in a narrative implies; (2) the understanding of change consequent upon knowledge; (3) the understanding of self implied by the very fact of "knowing."

To study the epistemology of recognition is to understand better how the theology of revelation has evolved and how revelation is mediated by the narratives of Scripture. The clearest movement traceable in this analysis is the shifting locus of recognition. Initially in Greek literature, recognition was a function of plot. Subsequently, it was perceived as an aspect of character. Eventually, literary theorists began to examine the recognition experience of the inscribed reader and the reader-audience. From information acknowledged, *anagnôrisis* became defined as gradual experiential apprehension.

In part II the works of literature selected for consideration are exemplary of distinct ways of understanding and different strategies for describing cognition. Chapter 2 begins with a consideration of how ancient Greek literature reflects Greek psychological understanding, for the Greeks not only used the recognition device throughout their epic and dramatic text, but also critiqued its use. Greek epistemology in literature can be analyzed by considering the relationship of the knowing self, the character, to the world "outside." These texts betray an imperative to bring the self into correspondence with the universe or reality that the self was to mirror. Generally, Greek dramatic characters change within a range of moral possibility that is essentially limited. Recognition for the Greeks, therefore, was judged to be a function of plot, rather than an event that could cause character transformation.

In the High Middle Ages Chrétien de Troyes (chapter 3) offers what for contemporary readers is still a puzzling narrative. It features a famous but almost indecipherable character, Perceval the Welsh, who changes from fool to knight to penitent in one bustling narrative sweep interlaced with the disparate adventures of Gawain. What is significant about the Perceval narrative is his almost-total character change during the story telling. Chrétien suggests that the self can change radically. That suggestion raises the question, What force was perceived to be powerful enough to alter character? What kind of awareness could so penetrate the soul as to subvert the inauthentic self? And what literary or religious justifications were available to the writer who described this kind of change? Perceval's self-discovery and conversion begin the modern search for identity.

The *modernity* of the search begins with the seventeenth-century Don Quixote, who must find the truth of himself within historical limitations—within, in fact, his own body. Writers after Cervantes learned from him how essential an ingredient time-bound reality was to the literary task. Chapter 4 considers the Cervantine problem: what is the relationship between language and the self? How does one know the true self? The engagement with real rather than mythical time is the beginning of a new kind of narrative and a new epistemological strategy. Its effect on a developing theology of revelation cannot be measured fully in this book, but we shall consider here its relationship to the revelatory event.

In chapter 5 I have selected the first of two texts that mark the transition into what we like to call modern literature. I chose them to exemplify the effects of what Erich Kahler has described as "the inward turn of narrative."[1] Both Jane Austen and George Eliot resorted to the time-bound reality invoked by Cervantes, one in a closed circle of space and time, the other according to a deepening sense of the directionality of history. In Jane Austen's *Emma* the central character must reflect privately on what has happened to her in the "outer world," so that she can interpret its significance and "know" what has happened to her. Her world is circumscribed by intimates who assist or deflect her knowing. The microcosmic historical time and place of her discovery and change is enclosed because the author has consciously resisted the romance-adventure structure with its open-ended possibilities. Truth in such a circle of time is finite, resembling information more than mystery; and information for the Austenite heroine—especially information that leads to self-knowledge—resolves somewhat neatly the more serious problems of living. Subsequently in literature those problems become less resolvable.

When the world of the novel opened into the social history of a nation (chapter 6), recognition became more than information or even mere self-knowledge; it became a question of understanding the self in its relationship to the human community and of making the kind of choices that acknowledge the self-in-relationship. Such self-understanding requires a continuum of experience. As sociohistorical time expanded in literature, the self opened into its own corresponding depths. "Interiority" became more and more a strategy as well as an epistemological problem in the depiction of character. George Eliot's Dorothea Brooke in *Middlemarch* "recognized" only after a longer and deeper struggle and a more complex

---

[1]Erich Kahler, *The Inward Turn of Narrative,* trans. Richard and Clara Winston (Princeton NJ: Princeton University Press, 1973).

relationship with others than anything Emma could have endured. The depiction of Dorothea Brooke reflects the Hegelian view of the relationship between the individual and society as well as Eliot's view of experience as an essential component of understanding.

After the nineteenth century, the subjective experience of truth seemed more aesthetically important than any inaccessible and questionable "objective" reality. Interiority became detached from the objective world, and with that dissociation came—not surprisingly—the "loss of self," the alienation of many modern literary characters. "Modern man," as Jung had argued before the days of gender-exclusive language, was in search of a soul. Walker Percy (chapter 7) has not been alone in mourning that loss of soul and in tracking the search for its recovery. His first published novel, *The Moviegoer*, depicts spiritual malaise and its possible resolution. To find the self, to recognize where it is and how it "connects," to use Forster's term, is the epistemological and theological issue Percy undertakes. Recognition for Percy is the rediscovery of authentic time, place, limit, and (therefore) self.

The postmodern movement (chapter 8) is distinguishable in part by a sense of the futility of search. Harold Pinter abandoned the depiction of subjectivity and tracked only the death of the subject, the disintegration of the ego, as timeless time becomes the measure of our lostness. The abyss has become the prison of its inhabitants, a labyrinth with no way out. Real time and place in fiction with its corresponding finitude—however shifting—had been the great literary achievement of Cervantes. When recognizable time and space are disallowed, knowledge has no magnetic pole for epistemological navigation. Harold Pinter's *No Man's Land* is a demonstration of a new kind of mimesis: the depiction of people with no past and space with no exit. How can one know in such a universe?

By contrast, recognition in the Gospels (part III) requires the acknowledgment of past and future and journey. Part of the task of the present book is to *sustain* a conversation between secular literature and the Gospel narratives. What we have learned to trace in the history of literature we can bring to bear on the Gospel texts. The word *conversation* is used pointedly here because, as David Tracy has argued, the back and forth of conversation is an appropriate paradigm for *any* event of understanding, especially in terms of its radical and finite character.[2]

The Gospels themselves tell us something about the particularity of revelation, its "nonabstractedness," its *incarnation* in history. Similarly,

---

[2]David Tracy, *The Analogical Imagination: Christian Theology and the Culture of Pluralism* (New York: Crossroad, 1981) 102.

"the classic text's real disclosure is its claim to attention on the ground that an event of understanding proper to finite human beings has here found expression."[3] Intensity and tragedy in the narratives of Western literature derive from the finitude of the characters and their discovery of that finitude. Gospel characters "recognize" only if they assent to the possible sacrality of finitude rather than its profaneness or horror. Mark depicted the experience of darkness, the hiddenness of the victory over the destructive forces of history, and the promise of vision. John proclaimed the presence of light, even in this place of darkness. The authors of the Gospel texts, moreover, consciously invoked their readers, modeling them within their narratives and calling them also to belief, even in their unbelief.

Critical theory now alerts us to the time-bound reality of the audience and to the angle of perception that reality imposes. Hence when we speak of recognition in literature, we are dealing with audience as well as with plot and character—and not only the fictional audience invoked by the author. My last chapter considers the audience of the Gospel as the locus of recognition. What theology of revelation allows the audience to recognize what the text discloses in a mode that is traditionally described as "hearing the Word"?

This study makes no claim to be a comprehensive theology of revelation or even a theology of conversion. It is, rather, a *poetics* of revelation because it attempts to describe how God's self-communication is apprehended in history and how literature models that apprehension. I would argue, finally, that to recognize the unhiddenness of God and to change, however gradually, is to hear the Word, however uttered in whatever scandal of particularity.

---

[3]Ibid.

REVELATION, TIME, AND TEXT

RECOGNITION: THE BEGINNING OF RELIGIOUS EXPERIENCE

For human concepts and human courses of action are products and expressions of acts of understanding, human understanding develops over time, such development is cumulative, and each cumulative development responds to the human and environmental conditions of its place and time.

—Bernard Lonergan, <u>Method in Theology</u>

There is an experience in life we call recognition. It is a kind of knowledge by which we apprehend meaning in a pattern of events or realize that the meaning we had once assigned to those events has been shattered. It is distinguished from simple cognition in which we become aware intellectually of a fact or an idea, but not necessarily of its implications. Recognition also differs from perception in that a fact or event is seen in a way that involves the whole of the perceiver's personal awareness, knowledge, values, and idea of existence. The assumption in this book is that the experience of recognition is the central humanizing and revelatory experience, the immediate cause of psychological and spiritual change. Recognition is thus at the heart of the literary text, both sacred and secular. To understand it is to have at hand a model of a theology of revelation. The advantages of models are clear from our experience of the use to which they have been put in scientific discourse as well as theological and religious language. Here, we are resorting to the recognition scene in literature as a model of the initial religious experience: the apprehension of revelation.

• The Meaning of Religious Experience •

The question of religious experience is always, "How do I know?" "How do I recognize a divine presence?" "What do I see when I see?" Or better, "How do I see?" The problem—and the first dimension of religious experience to be understood—is that the outwardly spoken word of God is mediated. We do not experience that word directly, but always through some other way in which God is disclosed. We can understand this by reflecting that we never experience *any* self directly. Merely being in the presence of another is not necessarily to know or to love whom we see. We observe *directly* the facial expression, the voice, the words, the gestures of another, and by these means the self of the other is mediated, the mystery disclosed. But what is more important to this comparison, the mystery of another can be disclosed only gradually, in time, through a series of encounters. To know another is to link experience to experience in such a way that pattern is found and a center of identity revealed. At the same time, we realize that each of us knows another in a different way. The child does not know his father as that father is known by his father—or his wife, brother, business associate, or employee. Each of us apprehends out of our own experience. In addition, knowledge of another is radically qualified by the circumstances in and by means of which the other is perceived. To apprehend the mystery of God, to experience God's presence, requires mediation, time, and the realization that our vision is always partial.

In addition to mediation, the second dimension of religious experience essential to an accurate understanding of its *religiousness* is that the recognition of God's self-disclosure causes change— somehow, some way, however gradual. A discovery that does not effect moral or spiritual transformation is not religious.

There are, then, two essential components of religious experience: (1) there is in such experience something revelatory, illuminating, or unifying mediated by a particular event or sequence of events. Some discovery occurs or some realization is deepened; (2) a transformation begins or continues. One is never the same afterwards. Although the two components cannot be separated completely, this book focuses primarily on the revelatory moment.

• Models of Religious Experience •

Those who have religious faith resort to analogues and models to express the kind of vision that faith brings about. The parables of Jesus and narrative pericopes in the Gospel text often function as such models. When

Matthew describes the disciples following Jesus into the boat, the rising storm, the terrified occupants of the craft, and the appeal to Jesus to save them from perishing, we have an early literary model of discipleship. To follow is not to be spared the storms and anxieties consequent upon companionship with Jesus. But Jesus is always present, always master of the storm, always there to save. When Luke describes two discouraged and despairing disciples leaving Jerusalem, walking away from the city toward Emmaus, and encountering another who discusses with them "the things which have happened," he tells of the hidden Jesus who is with his disciples on the way, who breaks bread with them, whose words make the hearts of the disciples burn within them. The pericope is a model of the Christian life, as the writer perceived it, and of Jesus' presence to his church.

Ian Ramsey, clarifying the nature of religious language, distinguishes between the picturing models used in the natural sciences, such as small-scale replicas, and the analogue or disclosure models used in theological discourse. To explain particular views of "atonement," for example, requires some kind of analogue, such as the freeing of a slave or the payment of a debt. Models used in theology have been especially necessary for discourse and sustaining intellectual exchange on such topics as grace, sin, heaven, or, as we have seen more recently, the Church and even God. The subject matter of theology is more than ordinarily elusive, and we are forced to locate comparisons in human experience that allow us to speak of God without stuttering finally into silence. A disclosure model, in other words, is not an explanation of the mystery, but an opening, a way into the mystery.[1]

A number of models have been used in recent literature to describe religious experience. John Wisdom gives us the gardener story to illustrate how people view reality in terms of the existence or nonexistence of God. Two people view an ill-kept garden. One believes in the existence of a gardener, however shabby his work. The other denies this possibility.[2] John Hick offers the change-of-aspect or duck-rabbit analogy. He supplies a sketch that can be seen alternately as a duck or a rabbit. Either

---

[1]Ian Ramsey, *Models and Mystery* (London: Oxford University Press, 1969) 151; see also Sallie McFague, *Metaphorical Theology* (Philadelphia: Fortress, 1982), which argues persuasively for the necessity of metaphors and models in religious/theological language as a way to circumvent the idolatry of literalism and the apparent irrelevance of much current religious/theological language.

[2]John Wisdom, "Gods" in *Logic and Language,* ed. Anthony Flew (Oxford: Blackwell, 1951) 193.

interpretation is possible. By analogy, we can look at the world: God/not God. Hick also proposes the "experiencing as" model: "All conscious experiencing involves a recognition which goes beyond what is immediately sensed; it involves interpretation according to concepts we already possess."[3]

But as Peter Donovan has argued, both "seeing as" and "experiencing as" contrast with normal kinds of experience.[4] Not all experience is ambiguous. To limit religious experience to ambiguity is not helpful. It is more to the point to suggest that religious experience is always an experience with its own meaning, which is not necessarily religious. To experience one's mortality or finitude is not necessarily a religious experience, but it could be. Everything depends upon how that experience is interpreted and to what it leads. Ian Ramsey proposes a comparison in which a bored judge recognizes the defendant as an old friend with whom he had shared many pleasant times years previously. A thousand memories surface as he realizes that the presumed stranger in the courtroom is actually someone who was once very close to him. The implications of the situation now alter radically. The whole atmosphere of the courtroom changes. What was impersonal becomes personal. The consequences of the defendant's presence in court are now vitally significant to the judge, even though, from all outward appearances, nothing has changed.[5]

The invisible dimension of the situation, in other words, affects our entire affective and intellectual response. It makes us more alert, sensitizes us to possibility, influences our actual participation, our engagement in events. Such is the way faith alters and qualifies our view of the situation in which we live. The experience is still itself; it is not God, but the context in which God is disclosed—the only context.

Similarly, John E. Smith sees particular moments of time as explanatory of the holy:

> For the encountering of God, we turn to the crucial events of life, to the occasions when the holy becomes manifest. . . . The problem of revelation is a central and inescapable one. But revelation or divine disclosure must not be set over against experience as if the latter were "natural" and the former "supernatural." For rev-

---

[3]John Hick, "Religious Faith as 'Experiencing As' " in *Talk of God*, ed. G. N. A. Vesey (New York: Macmillan, 1964) 23.

[4]Peter Donovan, *Interpreting Religious Experience* (New York: Seabury, 1979) 38.

[5]Ian Ramsey, *Religious Language* (New York: Macmillan, 1963) 20.

elation represents a further development of the experiential matrix of religion, since experience is the only medium through which anything can be revealed.[6]

The holy is discoverable, for us, only in the context of the profane. The beautiful can be distinguished only against the horizon of the unremarkable. The gift, the surprise, is only discernible within all else that is given.

In the language of process theology, Bernard Lee discusses the presence of God within which what he calls "drops of experience." The advantage of a processive view of experience is that God is not just passively present—to be discovered—but actually coproduces the experience. The problem is how to "crack open" the experience to interpret, to discover the component of it that is God's creativity, his motion, his call. The experience itself demands a hermeneutic.

> More needs to be said about the availability of God in drops of experience, in all experience, and in human experience in particular. Process theology presumes that every drop of experience is a co-production of God and itself. There is something which God offers, without which no moment of creativity can occur. God offers the world its possibilities. But a drop of reality presumes a subjectivity which receives the possibility and sets about doing something with it. God and itself are co-principles of each reality's emergence. Without God's offering there is no reality, and without self-causation also there is no reality.[7]

To assume that God is present, helping to create experience, is not to assume that God's creative presence contains an identical message to everyone in the same paradigmatic, or even the same actual, experience. The interpretation of an event shared by several people, for example, will depend upon each person's past and present values, worldview, and theology. The experience of discovery we occasionally undergo in life is not always and specifically a religious moment, even if it leads to new understanding of a specific situation. Only the religiously interpreted experience of discovery can be described as revelation, as Schillebeeckx argues:

> We see something against a background or horizon. The element of structure or form is not added on to our thinking, it is an intrin-

---

[6]John E. Smith, *Experience and God* (New York: Oxford University Press, 1968) 66.

[7]Bernard Lee, "A Process Theology of Religious Experience and Discourse," *Religion in Life* 48 (Winter 1979): 434-48.

sic element of our perception. So we see something in a different way and do not just interpret it differently. We can certainly take all the different perspectives together in theory, but we cannot see them all together at the same time. Thus the element of interpretation lies in the experience itself (one might say that we see "the interpretation," or better, we see interpretatively).[8]

But if all recognition is not religious experience, all religious experience begins with recognition, with discovery. This discovery is neither so subjective that it cannot be reflected upon or described, nor so objective and intellectually coercive that risk and loyalty are not required—risk, because the truths that are the most important to our living are often those with the least built-in certainty; loyalty, because what is realized is never self-evident. We are not loyal to facts. We simply acknowledge them.

Thus, to understand our personal experience fully, we have to go outside of that experience. To make sense of our own experience, we have to look at it against the horizon of the lives of others. We have to see personal experience not only in the context of all the events of our own life, but also within human history. For this reason, our encounter with the sacred can never be purely private. It will always involve others, insofar as we express it to them and interpret it in the light of what others also call the sacred. "We cannot speak in objectifying or descriptive terms of revelation," writes Edward Schillebeeckx, "apart from the faith of the community."[9] And we need to remind ourselves that communities exist in different places and at different moments in history.

To describe one's religious experience in an effort to "transmit" to another the new insight, the "feel" of the moment is to realize the inadequacy of language and to admit that language is all we have to tell of the vision. Words are the medium by which the mystery is disclosed.

• Religious Experience and Narrative •

I am using narrative not simply as a term to describe an account of a sequence of events, but as the deep structure of events, their "emplotment." Borrowing in part from John W. Dixon, Jr., I use *story* to mean "the recital of events as they develop in time" and *narrative* to mean "the

---

[8]Edward Schillebeeckx, *Christ, the Experience of Jesus as Lord*, trans. John Bowden (New York: Seabury, 1980) 53.

[9]Ibid., 48.

formal quality of experience," what I would describe as its causal connections.[10] Those connections are the stuff of literature.

The mystery of human experience, its deep structure, is the wellspring of literature as it is the environment of grace and revelation. Like music, literature can only be experienced in time, in a succession of moments; and we attend to those moments because of their promise of fulfillment. We are less attentive to a sequence of moments in our daily life because we are persuaded more often than not that those disparate events are devoid of a totality of meaning—at least that totality which art offers.

But we cannot live humanly without an effort to interpret those moments of experience that connect our days and design our history. Literature, of all the arts, offers a particularly effective means to compare our experience with that of others, to open ourselves to the interpretation of reality expressed by another, and to taste something of the order, beauty, and control against which chaos and powerlessness find their names. How narrative literature functions as a means to interpret the religious dimension of our lives is the problem we pursue in this book.

Narrative and Revelation

The recognition experience in literature is rarely the discovery of an answer. It is rather an apprehension of the enormity of reality—its unexpectedness, its openness, its menace. Readers or hearers of great literature can be brought to new awareness of the dimensions of human existence, to a sense of proportion between what one experiences personally and what there is or could be. The very existence of literature—the very existence of all great art—is a reminder that life apart from art is less than explicable, less than beautiful and ordered.

We fight off triviality and lack of structure in our lives by clocking and charting our time, by ritualizing part of our lives. By celebrating events, we recall and heighten significance. We reenact what we want to remember, we honor achievement, we mourn loss and reflect on our passages. Because of our structuring, life begins to have some design, even if it is only that which we impose through our calendars. These humanly constructed meanings or discoverable designs—the rhythms of light and darkness, seasons, birth, death, love, loss—help us to enter the mystery that engulfs our living. In a sense, everything in darkness, everything not known is a possible revelation. We can discover the hidden sources of motivation, the secret causes of hostility or fear, the unrecognized need

---

[10]John W. Dixon, Jr., *Art and the Theological Imagination* (New York: Seabury, 1978) 23.

or the undeclared love. There are patterns in history, in social behavior, in language, in politics, and all of these patterns can be studied, "recognized." Literature is a particular perspective of human existence, born not of data but of human experience and human imagining. It heightens the significance of events because it excludes consideration of what is irrelevant to the textual narration of events. It selects as life does not, and structures as life does not. In literature we know what to examine because it is there to be examined, and we look for revelation because the language exists for the purpose of disclosure. We are attentive to the play, the story, the words, the gestures because we sense that everything is supposed to mean something, to lead us to something. It offers us, as Lionel Trilling says, "the promise . . . of a significance."[11]

We know that everything is in someone's control and we expect to discover something—to learn of some event that will unify all that we are reading about or hearing, to discern something like our own human existence, but now ordered, interpreted, or probed for its ambiguity. Literature is "something like" our own existence, but at the same time it is "other." It is the otherness offered by great literature that enables us to transcend our limitations. "In this process of imaginative expansion and enlargement there is a difference between the new self which results from understanding the work, and the old self."[12] The critical heritage and contemporary psychoanalytic theory both testify to the formative and reformative effects of literature upon the self.[13] We enter into the literary experience by opening ourselves to possibility, by accepting a hypothesis and allowing ourselves to see where it can take not only the story but us.[14] The relation of life to literature is analogous to the relation of the profane to the holy. As a sense of the holy relieves and transfigures the profane, aesthetic experience relieves our dullness, intensifies and deepens our perceptions.

---

[11]Lionel Trilling, *Sincerity and Authenticity* (Cambridge: Harvard University Press, 1972) 136.

[12]Giles Gunn, *The Interpretation of Otherness: Literature, Religion, and the American Imagination* (New York: Oxford University Press, 1979) 121.

[13]See Marshall W. Alcorn, Jr. and Mark Bracher, "Literature, Psychoanalysis, and the Re-Formation of the Self: A New Direction for Reader-Response Theory," *PMLA* 100:3 (May 1985): 342-54.

[14]See Wolfgang Iser, "The Reading Process: A Phenomenological Approach," *New Literary History* 3 (1972): 279-99.

We recognize structure and meaning in plot because it has been designed for that purpose, but is it possible to transfer the experience of beauty and meaning to life itself, life unexpurgated of its tedium and insignificance? Not always. But if there is never a recognition experience in life, never a discovery of meaning to pattern, never a willingness to look at the other (that uncomfortable invasion of our comfortable awareness), then we are on the edge of one of the greatest of terrors: triviality and its concomitant, meaninglessness.

Literature means dealing with the other. Its particular challenge forces us to expand our capacity to imagine, to experience. It requires that we enter a world beyond our own, that we allow ourselves to see as another sees, that we discover pattern. By thus enlarging our own capacity to see and understand, we begin to experience a new self. Our ego, as Paul Ricoeur has suggested, is no longer alone.[15] Great literature does not merely offer us new things to see, although it does that; it can also change our mode of vision. This means that *we* are changed. This transformation models what happens when we encounter the self-disclosing God within human experience.

In narrative where the apparently irrelevant has a textual function, when, therefore, everything is significant, the experience of recognition is heightened. Time is compressed so that the moment becomes visible. But even in narrative, the moment is incomprehensible apart from the preceding events upon which its significance depends. Recognition is the climax of a series of events. It is not a disconnected flash of illumination. Recognition means that event is added to event and that discovery is consequent upon there being more than one event.

In William James's *The Varieties of Religious Experience,* for example, we read countless passages describing "waves of joy," "a sense of salvation," or an unexpected discovery of the oneness of the self and God. In those passages we may perceive a sense of suddenness—as if out of the ineffable, God revealed himself in some mysterious way, quite apart from the questioning and anguishing historical self—the self affected and shaped by study, by traditional religious and cultural influences, by human relationships, by despair even, or by a frightening sense of contingency. The passages in James's study are actually small narratives, frequently with initiating incident and rising action.

We read in one account, for example, "I went into town to do some shopping one morning, and I had not been gone long before I began to

---

[15]Paul Ricoeur, *Interpretation Theory: Discourse and the Surplus of Meaning* (Fort Worth: Texas Christian Union Press, 1976) 97.

feel ill. The ill feeling increased rapidly, until I had pains in all my bones."
The writer cited by James then goes on to describe her anxiety, her subsequent reflections on the "mind-cure teachings" she had been learning
about, her ability to resist complaining to a friend, a retreat into bed, a
refusal to call the doctor, prayer, and then: "I cannot express it in any other
way than to say that I did 'lie down in the stream of life and let it flow
over me,' I gave up all fear of impending disease." Finally, she says: "I
had no consciousness of time, or space, or persons; but only of love, and
happiness, and faith." The woman was healed; in the morning, the illness was gone.[16]

Are we to conclude from such a passage that the religious experience
consisted only of the momentary sense of timelessness and peace experienced by the writer of this account and not of the rising action? The experience of healing would not have been possible without the sense of pain
and dread that preceded it, nor without the less-sensational business of
"going into town to do some shopping" (or whatever "profane" activity she
would necessarily have been engaged in when her sense of her own health
diminished). The recognition of some transcendent healing power was not
possible, in other words, apart from a series of other experiences. And to
describe that recognition required a description of those other experiences,
required narrative. Recognition is not possible apart from history. The implications of this process for a theology of revelation are important. Revelation is not an announcement that drops into our laps or provides answers
to questions we have not asked. It is not something that will effect change
in us unless we apprehend it experientially.

Is this discovery of the divine dimension within our lives always an
emotional or affective climax? a moment we can identify? Here we have
to distinguish between a gradual, invisibly cumulative recognition that
constitutes sustained religious experience and a heightened sense of discovery, an epiphany that occurs occasionally and that often characterizes
the description of religious experience in modern literature. William James
speaks of "subconsciously maturing processes eventuating in results of
which we suddenly grow conscious."[17] This kind of suddenness, however, is not really essential to religious experience, although it does high-
light the dimension of "gift" and the sense of vision that are essential to
authentic religious existence. In other words, in the life of any maturing

---

[16]William James, *The Varieties of Religious Experience* (New York: Macmillan, 1961)
109.

[17]Ibid., 173.

person, there is a gradual— almost invisible—series of small choices, experiences, perceptions, judgments, and realizations that shape consciousness and develop what is an accumulated wisdom. In the life of anyone developing spiritually or religiously, there are comparable—and coincident—apparently insignificant choices, judgments, perceptions, and insights that shape the religious dimension of the personality. If the passages of one's life have been obscured or remain unacknowledged, it is only when one consciously looks back and traces the sequence of events that their meaning can become more intelligible.

We see such an analysis in the *Confessions* of St. Augustine. The first writer in Western literature to use memory for the purpose of examining the self achieved a view of events that was more than an accumulation of raw facts. He became aware of the movements of grace in his life and the power and beauty of the God who loved him from the beginning and whom he learned to love, as he said, "too late." We do not have the impression in reading the *Confessions* that Augustine's awareness of the presence of God in his life was either sudden or sheerly gratuitous. Even if his decision to become a Christian—the famous "take and read" passage—seems instantaneous, it was not. Long struggle preceded this graced locution and further struggle succeeded it. Paul Ricoeur argues:

> This book, indeed, attests to the fact that the attraction of the eternity of the Word felt by temporal experience is not such as to plunge the narration, which is still temporal, into a contemplation free from the constraints of time. In this respect, the failure of the efforts at Plotinian ecstasy, recounted in Book 7, is definitive. Neither the conversion recounted in Book 8, nor even the ecstasy of Ostia which marks the culmination of the narrative in Book 9, ever eliminate the temporal condition of the soul.[18]

Recognition in life will normally be a less-dramatic, less-heightened experience than recognition in narrative, where we are attentive to every event, every word. Life seems to straggle, to overflow with irrelevancies and apparent trivia, and it is open; we have the kind of freedom in life that is impossible in art, where every event has been predestined by its author. Within limits, we are free to choose the next event, which may not follow the present event in any logical or probable, or even plausible, sequence.

Our very freedom, the openness of our lives, can often preclude faith in the possible religious dimension of our experience. How can God dis-

---

[18]Paul Ricoeur, *Time and Narrative*, 3 vols., trans. Kathleen McLaughlin and David Pellauer (Chicago: University of Chicago Press, 1984) 1:29.

close himself within an event designed without any advertence to its religious possibilities? Here the term *sacred history* may need reexamination. Sacred history, we discover when we reflect on Scripture, was frequently less than sacred, by anybody's definition. Both Hebrew and Christian Scripture are shot through with failure, stubbornness, sin, folly, injustice—in short, every human corruption. If Scripture can be believed, all of history is the field of religious experience, not merely the moments identified as sacred.

• Narrative and Transformation •

Because recognition implies change, we need to examine what we mean by change. Conversion, because of its sometimes narrow application, is not always the most helpful term to describe what we are considering as the second component of religious experience. In the history of literature, the kind of change that follows recognition parallels the history of our understanding of consciousness. Studying what kind of character change occurs will clarify the nature of the recognitive experience that has been described.

What we have subsequently termed repentance is so familiar to the Western mind that it is sometimes startling to realize that such a concept was practically nonexistent in both Greek and Roman classical literature. One could change one's mind, but not one's character. The Hellenistic philosophers could urge a fool to alter his judgment, to correct a mistaken view, and a wise person could become wiser. But in Hellenistic literature, as well as in earlier Greek texts, there is no understanding of what the Septuagint called repentance, "turning back" (*epistrephein*) and of what the Christian texts called *metanoia*. New facts could alter the course of events, but a new view of events that implied radical character transformation and a new relationship to events was not part of the classical understanding of consciousness. Achilles did not alter his character or his personality when he decided finally to go into battle against the Trojans. He learned, rather, that Patroclus had been killed, and that realization was the occasion of a decision to act. He relinquished for the moment his sullen refusal to cooperate with the Greek effort, but he scarcely repented. He matured.

The Greek understanding of consciousness was clearly influenced by the Greek understanding of truth. Even though it is always a little deceptive to generalize about the Greeks, we nevertheless can trace their understanding through the great epics and drama, and sense how distinctly their narrative possibility differed from that of the Hebrews. The Greeks revered truth, *aletheia*. The very word itself—meaning "unhiddenness"—suggested the possibility of concealment and unknowing, and the necessity of waiting. Imaginative literature diminished when they began to struggle for more intellectual control of reality in the fourth century. In the great moments of epic and drama, the Greeks were profoundly aware of their limitations, their lack of control.

To discover the sweeping force of reality outside themselves was triumph only insofar as one could be heroically responsive to such a recognition. But the truth the Greeks discovered was impersonal. It could bear down and destroy, attract, repel, terrify; always the individual was somehow at its mercy. It would be disclosed, possibly, in time, which was rarely the time of need. Hence recognition in Greek culture was crisis; but when it occurred, it was often too late to change, too late to prepare oneself, too late to recover. One could only submit to the irresistible, the now-unhidden truth of things. Such a view precludes substantial character change or radical interior transformation, and it would be centuries before Western imaginative literature could see such a possibility as part of narrative structure.

When we contrast the character of Job with the characters of Greek literature, we see a different understanding of what can happen to a character because we are in the presence of a different concept of truth. For the Hebrews, truth was not so much a cognitive reality as a relationship. What Job experiences in his recognition is a change in perspective, a change in relationship to a person; he is transformed by his realization that Yahweh is an Unknowable Presence, that he is identified with the questions of a universe whose mysteries transcend Job's private existence and even his power to question. His response to the dark revelation of the interrogating Yahweh is "I repent." The word is important to an understanding of the different concept of character we have in this dramatic narrative.[19]

---

[19]Meir Sternberg, discussing the passage from ignorance to knowledge in Hebrew literature, emphasizes that merit in a biblical character "consists less in innate virtue, than in the capacity for acquiring and retaining knowledge of God's ways: less in a state of being than in a process of becoming, by the trial and error of experience." He adds that recognition was essential to Hebrew narrative, not merely a plot possibility as with the Greeks. See *The Poetics of Biblical Narrative: Ideological Literature and the Drama of Reading* (Bloomington: Indiana University Press, 1985) 177. Sternberg's analysis of the play of perspectives is especially helpful in clarifying how biblical narrative was unique in the ancient world and how in its *differentia* it anticipates the art of modern fiction "with its turn inward to focus on the workings of viewpoint and consciousness."

The Hebrew words *naham* and *shub* mean "to regret" or "to repent." *Shub* originally meant simply "to turn back," but it gradually acquired the meaning of conversion. The Hebrew prophets appealed over and over again for interior change: "Rend your hearts, and not your garments"; "turn to me and be saved." In Psalm 119 we sense the turning away from delusion and the interior change that accompanies repentance:

> *Down in the dust I lie prostrate:*
> *revive me as your word has guaranteed.*
> *I admitted my behavior, you answered me,*
> *now teach me your statutes.*
> *Explain to me how to keep your precepts,*
> *that I may meditate on your marvels.*
> *I am sleepless with grief:*
> *raise me as your word has guaranteed.*
> *Turn me from the path of delusion,*
> *grant me the grace of your Law.*
> *I have chosen the way of fidelity,*
> *I have set my heart on your rulings.*
> *I cling to your decrees:*
> *Yahweh do not disappoint me.*
> *I run the way of your commandments,*
> *since you have set me free.*   (Psalm 119:25-32)

This understanding of possibility was extended into early Christian literature. In the first chapter of the Gospel of Mark, we read, "and so it was that John the Baptist appeared in the wilderness proclaiming a baptism of repentance for the forgiveness of sins" (Mark 1:4-5), and then "after John had been arrested, Jesus went into Galilee. . . . 'The time has come,' he said, 'and the kingdom of God is close at hand. Repent.' " In the beginning of Christian literature, we see the classic prophetic call to "turn back to God." This call meant, at the same time, "turn away from your sins." Luke, describing John the Baptist, spells out some of the changes in ethical behavior that repentance implied: "Share your clothing and your food with those who have neither"; to tax collectors: "Exact no more than your rate"; to soldiers: "No intimidation. No extortion. Be content with your pay" (Luke 3:14-15).

The demand to adjust one's ethical behavior to the requirements of morality and to turn to God was not a novel announcement. John the Baptist called for repentance, but his strictures were not radically different from those of the great prophets, who had never ceased demanding that their hearers purify their ethics as well as their rituals of worship.

When Jesus begins preaching, however, more than ethics is involved, more than a quick or even drastic moral shaping up. He called for a whole new way of regarding the world, God, and one's fellows, and, like the author of Job, offered a new way of looking at good and evil. If one believed this Jesus, nothing could ever be the same again.

It was this concept of change that eventually affected Western literature. Even in situations where the Judeo-Christian notion of *metanoia* was of no concern to a writer, the understanding of consciousness that *metanoia* implied became part of the Western philosophical and literary tradition.

To understand the change of consciousness demanded by Jesus, we could consider the significance of his parables. We do not have all of these stories precisely as he related them since most of them were transposed into church situations of the next generation, but we do have the sense of what kind of shock those parables evoked in their original telling. Jesus' audience was asked to consider a publican justified by his prayer for mercy, a Samaritan who could be compassionate, one-hour laborers in the vineyard being paid as much by a generous landowner as those who had worked all day— (and the landowner wondering amiably why the latter are disturbed), a banquet to which the lame and the outcast are invited, a wheat field where thistles are allowed to thrive. Jesus' stories often demanded violent disruptions of logical thinking.

Picture a world in which all values are reversed, where prostitutes and taxpayers eat at the tables in the Kingdom, where the righteous will be last. The parables called for a new kind of vision, an admission that one's preconceptions about how things should be might well consist of tragic and eternally consequential misconceptions. The parables required a surrender of the obvious and preparation for a God never imagined, a God "who is who he is" and hence neither a product of the poverty of human desire nor the projection of human self-hatred.

Narrative and Interiority

What we do not have in Christian narrative is the interior debate of the people who heard these stories, of those who observed the Jesus who called for this change of thinking. We see most of their actions from the outside: the swift decision, the hasty observation, the simplistic question. We read that Peter wept, that the women of the tomb were frightened, that Pilate was puzzled and Herod curious. Apart from the stylized "we" passages in Acts, the only first-person accounts we have in Christian Scripture are the narrative passages in the Pauline epistles, but even these tell us very little of Paul's inner life. We can understand better the kind of change implied in the term *metanoia*—in its Christian rather than classical sense—by studying what is meant by interiority, consciousness. Western literature helps us here, especially as this literature reflects the persistent and primordial struggle to know 'Being.'

John E. Smith has suggested that there are only two fundamental currents in this struggle: the Aristotelian and the Platonic-Augustinian.[20] In the Aristotelian model, recognition of truth is a matter of adequation. The mind must adjust to "see" reality outside. It does not, of itself, create or shape truth. Its function is to reflect, to recognize what is *there*. The Platonic-Augustinian model requires individual insight and more direct, less-cognitional experience. Aristotelian views of truth lead to exposition and assertion; the Platonic-Augustinian to dialogue and eventually narrative. This Aristotelian notion of access to truth, which has implications for a theology of revelation, has suffered repeated assaults not only from different philosophical traditions but especially from writers of imaginative literature.

M. H. Abrams has focused our attention on the shift of the mind from reflector to lamp in the late-eighteenth and early-nineteenth centuries. When the Romantics discovered the imagination, they discovered a new relationship to reality.

> A number of romantic writers . . . whether in verse or prose, habitually pictured the mind in perception, as well as the mind in composition, by sometimes identical analogies of projection into, or of reciprocity with, elements from without. Usually in these metaphors of the perceiving mind, the boundary between what is given and what is bestowed is a sliding one, to be established as best one can from the individual context.[21]

In the post-Romantic period the emphasis on the subjective, leading eventually to the use of stream of consciousness, became more and more evident. It was not so much reality that affected the mind but the mind that qualified reality. After the Realists, the objective world outside the literary character was often devoid of significant content.

The term *epiphany* in modern literature was popularized by James Joyce to describe a "sudden spiritual manifestation, whether in the vulgarity of speech or of gesture or in a memorable phase of the mind itself."[22] An epiphany is not the result of information received or great events experienced. It is not a conclusion. Epiphany is characterized rather, as Morris Beja observes, by the irrelevance and apparent triviality of the incident

---

[20]Smith, *Experience and God*, 115.

[21]M. H. Abrams, *The Mirror and the Lamp* (New York: Oxford University Press, 1974) 62.

[22]James Joyce, *Stephen Hero*, ed. Theodore Spencer, rev. John J. Slocum and Herbert Cahoon (Norfolk CT: New Directions, 1963) 211.

that triggers it.[23] This emphasis on the random and insignificant distinguishes the experience of recognition in modern literature from its nineteenth-century counterpart and, according to Beja, expresses the loss of faith in the truth and absolutes of the past. Earlier writers had included such flashes of discovery in their novels, but they had not used these moments as keystones of their art. Presumably Beja is referring to the quality of religious experience that the mainline churches seemed capable of evoking, or even considering as a possibility, when he notes that this emphasis on random moments of intensity emerges as a result of disillusion with religion, as well as "an equally great loss of faith in reason." He adds, "The conviction that enlightenment is no more likely to come from rationalism and logic than it is from God makes the need for instantaneous, intuitive illumination seem all the more critical."[24]

Based on the above, epiphany—as a literary device—seems irreligious and is described by Beja as such. In fact, though, it represents a possible theological viewpoint. Rationalism and logic have never produced enlightenment that reaches into the human person and touches emotions of loyalty and love while evoking radical awareness. Pascal, long before the advent of modern fiction, spoke of the God of Abraham, Isaac, and Jacob as "the fire," the presence, which he knew to be transcendently different from "the god of the philosophers." But, according to the literary notion of epiphany, enlightenment does not come from God either. At least, it does not come from the god so many modern writers seem to have understood as God: that is, a remote and irrelevant god of uninspired religion, a god of propositional revelation alone, a god preached by the spiritually inept. To turn away from such religion—as well as from logic and rationalism—was often to escape to privatized intuition, to subjective consciousness, which seemed only tenuously connected to the world of time and situation.

In the modern concept of epiphany, with its emphasis on subjective significance, we are far away from the Greeks' understanding of recognition as part of plot. Their sense of interiority was also quite different, for they did not really understand consciousness in the modern sense of that word at all. But in the modern novel, we are also close to a contemporary theology of transcendental revelation. Quite simply, how does one apprehend a revealing God—supposing that God reveals himself— apart

---

[23]Morris Beja, *Epiphany in the Modern Novel* (Seattle: University of Washington Press, 1971) 17-21.

[24]Ibid., 21.

from the structures of the human mind, which must always deal with the finite and cannot apprehend any universal apart from finite experience?

The theology of Karl Rahner is especially helpful in this context. Recognizing that anthropology is the key to understanding how God is disclosed, and supposing that God chooses to reveal his mystery to humankind, Rahner begins with the nature of the human subject to whom truth is revealed. We know God as we know anything else, that is, through our "spirit in the world," our corporeality *inspirited*. The mind reaches to the infinite through the finite. The fact that we long for the infinite is itself suggestive of a call from Infinite Being. Rahner speaks of our capacity to hear that call as our "obediential potency."[25] The tension between the abyss that is God and the finite human person struggling to apprehend him results in what Avery Dulles describes as a "dualism of the explicit and the implicit, the thematic and the unthematic, the datum and the horizon in all revealing experience."[26]

Thus, the human person requires not propositional language only, for that is inadequate to the abyss that is God, nor isolated ecstasy and privatized intuition only, for such experience is often uninterpretable, but "mediated immediacy," that is, *symbol*. If God cannot be apprehended and loved simply from propositions about him, and if events seem connected to one another but not to anything else, some kind of "sheer intuition" would seem the only way to faith. But the sheer intuition of an epiphany— religious or not—is less "sheer" than its practitioners claim. To insist on the significance of the insignificant is to weight every event with a possible "hidden splendor," and that assumption is scarcely antireligious.

To pit the insignificant against the significant is to return us to spirit, to the unexpected, to openness and freedom, to the cosmic significance of the human mind itself as well as to that reality which is as present in a whisper as in a whirlwind. If we interpret religious experience as requiring an intersection between person and event, an intuition triggered by an insignificant event is no more necessarily devoid of God than David's conversation with Nathan about a farmer and his ewe lamb. Nor is epiphany in life as disconnected from experience as some writers suggest. Only in its surface structure can we assert disconnectedness and triviality.

William James argued long ago for the force of the subliminal structure of the mind, since apparently disconnected and trivial events may

---

[25]See Karl Rahner, *Foundations of Christian Faith* (New York: Seabury, 1978).

[26]Avery Dulles, "The Symbolic Structure of Revelation," *Journal of Theological Studies* 1 (March 1980): 51-73, at p. 69.

trigger an epiphany. The subliminal mind has its own symbol-making power, which—like Whitman's gossamer filament—can catch somewhere and cling with ductile strength. The modern notion of epiphany is irreligious only to the extent that the finite is perceived as ultimately significant, rather than significant against the horizon by which it is identified as finite. Even the final epiphany in Joyce's *Portrait of the Artist*, the imagery of priesthood to which it leads, assumes meaning only against another concept of priesthood that gives the notion of the artist in Joyce's work its particular beauty.

The movement toward interiority in literature was prophetic to a developing theology of subjective revelation. For this reason, it can be studied as a clue to how revelation itself is presently understood.

Propositions, dogma are "after the fact" of revelatory experience. They cannot constitute the experience itself (or substitute for it). By the same token, historical events alone, in their factual sense, are not in themselves revelation. It is the *response* to events, which "by their *symbolic* power grasp and mold the consciousness of the religiously oriented interpreter," that constitutes revelation.[27] Thus the key to understanding revelatory experience is the concept of *symbol*. Revelatory experience can be described as symbolic knowledge because, unlike mere facts or incommunicable tremors, such experience is transformative, existential, and participatory. It is transformative because we are changed by such experience; it is existential because it happens in time and place; it is participatory because it affects our relationship to the world and to other human beings.[28]

In the following chapters we shall consider a form of revelatory experience known in literature as "recognition" and we shall examine how the narrative experience of recognition can evoke in readers a comparable transformative experience. The understanding of recognition that we achieve through analysis of secular classics can then be brought to a reading of two religious classics so that we perceive how Scripture can be a symbolic expression of the divine-human encounter and bearer of the self-disclosing God. The Christian Gospel, like much of Hebrew Scripture, has been grounded in narrative. It proposes to lead its audience to a recognition of a person—Christ—and to an experience of the Christ-event. A consideration of recognition in Scripture could shed light on the kind of revelation that the Gospel offers and how readers and hearers respond to

---

[27]Ibid.

[28]Ibid., 63.

that revelation: for when they do respond, when they "hear the Word," as the language of believers expresses it, they testify that they have recognized the Christ. In theological terms, they have subjectively apprehended revelation.

To describe the experience of revelation and to appeal to that experience as a means of evoking a new experience of revelation in the audience requires narrative. The Gospels are narratives that have as their purpose the evocation of recognition in those who hear and read of the Christ-event in history. The Gospels describe an event and can create a new event. How they do so forms the conclusion of this book. Both contemporary literary theory, especially hermeneutics, and our present understanding of how we "know" bears upon the Gospel described as revelation.

One of the more unfortunate consequences of the Christian effort to clarify the noetic dimension of the Christ-event was the assumption, especially on the level of popular piety, that the exposition of the content of revelation could be revelation, and that to say yes to that content was to "believe." That confusion was accountable not to Scripture, which had never suggested such a notion of faith, but to epistemological confusion about the meaning of truth and access to knowable Being. We have to admit also the tendency of all religions to become mechanistic, to reduce the primordial religious event to something that can be acquired without sacrifice. It is tempting to look for truth without struggle or commitment. But neither Jewish nor Christian writers of the sacred texts nor imaginative writers of any generation suggested that self-disclosing Being was not also hidden.

The kind of interiority begun in Hebrew and Christian Scripture did not emerge in Western imaginative literature until the twelfth century with what Chenu has called *l'éveil de la conscience*. Peter Abelard, in fact, has been described as "the first modern man" because he was the first theologian to discuss the effect of the degree of the interior consent on the morality of an action.[29] And Chrétien de Troyes in the same century created the first character in Western literature to undergo a complete change of consciousness. Considered in this sense, modern literature begins with Perceval; from this twelfth-century narrative, we can trace the move-

---

[29]M.-D. Chenu, *L'éveil de la conscience dans la civilisation médiévale.* Conférence Albert-Le Grand 1968 (Montreal: Institut d'Etudes Médiévales, 1969) 17.

ments that marked the passage to the modern understanding of consciousness.

We must begin with the Greeks, however, for they mark the initial Western effort to examine the relationship of men and women to the reality they had to interpret if they were to sustain their humanity.

· P A R T I I ·

RECOGNITION
IN
WESTERN LITERATURE

THE GREEK EPOCH:
RETURN AND RECOGNITION

Of all the extensions in which the World and our own person develop, of the historical phases and physical conditions of our return to God, we know practically nothing at all. We are moving through darkness towards a luminous point; and if we do not defend our vision with real determination, if at every moment we do not recapture it, the very sight of the star will escape us.

—Pierre Teilhard de Chardin,
<u>The Heart of Matter</u>

To study even briefly that great period in Western history from Homer to Euripides and Aristotle is to be overwhelmed by the struggle of the Greeks to come to terms with reality, alternately to submit to and attempt to control it, and finally, to try to comprehend the human mind itself. We cannot understand our own mode of vision unless we know something of the origins of what we now call the Western mind. Those in the Judeo-Christian tradition have scarcely escaped the Greek mode, for their Scripture and their faith have come to the contemporary world through the language and thought structures of the Greeks. We have gone beyond those structures to a large extent, retrieving on the one hand Semitic concepts and reappropriating, on the other, an understanding of phenomena that the Greeks seemed not to have grasped completely. But we are indebted to this people to an extent that is scarcely measurable anymore, so deeply rooted in our consciousness is their mythic vision, their sense of beauty, and their longing for the truth of things. It is that longing we need to trace. It helps to explain us to ourselves. The Greek attempt to penetrate the hiddenness of reality is the beginning of our own struggle. Their way of seeing became for centuries, in large measure, our own.

• The Return of Odysseus •

When, after ten years of fighting and ten of wandering, Odysseus returns to Ithaca, "the brightest of stars," writes Homer, had come—"that star which ushers in the tender light of dawn. The ship's voyage was done."[1]

There is no Homeric moment that captures so completely the density of the Greek concept of return and its destiny as an idea. Of all the returns (*nostoi*) from Troy, that of Odysseus was the most perilous and the most triumphant because Odysseus, unlike any of his men, "never forgot his homecoming."[2]

His return was an escape from every force that would have deprived him of humanity, of memory, of personal identity, and of life. Immediately preceding the description of the arrival in Ithaca, we see Odysseus "in sleep delicious and profound, the very counterfeit of death." The Phaeacians, upon entering a harbor, deposit the still-sleeping Odysseus on the shore of his homeland. The sun has risen, but the mist cast by Athena still covers the countryside. Returning to consciousness, Odysseus does not at first recognize where he is, and only when Athena in disguise tells him, can he rejoice. "He revelled in the knowledge that he was on his native soil."

There is considerable evidence that the word for return in Homeric Greek (*nostos*) is akin to the very quality in Odysseus that accounted for his survival: his capacity to see a situation, his *noos*. And *noos* (subsequently nous) has a long linguistic history, a history important to us because it is so closely related to our contemporary understanding of vision, recognition, and of mind. To come home again (*neomai*) is somehow to

---

[1]Homer, *The Odyssey*, trans. E. V. Rieu (1946; rpt., Baltimore: Penguin Books, 1970) 13.207, p. 204. All subsequent citations are taken from this edition.

[2]Douglas Frame, *The Myth of Return in Early Greek Epic* (New Haven: Yale University Press, 1978) 35ff. Frame cites a passage from Theognis that illustrates the relationship between intelligence and the return from death. Lethe, or oblivion, is consistently associated with death in Greek literature. "Sisyphus the son of Aeolus, who came up from the house of Hades by means of his *great intelligence*, persuading Persephone with wily words, *she who gives forgetfulness to mortals, unhinging their minds*—no other man had ever devised this thing once that black cloud of death covered him over and he had come into the shadowy region of the deceased, passing by the dark gates which restrain the unwilling spirits of the dead. But even from that place Sisyphus came back into the light of the sun by means of his *great shrewdness*" (702ff.).

recognize one's situation (*noein*) and to have come back from death.[3] But the curious part about this scene is the sleep of Odysseus, the most cunning and alert hero of the ancient world. Why is he asleep at the very moment of return, the moment he has been struggling to achieve throughout his epic journey? Homer's scene is an extraordinary artistic paradigm of the experience of discovery. The struggles of Odysseus had been struggles *against* oblivion; his triumphs were the victories of mind. But his return home was a gift. The Phaeacians brought him on their own ship and deposited him gently on his native shore. Recognition of his homeland followed a night of darkness, the quasi death even of his reasoning powers. Discovery was rediscovery. Avery Dulles, commenting on cognitive theory as correspondent to a theology of revelation, writes of the probing, struggling phase of thought, then the relaxation period, the surrender, and finally the often sudden arrival of the unbidden idea, delivered from the unconscious. Is the idea "discovery" or "revelation"? Achievement or gift?[4] We begin to understand why Greek storytellers, knowing that the rational processes alone could not bring them to their destination, called on the Muse for inspiration. How shall the hero return? How shall his people know him? And most important, how shall the song be sung?

A cosmogony that antedates the stories of the returns from Troy may help to explain the appeal of these tales, apart from their sheer power as narrative to fascinate us. In the first millennium B.C.E. (the Bronze Age), in the mythologies of both the Orient and the Occident, "the meeting of the Sun and Moon" was a recurring image. In the diurnal sequence, the sunset, according to Joseph Campbell, symbolized "the inward turning of the mind,"[5] a gaze that resulted in the discovery of a microcosm—the individual—which then became identified with the macrocosm—the universe. Two principles were thus brought together: eternity and time, sun

---

[3]Ibid., 31.

[4]Avery Dulles, "Revelation and Discovery," in *Theology and Discovery*, ed. William J. Kelly (Milwaukee: Marquette University Press, 1980) 1-29. Dulles draws from Michael Polanyi, *Personal Knowledge* (New York: Harper Torchbooks, 1964) 121-31, and Henri Poincaré, *l'Intuition et la logique en mathématique* (1900). According to Poincaré's theory discovery is a four-stage process: wonder, or seeing the problem, incubation, illumination, and confirmation. Odysseus has seen the problem; he has been prevented from getting home. Most of the epic is about that problem. Its triumphal conclusion makes it a story of recognition.

[5]Joseph Campbell, *The Masks of God: Occidental Mythology* (New York: Viking Press, 1970) 163.

and moon, male and female, Hermes and Aphrodite (Hermaphroditus), and the two serpents of the caduceus. The warrior must return from the outer to the inner world—from the conquest of Troy to his wife and home—or in Jungian terms, from the conscious to the unconscious, which waits actively. Penelope, weaving and unweaving, is the rhythmic moon.

Citing Heraclitus's term *enantiodromia* ("running the other way"), Campbell interprets the themes of the two Homeric epics:

> . . . as an example of the process no better instance could be sought than that supplied by the two contrasting epics of Homer on which Heraclitus and his whole generation were raised: on the one hand, the *Iliad*, with world of *arete* and manly work and, on the other, the *Odyssey*, the long return, completely uncontrolled, of the wisest of the men of that heroic generation to the realm of those powers and knowledges which, in the interval, had been waiting unattended, undeveloped, even unknown, in that "other mind" which is woman: that mind in the earlier Aegean day of those lovely beings of Crete had made its sensitive statement, but in the sheerly masculine Heroic Age had been submerged like Atlantis.[6]

Further, the mythic and temporal references of the *Odyssey* are based on the cosmogonic imagery of the solar hero guided by Hermes, "patron of rebirth and lord of the knowledges beyond death."[7] The Trojan War had lasted ten years and the voyage of Odysseus to Ithaca another ten. The most persuasive analysis of Homer's timing is Gilbert Murray's: The lunar calendar consisted of twelve lunar months of 354 days plus a few hours; the solar calendar, 364 days and a few hours. Every nineteen years the two calendars intersected, a cycle that was referred to by the astronomer Meton as the "Grand Cycle of Nineteen Years." Odysseus returned to Ithaca at dawn. He rejoined his wife at the end of the nineteenth year, at the time of the new moon, which was also the day of the Apollo Feast, or solstice festival of the sun.[8]

The story of the "return and recognition" has, therefore, a profoundly significant component: the rediscovery of an inner world, which, in the Greek understanding of that concept, was a universe in shadow.

---

[6]Ibid., 160.

[7]Ibid., 162.

[8]Gilbert Murray, *The Rise of the Greek Epic*, 3d ed., rev. and enl. (Oxford: Clarendon Press, 1924) 211. Cited in Campbell, *Masks of God*, 163.

We can look to the epic tradition as the presumable source of recognition scenes in later Greek drama, for the earliest scenes still extant are those in the Homeric corpus. But as Homer uses such scenes, they are already conventional. Odysseus has recognized his own land. But will those at home recognize and receive *him*?

In the *Odyssey* the disguised hero is often struck or insulted (bks. 17, 18, 20), or made the target of physical abuse. Antinoos ("Antimind"), the chief suitor, throws a stool at Odysseus; the maids are flippant; Melanthios, the goatherd, insults him; and during dinner, Ctessippus hurls a cow's hoof at the disguised Odysseus. "These incidents," writes A. B. Lord, "are multiforms of a single theme four times repeated, whose meaning, deeply bedded in the myth underlying the story is that the resurrected god in disguise is rejected by the unworthy, who cannot recognize him. These episodes are actually testings."[9]

However conventional the recognition scene became by the eighth century, the homecoming of Odysseus is suspenseful and touching by any standards, the more so as the audience is made aware of Odysseus's scheme and the extent to which it depended on the loyalty and trust of those who had spent twenty years waiting for him. The pain of not being recognized, as well as its strategic advantages, is exploited completely in the climactic book 23. And in a particularly effective moment, we grasp fully the character of Penelope, who must determine beyond any doubt who it is that claims to be Odysseus. The pleasure of the audience is heightened by its own awareness of the presence of Odysseus to his wife.

"Come, Eurycleia," says Penelope in an instruction that exasperates her usually temperate husband, "make him a comfortable bed outside the bedroom that he built so well himself. Place the big bed out there, and make it up with rugs and blankets, and with laundered sheets" (p. 345).

When Odysseus, in a fit of justifiable exasperation, describes the immovability of the marriage bed he had constructed, Penelope yields—finally—to evidence. Her refusal to act while in doubt exemplifies her resistance to ambiguity. To betray her husband, even by error, would be to strip them both of their identity, imaged by the bed constructed from an olive tree rooted in the earth.

In a sensitive analysis of this scene, Norman Austin writes that Penelope had twice invoked the epiphany and twice recoiled from it. Mysterious suffering preceded recognition because acknowledgment would

---

[9]A. B. Lord, *The Singer of Tales* (Cambridge: Harvard University Press, 1960) 175.

be consequential. Penelope had left the room when Eurycleia bathed Odysseus, the old nurse experiencing her own shock of recognition at the sight of the visitor's scar. The test of the bow had been proposed by Penelope out of her subconscious intuition, but fearing the results of the contest, she had again left the room, knowing full well what was at stake. Only Odysseus had ever been able to draw the bowstring of his own weapon. Any competitor who could do so would make himself or "prove" himself her husband. The risk was more than she could endure to watch. In the final scene Penelope subjects Odysseus to the last test, heroically restraining her own longing. There would be no ambiguity, no masks. For the hearer of the story, the suspense is comparably unendurable. But when Odysseus, stung by the suggestion that the marriage bed could be moved, bursts into an angry (and revelatory) disclosure of their mutual secret, thus truly identifying himself, husband and wife finally face each other without disguise. "It is hardly man and woman . . . facing each other now," writes Austin, "but mind looking into mind, and seeing there the reflection of itself."[10]

Drama had neither the length nor the narrative distance to develop recognition scenes so completely as was possible in the final chapters of the *Odyssey*. Nor was it usually possible in fifth-century drama to link a recognition scene so completely and so seriously to the theme of the entire story. (*Oedipus the King* would constitute a conspicuous exception.) Odysseus returned home alive because he never forgot his origins or who he was.[11] He had learned when it was possible and to whom he could reveal his name. He had learned to recreate new versions of his identity when he was vulnerable and to assert himself only when he was strong. Those in Ithaca who were his enemies recognized him too late.

Recognition in Greek Drama

Three hundred years after Homer, the great tragedies of the fifth century would continue to draw their inspiration from the epic cycles. When and how tragedy developed as an art form is historically obscure, although theories about its origins have not been denied us—from Aristotle to our own day. We know that drama flourished in the City Dionysia in the great festivals of Athens and that when we discover it, we are already in the grip of masters: Aeschylus, Sophocles, Euripides. We have

---

[10]Norman Austin, *Archery at the Dark of the Moon: Poetic Problems of Homer's "Odyssey"* (Berkeley: University of California Press, 1975) 238.

[11]See J.-P. Vernant, *Myth and Thought among the Greeks* (London: Routledge and Kegan Paul, 1983) 75-105. Ch. 3 is especially pertinent.

never really recovered from their influence, for they gave us the kind of greatness in theater against which we have measured every other effort.

The dramatists of the fifth century often used the recognition scene with considerable sophistication. Its function in the drama had a great deal to do with the use of evidence, its inadequacy, and the hiddenness of truth. The protagonist could be persuaded or not by the evidence, depending on the congruence of mind to what was offered as testimony.

The evidence in the Electra/Orestes recognition scenes created by Aeschylus and Euripides does not force a conclusion. Electra in both plays responds to evidence in terms of her own faith, expectations, or fears; and in both versions, her character is fixed.[12] In Aeschylus's *The Libation Bearers*, Orestes has returned, has placed a lock of hair on his father's tomb, an act that is religiously significant because it suggests an effort on the part of one who loves, to communicate with the dead. Electra, finding the lock and noting that it matches her hair, must struggle to conclude that Orestes has returned to Argos. An enemy, after all, could be mocking her. But she wants to believe and, in fact, does so:

> Electra: Someone has cut a strand of hair and laid it on the tomb.
> ....
> It seems that it must be nobody's hair but his.[13]

The footprints that match her own are even less conclusive than the lock of hair:

> Electra: But see, here is another sign. Footprints are here. The feet
> that made them are alike, and look like mine . . . I step where
> he has stepped, and heelmarks, and the space between his
> heel, and toe are like the prints I make. Oh, this is torment,
> and my wits are going.   (205)

Orestes' actual appearance and his further proof—he has a piece of her weaving—complete the scene. But Electra was prepared already to believe.

Euripides' version of the discovery of Orestes is both commentary on Aeschylus and a reinterpretation of the significance of evidence. Pucci notes that Euripides suppresses the religious meaning in Aeschylus of the

---

[12]Pietro Pucci, "Euripides Heautontimoroumenos," *Transactions and Proceedings of the American Philological Association* 98 (1967): 365-71.

[13]Aeschylus, *The Libation Bearers*, trans. Richmond Lattimore in *The Complete Greek Tragedies*, vol. 1, ed. David Grene and Richmond Lattimore (Chicago: University of Chicago Press, 1959). All citations are taken from this edition.

lock of hair on the tomb; Euripides' Electra rejects any suggestion that Orestes has secretly returned, arguing that he would never return except as a public hero. On the basis of her expectations, she discounts both evidence and testimony of his return. Even when talking to Orestes, she does not recognize him. She is so persuaded that he will make his appearance in another way, and so convinced that the evidence at her disposal is utterly inconclusive, that she is blinded to reality by her own logic:[14]

> . . . how could a lock of his hair match with mine?[15]
> ....
> . . . how could rocky ground receive the imprint of a foot? And if it could be traced, it would not be same for brother and for sister. . . .   (534-36)

Only when another character calls her attention to a scar on her brother's face does Electra yield to material proof. Euripides' purposes are clear: he uses the recognition scenes in his play both to criticize Aeschylus for naive faith, a faulty use of evidence, and at the same time to point to the naïveté of those who consider evidence as self-supporting. Euripides' editorializing is consistent, especially in his *Electra*. Human reason is deceptive. To trust in one's rational processes is to be quite unenlightened to the preconceptions, the obsessions that influence our response to reality. Electra's character in the Euripidean version is not changed by the forceful assertion of material evidence. By her reactions in this regard, readers recognize her fixed character: her obsession with vengeance, her inflexible point of view.[16]

Oedipus the King of Sophocles had offered a different account of the problem of recognition: Oedipus, too, had what may be called an inflexible point of view. But he had good reason. He had been given the wrong information, evidence enough to conclude quite justifiably that the murderer of Laius was someone other than himself. If to the audience his anger at Teiresias seems excessive, we have to recall how thoroughly inaccurate was his knowledge of his origins. The problem was the essential problem of conversion. How does one abandon the framework out of which one's conclusions are normally established?

---

[14]Pucci, "Euripides," 371.

[15]Euripides, *Electra*, trans. Emily Townsend Vermeule in *The Complete Greek Tragedies*, vol. 4, ed. David Grene and Richmond Lattimore (Chicago: University of Chicago Press, 1960). All citations are taken from this edition.

[16]Pucci, "Euripides," 371.

Sophoclean characters are generally thinkers, arguers whose reasoning processes are quite thorough (we can exclude Antigone), even sensitive. Their problem is not always or exclusively with themselves but with a universe larger than their possibilities, with events that exceed their measuring. Oedipus experiences tragedy, not because he is wrongly obsessed with his innocence, but because he insisted upon knowing the truth, the reality that had exceeded his imagining. Jocasta is less than heroic and not really tragic: "Do not concern yourself about this matter," she suggests. "So clear in this case were the oracles, so clear and false. Give them no heed."[17] Oedipus was heroic before he knew of his origins. He was heroic at the moment of recognition, and he sustained his courage before the gods and his enemies to the end. Truth had indeed been hidden from him, but not because of guilt on his part. He had searched relentlessly and argued faultlessly. If the truth eluded for a time his discovery, it was because Oedipus worked with the only evidence at his disposal. "If someone tried to kill you here and now," he asks in *Oedipus at Colonus*, "what would you do, inquire first if the stranger was your father?"[18]

Greek playwrights, as well as their epic precursors, were aware that recognition is not usually preceded by a reasoning process adequate to the new truth to be apprehended. This principle is fundamental to any understanding of discovery in human sciences, as well as in religious experience. Commenting on the kind of dilemma this incongruence supposes, Avery Dulles writes, "In discovery . . . the clues cannot be explicitly attended to, or the solution will disappear."[19] Even words that convey accurate information are not necessarily revelatory because the hearer will interpret them in terms of an existing framework of understanding or expectation. As in the Oedipus myth, it is often that "preconception" that needs to be subverted.

Sophocles includes three recognition scenes in his version of the Electra myth, each a shattering reversal of such a preconception. Electra does

---

[17]Sophocles, *Oedipus the King*, trans. David Grene in *The Complete Greek Tragedies*, vol. 2, ed. David Grene and Richmond Lattimore (Chicago: University of Chicago Press, 1959) ll. 706, 725.

[18]Sophocles, *Oedipus at Colonus*, trans. Robert Fitzgerald in *Complete Greek Tragedies*, vol. 2, ll. 991-93. All citations are taken from this edition.

[19]Dulles, "Revelation and Discovery," 10. See also Kathy Eden, *Poetic and Legal Fiction in the Aristotelian Tradition* (Princeton: Princeton University Press, 1986). "The best recognitions [according to Aristotle] are *entechnic* [based on probability] . . . not only because they are likely to happen, but because their probability, like the *peripeteia* itself, emerges contrary to intention and expectation" (22).

not believe the report of Chrysothemis that Orestes has arrived because she has just been informed that he had been killed in a chariot race. "You do not know where you are," she says to her ecstatic sister, who reports his arrival, "nor where your thoughts are."[20] When Orestes finally reveals himself to her, offering as proof his signet ring, she responds with no hesitation, "O happiest light! / . . . dearest of women, fellow citizen / here is Orestes that was dead in craft, and now by craft restored to life again" (1222, 1227-29).

As brother and sister enter the palace, she comments, "There is no chance of your recognition." And the next moment of truth is Clytemnestra's. She had no reason to fear because she also believed Orestes dead. We hear from offstage: "My son, my son, / pity your mother" (1410).

Aegisthus is equally misinformed by Electra's ambiguous words:

Aegisthus: Where are the strangers then? Tell me that.

Electra: Inside. They have found their hostess very kind.

(1450-52)

Aegisthus then experiences the reality of his own situation. Uncovering the face of the dead Clytemnestra, he knows. "This is my end then" (1482).

In each case, knowledge comes quickly with irrefutable evidence. The signet ring, scarcely adequate proof to a modern, was a classic sign of personal identity. Electra could not have questioned it.

In Sophocles, understanding one's situation and one's "fate" was clearly a matter of surrendering to eventual irresistible evidence, but that evidence is never forthcoming at the time of need. Words do not give access to truth, for the testimony of human beings and even of the gods is ambiguous. In *time*, events will declare the real truth of the situation. Recognizing truth is a matter of waiting and finally experiencing. The order of the universe will be reasserted.

Euripides, of all the Greek playwrights, was least convinced of that order. It was he who probed most intensely whether such an order even existed and, if it did, was it benevolent? He was no friend to the pious believer, nor was he as convinced of the rule of reason and the eventual triumph of harmony as was Sophocles. Self-knowledge, for him, included a realization not just of "nature" or the telos of nature, but of passion, of the violent forces that can destroy reason, however much one asserts the possibility of a reasoned control over them. In play after play,

---

[20]Sophocles, *Electra*, trans. David Grene in *Complete Greek Tragedies*, vol. 2, l. 921. All citations are taken from this edition.

he describes the triumph of the irrational and, in doing so, urges respect for the limitations of reason. The most terrifying recognition scene in Greek drama is unquestionably Agave's realization in *The Bacchae* that the head she has impaled on her staff is that of her son. In her Dionysiac madness, she had killed Pentheus, imagining him to be a wild beast:

Cadmus: And whose head do you hold in your hands?

Agave: (averting her eyes) A—lion's head—or so the hunters told me.

....

Agave: No, no, it is—Pentheus' head—I hold—[21]

Agave has recovered from her madness to look upon the deed she has done, the violence and savagery of which she was capable. Euripides' Hippolytus had been destroyed because of his refusal to honor Artemis or—in Euripidean terms—the force that Artemis represented. Agave, the women, and Pentheus in *The Bacchae* are destroyed for a comparable reason: they refused to come to terms with the reality of Dionysus in their midst. Their blindness is magnificently epitomized in Pentheus's dialogue with the god in disguise, especially the final words:

Dionysus: He is here now and sees what I endure from you.

Pentheus: Where is he? I cannot see him.

Dionysus: With me. Your blasphemies have made you blind.

(480-501)

Once again the hidden god is present and unseen. But this is not a god who brings order. This is the god within, the passion that thrills and blinds and maddens, the power one must acknowledge or risk the most profound deception. Euripides could see no homeland for the human wanderer, neither in an inner nor in the outer universe. His characters, like those of Sophocles, may discover the truth, may recognize their situation, but never in time, never soon enough. A future is always denied them. Recognition does not alter their characters; it only makes their fate more painful.

When, in the fourth century, Aristotle described the structure of tragedy, his exempla were the plays of the previous century. Among the three formal elements of plot, the "soul" of tragedy, he included "recognition," or in his terminology *anagnôrisis*. It was, we read, "as the very word

_____

[21]Euripides, *The Bacchae*, trans. William Arrowsmith in *Complete Greek Tragedies*, vol. 4.

implies, a change from ignorance to knowledge, and thus to either love or hate, in the personages marked for good or evil fortune."[22] Recognition is one of three formal elements of a complex plot, reversal and suffering being the other two.

Aristotle preferred a plot such as that of *Oedipus the King* in which recognition occurs together with reversal (*peripeteia*). He adds in the eleventh chapter of the *Poetics* that recognition can be directed simply to an inanimate object or it can be the discovery that "someone has or has not done something." But usually, recognition in drama is of a person, although it may sometimes be limited merely to identification of one party by another or of both parties by each other. The recognition scene makes a plot by definition *complex,* for it accomplishes a change in the action, from friendship to hostility or the reverse. When recognition of persons results in a change in the direction of action, the intended effect on the audience is surprise, and when the plot is fatal, that surprise is accompanied by pity and fear.

That recognition in Greek drama and narrative is a *function of plot and not of character* is the single most important observation to make in this consideration of consciousness in ancient literature. To moderns accustomed to looking at Oedipus, for example, with a postromantic awareness of self, it is strange to note that the character of Oedipus does not really change when he discovers the reality of his situation. He does not reevaluate his personality or repent of his decisions. His life changes, not because he repents but rather because the force of reality bears down upon him. He responds to the impact of attaining accurate knowledge, finally, of his origins and his identity. Fortune changes, and Oedipus reappraises his situation, now recognized as tragic.

We should briefly examine what in Greek culture and cognitional theory accounts for this emphasis on plot rather than character in the literature of the period. We are so accustomed to character development in modern literature, even character discontinuity, that we may be puzzled by Hegel's assertion that the more titanic characters in Greek literature were proud to be guilty.[23]

---

[22]Aristotle, *Poetics,* trans. Ingram Bywater (New York: Modern Library, 1954) 1452a.30. Bywater uses the term *discovery* for *anagnôrisis.*

[23]Georg W. F. Hegel, *The Philosophy of Fine Art,* vol. 4, trans. F. P. B. Osmaston (London: G. Bell and Sons, Ltd., 1920). Cited in Bernard F. Dukore, *Dramatic Theory and Criticism: The Greeks to Grotowski* (New York: Holt, Rinehart and Winston, 1974) 540.

Bruno Snell, influenced by Hegel and thus comparably evolutionary in his analysis, had traced the origins of the European mind through the various strata of Greek culture, especially literary and historical texts, to show how slowly such concepts as 'mind' grew from Homer's understanding, for example, of psyche (breath, probably cold, moist), to the idea of nous in Aristotle.[24] (It would be generations before we could talk about a psychological self.) However controversial, Snell's work has profoundly influenced subsequent scholars. We can understand Greek tragedy better if we understand something, at least, of the fifth- and fourth-century concepts of mind and truth, and of access to truth. And those concepts are embedded deeply not only in the Greek understanding of time and being, but, necessarily, in the history of language itself.

In Homer, the narrative voice describes the inner life of his heroes by means of "personified interchanges."[25] Odysseus talks to Athena, to the river god, or to his *thymos,* and we have access to his inner life. Knowledge comes to the Homeric hero by perception or report, or sometimes by omen. The Muses or the gods knew everything, and they could communicate what they knew if they chose to do so. Eurycleia knows Odysseus by the scar on his leg; Penelope (perhaps) by a dream that Odysseus, in disguise, affirms. Her intuition, however, must be tested. Only Odysseus knows how the marriage bed had been constructed and that it could not be moved. Penelope was wary enough to know that deception was possible and that her desires could be manipulated. The truth of Odysseus's return had to be objectively demonstrable. It is typically (early)

---

[24]Bruno Snell, *The Discovery of the Mind: The Greek Origins of European Thought,* trans. T. G. Rosenmeyer (Cambridge: Harvard University Press, 1953). See also K. von Fritz, "*Noos* and *Noein* in the Homeric Poems," *Classical Philology* 28:2 (April 1943): 79-91, and T. B. L. Webster, "Some Psychological Terms in Greek Tragedy," *Journal of Hellenic Studies* 77 (1957): 149-54.

Norman Austin argues that the mental life of an individual in Homer is a shadowy replica of his or her social life. See especially ch. 4 of his *Archery,* 179-238. The Austin/Snell discussion is continued (in defense of Snell) in W. Thomas MacCrary, *Childlike Achilles: Ontogeny and Phylogeny in "The Iliad"* (New York: Columbia University Press, 1982).

[25]Joseph Russo and Bennet Simon, "Homeric Psychology and the Oral Epic Tradition," *Journal of the History of Ideas* 29 (1968): 487. The authors note that the use of "personified interchanges" suggests not only Greek psychology but the devices that were customary in oral epic tradition. See especially E. R. Dodds, *The Greeks and the Irrational* (Berkeley: University of California Press, 1951), and Lord, *Singer of Tales.*

Greek that the truth of the present is discernible only by means of a link to the past.

What we now call characterization in Greek drama was affected by the fifth-century dramatists' understanding of ethics and the role of knowledge in human life. Homer's characters, as those of Aeschylus and Sophocles, had to relate to the world and to the gods, to an outside order. The external world impinged upon them and required their response. To discover and achieve their being, they needed information. Oedipus must determine his real parentage. Electra must learn whether her brother has returned. Agamemnon's fate is not to know his wife's plans. Ion must find out who his mother is or she will die. Creon must realize Antigone's implacability if he is to avoid disaster. Only in Euripides do we begin to see a probing of motives, rather than knowledge or ignorance, as the pivotal issue. But this beginning was never fully exploited in Greek drama. It was not to be probed, in fact, for centuries.

It was Hegel, and later Kierkegaard, who pointed out how profoundly Greek drama differed from modern drama in its understanding of the consciousness of characters. The modern reader or spectator, aware of the role of intentionality in assessing the morality of human actions, sees Oedipus quite differently from the way the Greeks viewed him. According to Hegel, "The plastic nature of the Greek . . . adheres to the bare fact which an individual has achieved, and refuses to face the division implied by the purely ideal attitude of the soul in the self-conscious life on the one hand, and the objective significance of the fact accomplished on the other."[26] Any division between exterior behavior and the interior disposition weakened action, diminishing its greatness and thereby the greatness of the actor. Conflict in Greek drama is "within," but that inner debate does not constitute the tragedy. The tragedy is what happens when the inner conflict is resolved. In such a world one treads carefully. It is important to acquire correct information and to be wise enough to concede that the information one has may not be either accurate or complete.

In such a world the hero or heroine does not repent. How can one repent if action has been taken on the basis of necessity and on the available information? One can experience shame or psychological guilt in this culture, but not the kind of repentance or sense of moral guilt that alters the soul or changes self-understanding. Characters can achieve wisdom through their sufferings, wisdom flowing from an accumulation of ex-

---

[26]Hegel, *Philosophy of Fine Art;* cited in Dukore, *Dramatic Theory and Criticism,* 539.

perience, but their moral characters remain static. Deeds always count, despite motives or circumstance. This is one reason that Aristotle speaks of beginning a drama with the imitation of action and then conceiving of the kind of character who would perform such action, rather than beginning with a character and imagining what that character would do. Greek drama is concerned about what the protagonist *does* and what follows logically or probably from what he or she does, what follows from "outside." And it is the problem of the hero or heroine to determine what *is* outside and to discover it in time.

· The Time of Recognition ·

Tragedy is possible not only because things happen to a character in some critical relationship to that character's goodness and knowledge, but because these things happen so quickly.[27] It has been said that the Greeks discovered time in the fifth century. Indeed, it is not coincidental that tragedy emerged and reached artistic perfection during that same period. Tragedy can be seen as a kind of monumental change that occurs to a character within a brief passage of time. The subject matter is always "one great event, which overthrows all that existed before: it means death, destruction, reversal of fortune; its strength rests on contrast between before and after; and the deeper the contrast, the more tragic the event."[28] Changes occur within an epic also, but the sense of change is less sensational because time is extended. The change that occurs within the time span of a tragedy can shock us into the awareness of possibility. Emotions are quickly engaged and that very swiftness, the brevity of the performance, alerts the audience to the significance of each event, an alertness that normally is not brought to other events of life. The action of a tragedy is, in Aristotle's words, "serious and complete." A single revolution of the sun does not seem to bring such seriousness or completion to daily life. Even when a single serious event does occur, it is not isolated as it is in tragedy, enclosed in a universe of meaning. In tragedy, time is charged with the promise of significance.

In Aeschylus, time "teaches," and it does so by punishing. The justice of the gods will work itself out "in time." And if this is the case, one waits not for surprises or new information, but with certainty and anguished

---

[27]See Jacqueline de Romilly, *Time in Greek Tragedy* (Ithaca: Cornell University Press, 1968), and J. de la Harpe, "Le progrès de l'idée de temps dans la philosophie grècque" in *Festschrift zum 60 Geburstag von A. Speiser* (Zurich, 1945) 128-37.

[28]Romilly, *Time in Greek Tragedy*, 5-6.

uncertainty, for one never knows what exactly will come or when, only that it *will* come. Meaning becomes available when the disaster arrives and purification (*catharsis*) is achieved. Because the justice of the gods is a result of misdeeds of the past, it is to the past that one must go for meaning. The pattern of the *Oresteia* trilogy is the supreme example of such a view of time and meaning.

In the plays by Sophocles, time is not the field where justice is accomplished, but the field of mutability, the dimension in which change of fortune can occur and where men and women must respond somehow to that change. What occurs is not rooted in a decision of the gods, but rather in the nature of things.[29] Not only do "things" change, so too do feelings of human beings. Tragedy in Sophocles is frequently the result of the central character's refusal to yield to the passage of time and the presumable diminution of energy or shifting emotion that such movement generally brings.

Commenting on the relentless eternalizing of the present moment, the refusal to let the past be past in Sophoclean tragedy, Charles Segal observes that it is civilization that mediates "between the limitless time of eternity or death and the measurable span of the individual life with its finite sorrows and satisfactions."[30] Civilization breaks down all time into meaningful, graspable units. Tragedy, according to Segal, "threatens those structures and forces man to confront again the threat of meaninglessness raised by the endless cycles of nature or the undifferentiated time of eternity."[31] It is perhaps closer to the point to note that tragedy (and thus recognition) occurs at the intersection of time and eternity. The exigencies of the present moment do not break the will of the Sophoclean hero or heroine to remain fixed in some eternal value or intransigent conviction. It is in the clash between mutability of the world and the immovability of the central character that power is displayed and catastrophe occurs. Time, in other words, "is where the real nature of things and of people comes to light."[32]

The contrast between timelessness and mutability is expressed most poignantly by Oedipus, the aged king in exile:

---

[29]Ibid., 93.

[30]Charles Segal, *Tragedy and Civilization: An Interpretation of Sophocles* (Cambridge: Harvard University Press, 1981) 265.

[31]Ibid.

[32]Romilly, *Time in Greek Tragedy*, 107.

The immortal
Gods alone have neither age nor death!
All other things almighty Time disquiets.
Earth wastes away; the body wastes away;
Faith dies; distrust is born.
And imperceptibly the spirit changes
Between a man and his friend, or between two cities.
For some men soon, for others in later time,
Their pleasure sickens; or love comes again.
And so with you and Thebes: the sweet season
Holds between you now; but time goes on,
Unmeasured Time, fathering numberless
Nights, unnumbered days; and on one day
They'll break apart with spears this harmony—
All for a trivial word.   *Oedipus at Colonus* (607-21)

The concept of time in Euripides is affected by his pessimism. As in Sophoclean drama, the world is mutable. Euripides stresses not only the unpredictability of events, but their swiftness. In a single day, anything can happen. Euripides does not call his protagonist or his audience to respect for order, but to an acknowledgment of the power of the nonrational. He urges not only pliancy of feeling, but openness to a different perspective on reality, a reality that often escapes cognitive control. The logic of Electra and the rigid complacency of Pentheus are not commended.

Given the threat of time to men and women, the Greek playwrights generally reinforced the concept that outside of human experience the cosmos proceeded in some kind of everlasting harmonious cycle. One of the functions of the chorus was to recall the audience to a sense of this movement. By evoking the past, the chorus could connect or even identify events. Sophocles, in particular, used the chorus to universalize meaning. The songs of the chorus could often provide the kind of meditative pause that released the audience from the urgency of events and thus from the afflictions of time itself. The universe remained nontemporal, despite its appearance of mutability. A Sophoclean play especially, in its structural balance between time and timelessness, between mutability and stillness, represented an intersection where truth—*aletheia*—was unveiled.

• The Place of Recognition •

Because the recognition experience in literature is a mirror to the audience, its aesthetic function correlates closely with the aesthetic effect of the entire text. Aristotle had argued that tragedy is presented "in a dramatic, not in a narrative form; with incidents arousing pity and fear,

wherewith to accomplish its catharsis'' (ch. 6, *Poetics*). We cannot pre-
sume scholarly agreement on Aristotle's meaning here. Every library offers adequate testimony to the multiple disagreements of classicists with
one another on the meaning of catharsis, as well as their occasional disagreements with Aristotle himself. With this caveat the Aristotelian theory can be considered. Drama clearly has something to do with the
imitation of human beings in action, as Aristotle had noted, and clearly
that imitation has as its central purpose to accord pleasure to other men
and women. How and why one experiences pleasure in attending a performance of human beings acting is at issue in Aristotle, and critics of every
century have offered to explain what he meant. We have learned to dis-
miss some of the less felicitous theories. Others we have to consider more
seriously, but only in large terms here, for we are dealing not just with
tragedy but with narrative in general. Aristotle's theory of catharsis is
helpful to an understanding of how all forms of narrative literature work,
how they mirror and illumine.

Tragic pleasure does not result simply from watching pain, but rather
from watching how events, even tragic and painful events, are connected. The structure of an art form such as tragedy provides a compre-
hensible link from event to event, the kind of link that life unedited does
not provide. There is an emotional reaction to life and an emotional reaction to art: they are not the same, and Aristotle analyzes the difference.

Two principles help to explain the function of narrative as mediating
awareness. First, narrative and drama usually involve the audience emotionally, catch the reader up into a universe imitative of life but not life,
a place where connections are supplied, control of emotions is offered,
significance is graspable. Even when art represents nonsignificance, such
nonmeaning is apprehensible only against a possibility of structure and
meaning that the literary form itself declares. Second, the emotions evoked
by an encounter with the text are pleasurable because the structure of the
work enables the reader to control response and to extend particular meaning to the universal. The struggle to image the world in art has always been a struggle to bring the audience to experience the world in a
new way. Like every sign system, narrative mediates awareness.

In classical Greek drama recognition usually occurs onstage in the
world of the characters, who discover or fail to discover someone's identity. Recognition is one of the important elements composing the whole
dramatic experience because it functions as a paradigm of a character's
access to reality, of the kind of obstacle experienced in struggling to
"know," and of the tragic effects of nonperception. In modern drama,
recognition can be displaced to the audience almost completely, as we see

in Sean O'Casey's *Juno and the Paycock,* or in most of Chekhov's plays. Even in Greek drama the audience can be, in a sense, part of the tragic world—not admitted completely to the secret of the artist-in-control and thus made to live through recognition on the same level as the other characters, superior only to the chorus and to the nonheroic personages.

Oedipus at Colonus is such a play. It is a unique drama of recognition—if that term is used in a broad sense—a drama in which the primary experience of recognition is that of the audience. It is considered here because it is a compelling example of the power of narrative to affect the way an audience sees.

• The Audience as Locus of Recognition •

"I see a man now. . . . "

In *Oedipus at Colonus* Sophocles did not use any of the traditional recognition devices and may not have considered the play a study in recognition in the traditional sense at all. But we have in this last and magnificent Sophoclean effort a profound analysis, not of character, but of perception of character. Oedipus is first presented to the audience as a helpless, feeble, disreputable-looking old man, dependent upon a young girl for guidance. In the first of numerous topographical references, he seems not to know where he is:

What place is this, Antigone? What people? Who will be kind to us
this evening?   (sc. 1, 3-4)

There is a hint that time has brought serenity:

Suffering and time;
Vast time, have been instructors in contentment.   (6-7)

He suggests that he is submissive:

We must learn from the local people and do as they direct.   (12-13)

Antigone is ever looking away and struggling to discern. In lines that foreshadow the revelation we shall soon experience of Oedipus himself, she says:

The towers that crown the city still seem far away   (14-15)

I see a man now, not far away from us.   (29)

And later, as Ismene arrives:

I don't know! Is it or isn't it? Or am I dreaming?
I think so; yes! No, I can't be sure.   (316-17)

Oedipus consistently reveals the strength of his own conviction about himself. However defeated, he is able to say, "How was I evil?" The chorus expresses the essential tension of the play, the doubt that exists outside of the central character:

> We pity him for his misfortune;
> But we tremble to think of what the gods may do   (255-56)

Ismene is the first to relate what the gods intend to do. She arrives with the report of the struggle of Eteocles and Polyneices for power, the banishment of Polyneices to Argos, and the subsequent prediction of the Oracle that the gods will sustain Oedipus. "The proof of their blessing," she adds, "is that Creon is coming to you" (396).

Oedipus, already convinced of his innocence, with or without the Oracle, comments finally, "Ah, then! No god's assistance is needed in comprehending." But now his enemies know that the gods are with him. His fortune is changing.

To Creon, who demands his return to Thebes saying, "Bury the whole thing now; agree with me," Oedipus reveals his own perception of Creon's real motives:

> You come to take me, but not to take me home;
> Rather to settle me outside the city
> So that the city may escape my curse.   (784-86)

And now we recognize the real power of Oedipus's actual vengeance:

> Now who knows better the destiny of Thebes?
> I do, for I have the best informants.   (791-92)

When it seems that the real crisis of the play has passed, when Ismene and Antigone have been rescued from Creon's attempt to use them as hostages, when Oedipus has expressed his gratitude to Theseus in words that reflect his sensitivity to his own outcast position, a third visitor arrives wishing to speak to Oedipus.

The chorus sings of the burden of life and the pain of "strengthless age" (1235). "This is the truth," they say, "not for me only, but for this blind and ruined man" (1240). But what we see in the next moment is quite other than the despairing truth proclaimed by an uncomprehending chorus. Oedipus is far from strengthless as he encounters his son Polyneices, now driven from Thebes by his brother and arguing his case before an unyielding and enraged parent.

"If we can put any trust in oracles," he pleads, in a peculiarly antireligious and essentially political observation, "they say that those you bless

shall come to power" (1331-32). He attempts to compare his situation with
that of his apparently desolate father:

> Are we not beggars
> Both of us, and exiles, you and I?   (1334-35)

But it is, after all, only Polyneices now who is the beggar.

And Oedipus finally speaks. In fifty-four lines of excoriation, he dem-
onstrates a soaring strength, an unassailable claim to the justice required
by a betrayed and dishonored father:

> I abominate and disown you!
> You utter scoundrel! Go with the malediction
> I here pronounce for you: that you shall never
> Master your native land by force of arms,
> Nor ever see your home again in Argos,
> The land below the hills; but you shall die
> By your own brother's hand, and you shall kill
> The brother who banished you. For this I pray.
> And I cry out to the hated underworld
> That it may take you home; cry out to those
> Powers indwelling here; and to that Power
> Of furious War that filled your hearts with hate!
> Now you have heard me. Go: tell it to Thebes,
> Tell all the Thebans; tell your faithful fighting
> Friends what sort of honors
> Oedipus has divided among his sons!   (1383-96)

This is hardly the tottering and submissive Oedipus we saw in the beginning of the play. And if Polyneices is informed so bluntly both of his
fate and of his underestimation of his father, the audience is brought to
a recognition of the power and greatness of this man. Antigone, trying to
nullify the curse, urges Polyneices to change his plans. But Polyneices remarks, "It is shameful to run," and adds that he has no intention of men-
tioning this "trifle" to those who are now about to follow him into disaster.
The chorus, incapable of dealing with the destructive purposes of Polyneices, laments, "I am not one to say, 'This is vain / Of anything allotted
to mankind,' " and turns the whole mystery over to Time, "who watches
all things steadily" (1455).

We are prepared now for the final blessing of Oedipus over Athens,
the favored city, for his superior understanding of the events that pre-
sage his death, for the control he exercises over everyone in his final moments, for their dependence upon him to explain and even to lead them
to his final "holy and funereal ground."

"What has happened," says the messenger to the citizens of Athens in the final scene, "was no simple thing." The last (oblique) view we have of Oedipus is that of the messenger describing Theseus, in the presence of the dying king, "shading his eyes as if from something awful." "Indeed," says the messenger, "his end was wonderful if mortal's ever was" (1664-65).

The sense of mounting power that Sophocles creates from the opening scene to the climactic apotheosis of Oedipus is evidence of the playwright's extraordinary capacity to control his audience's perspective. It is only by contrasting the opening and closing scenes that we begin to realize what he has done. By intensifying his focus, by bringing Oedipus nearer and nearer into our own vision, by repeating the assaults upon Oedipus's essential dignity, Sophocles draws the audience into an experience of human greatness where the justice of the gods seems vindicated and the injustices and violence of men overwhelmed. We have been brought to an experience of wonder in a world that, despite the chorus's final appeal, is still very much with us. Antigone leaves in the naive hope that she can stop the bloody war between her brothers, and the chorus urges, "Now let the weeping cease; Let no one mourn again." We are quite aware that we shall indeed mourn again, but Sophocles, by controlling our vision and expectations, has shown us something of their peculiar limits. That sense of darkened vision is in itself recognition, a reknowing of our own experience, such that we pity in another what we fear for ourselves. We taste the mystery of time. This kind of aesthetic experience is what Aristotle called catharsis. It is the total effect, the final cause of the text. It represents the function of all art: to give a particular experience of beauty and so to heighten awareness of what we already know and what there is yet to see.

The Greek poetic achievement reveals to us, as no other literature does, the fragmentary nature of vision, the importance of time, and the power of narrative to disclose the consequences of resistance to truth. Truth was what could break into the present, what could be finally "unhidden." Recognition of truth occurred where worlds joined: sun and moon, time and eternity, past and present. Recognition was the return to one's native country and thus to a finally acknowledged identity.

PERCEVAL:
THE WORD FROM ABOVE

When first I knew you, you raised me up so that I could see that there was something to be seen, but also that I was not able to see it. I gazed on you with eyes too weak to resist the dazzle of your splendor. Your light shone upon me in its brilliance, and I thrilled with love and dread alike. I realized that I was far away from you. It was as though I were in a land where all is different from your own.

—*St. Augustine*, Confessions

Greek epic and much of Greek drama is born from the struggle to return. When the native land was recognized or identity acknowledged, that return was complete. We may describe the beginnings of modern literature not as return but as quest, as a longing to leave Ithaca, to find identity, to delight in mutability. The modern Ulysses says to his men: "'Tis not too late to seek a newer world."[1]

The protagonist in medieval literature sets out on a journey to forge an identity by *means* of deeds, the *res gestae* of early biographers. Identity was public rather than private property.[2] But in twelfth-century literature and theology, the tension between public identity and personal awareness or interiority begins to be evident. The world was the field of both achievement and self-discovery. It was not enough to perform deeds: one had to be personally motivated to act. It was not enough to see the world: one had to see *through* it with purified vision because spiritual truth was hidden behind the veil of sensory appearances. The world mirrored that which transcended the world.

---

[1]Alfred Lord Tennyson, "Ulysses."

[2]See Hugh Richmond, "Personal Identity and Literary Personae: A Study in Historical Psychology," *PMLA* 20 (March 1975): 209-21.

Nowhere is the tension between private and public identity more clear than in the twelfth-century story of Perceval. And nowhere is the epistemology of recognition more affected by the intersection of sense and spirit. Perceval "knows again" the Christ his mother had once described to him, but only his second knowing urges him to respond to what he is told. Only after his encounter with a mystery beyond worldly experience, beyond simple instruction, was he prepared to know "JesuChrist" and to recognize his own story and the mystery of his own identity in the story of the god who died. He had tried to create his own identity by deserting his mother, his past, his childhood in the "Waste Forest." He created a false identity by imitating others, by assuming the gestures and the clothing of others. To be who he is, Perceval must reject the false identity he assumed after his repudiation of his mother. He must die to the false self, reappropriate his true self, and affirm that self by public (sacramental) repentance. His "return" is both character change and public conversion.

Such character development was new to imaginative literature. It corresponds to the change in the understanding of consciousness in the late Middle Ages and contrasts with the theory of consciousness that had shaped earlier literature. Revelation in the story of Perceval is not information alone, nor evidence, finally, but transcendent reality *showing through* material or sensible reality, piercing the exterior consciousness and transforming the inner self. The story of the conversion of Perceval, as Chrétien de Troyes tells it, is a pivotal example of the religious issues of the twelfth century. Knowledge was veiled, and the one who would see had to be purified by contrition (Abelard) and by love (Bernard of Clairvaux).[3] One who would find God had to seek, and the quest became the literary model of the Christian journey.

Part of the sense of quest in medieval literature derives from the story-teller's control of time. He begins, much more often than do the Greek writers, at the beginning rather than in medias res. One story may interrupt and suspend another, but we are rarely so dependent on the past that the sequence of events is incomprehensible without a revelatory disclosure or exposition of previous events. Because of this structure, we are prepared for something new to happen. The word "adventure" itself, from *adventurus* in Latin, means "that which is to happen."

---

[3]M.-D. Chenu, *Nature, Man, and Society in the Twelfth Century: Essays on New Theological Perspectives in the Latin West,* ed. and trans. Jerome Taylor and Lester K. Little (Chicago: University of Chicago Press, 1968). See esp. 99-145.

The beginning of adventure in Western literature tells us something about the people who longed to hear stories of the unexpected. It suggests a particular way of looking at reality and time and noting how time affects us. If Greek character did not change fundamentally but could only respond to what time disclosed (and what time disclosed was somehow always there—in the past, which could become the present truth), character in Western nondramatic literature began in the twelfth century to have new possibilities. One of these was change. This development happened for several reasons: first, Western literature was shaped much more by the concept of linear time, of passage into a new world, than was possible in the Greek view of time. If new events could occur in the future, the unexpected lay in the future rather than in a discovery of a secret past.

In addition, the twelfth century discovered the biblical concept of interior conversion. Time did not just affect simply the course of events, but could demand a new kind of response. One need not be simply buffeted and broken by reality; one could re-create it by seeing it in a new way. The Hebrew God had said that even the pain of the past could be mitigated. He could himself choose to remember or to forget. He had power over both the future and the past. In such a world one is not merely a victim struggling—however heroically or nobly— to deal with a reality one could not affect and could perceive only by assuming heroic risks. With a linear view of time, with the realization that there is such a thing as "salvation history"—the coming together of person and event so that the occasion is unique—each moment is weighted with possibility. There is kairos as well as chronos. To move from cyclical time to linear time is to reshape the structure and the perception of reality.

Western imaginative nondramatic literature begins slowly. It is centuries away from its Greek and Roman antecedents as well as its religious and mythical origins. But when in the twelfth century Chrétien de Troyes's Perceval emerges from the Waste Forest, his own particular wilderness, an audience was ready to understand that a man or woman could begin life in ignorance, learn, develop, succeed, fail, and change.

The troubadours had taught readers about adventure and love. Scripture and St. Augustine had taught them about interior conversion. This was an audience developing new sacramental ways of dealing with personal sin, of understanding what constituted sin and its degrees. The sacramental system itself had been part of and partly causative of a growing sense of symbol, a sense that "all natural or historical reality possessed a signification which transcended its crude reality and which a certain symbolic dimension of that reality would reveal to man's mind."[4] Colors, numbers, names, the elements of the universe were all bearers of hidden meaning, and perception of that meaning was a question of discerning the secret connection between an invisible mystery and a visible, tactile, even gustatory reality. An audience sensitive to time, to interiority, to symbol, learning to delight in the unpredicted, could respond to Chrétien's imagination and this Perceval, whose character was not fixed at the beginning of the story but rather discovered only gradually.

• Perceval: The Youth[5] •

Chrétien's Perceval, distinct from subsequent versions of the character, begins in the Waste Forest at a time when, as the storyteller says, "meadows turn green and birds sing sweetly in Latin." The hero is described merely as "the son of the widow." His one skill is hurling javelins. His name is not revealed. When five knights appear in the forest, the young man is incapable of interpreting who and what they are. The noise their hauberks make leads him to think they are devils, but soon enough he decides that they are angels and that at least one of them is God—a hint of subsequent ambiguities. The young man's questions are ceaseless: "Are you God?" "What is this you hold?" "What is this you are wearing?" And finally, "Tell me of the King who makes Knights."[6]

When Perceval becomes fascinated with weapons and clothing and the means to acquire them, his adventures begin. Despite his mother's resistance, he decides to become what he suddenly began to worship. After receiving brief instructions from his mother about his behavior towards women and his obligations to pray, he sets out across the bridge to the outside world. Behind him, his mother collapses in death, but Perceval, looking back, interprets her fall as a swoon. Pressing his horse to continue, he sleeps that night in the forest, away from everything he has known and already confused about reality.

His subsequent adventures suggest that Perceval is crudely obedient to his mother's final instructions, but stupidly incapable of interpreting

---

[4]Ibid., 102.

[5]Because Chrétien de Troyes's story of Perceval in the twelfth-century *Li Contes del Graal* is not easily accessible, a summary of the story is included in this analysis.

[6]Chrétien de Troyes, *The Story of the Grail*, trans. Robert White Linker (Chapel Hill: University of North Carolina Press, 1960) 5. All citations in the analysis of the Perceval story are from this translation. The old French text is that edited by Alfons Helku (*Li Contes del Graal*).

what he sees or of accomplishing anything with finesse. After relating a series of his gaucheries, the narrator observes mildly: "It is a very heavy thing to teach a fool" (28). This unexpected voice of the narrator draws the audience into a tutorial relationship to Perceval. He is, indeed, a foolish youth. When is he going to learn? More especially, when is he going to learn what the storyteller and his hearers together understand to be common sense? The narrator clearly distances himself from Perceval and allies himself with the audience, now made to feel superior to the hero of the tale.[7]

But Perceval does begin to learn as Gornemant de Goort, whom he meets in his travels and perceives as a wise man, teaches him how to handle his weapon and cautions him not to be too talkative. Gornemant further urges him to pray. Perceval finally consents to give up the rough garments made by his mother and to dress completely as a knight. The adoption of a new identity begins.

• Perceval: The Knight •

Perceval later proves the value of his education by rescuing Blancheflor and her castle of Belrepaire from the siege of a certain Clamadeu. But Perceval refuses to stay at the castle, arguing that he must return to the Waste Forest to find his mother. He seems not to know the way back, however, and in his wanderings reaches a river that he cannot cross. The next adventure is crucial. The young knight, unable to ford the river, calls to two men whom he sees fishing from a small boat. One of them offers hospitality in a house to which Perceval is directed. Initially, when Perceval travels to the top of the hill, he cannot see the castle, but then the top of a tower appears and the features of a beautiful castle become visible.

The existence of the castle is problematic since it appears in a valley where, we are told later, there is no dwelling at all. Perceval's experience lies somewhere between vision and reality, and the narrator makes no effort to distinguish between the two.[8] Entering the castle, Perceval is received graciously as new clothing is offered and food brought. His host, who cannot walk, is a textual surrogate of Perceval's own father, who had been wounded in the legs and had to be carried in a litter.

---

[7]*Li Contes del Graal* was written to be read to an audience gathered for a social occasion. This audience is implicitly, and sometimes explicitly, invoked throughout the story.

[8]Edwin Williamson, *The Half-Way House of Fiction: Don Quixote and Arthurian Romance* (Oxford: Clarendon, 1984) 6.

But Perceval, despite his education and his acquired prowess, is still capable of bad judgment. Just as he had once refused earlier to relinquish the clothing his mother made for him and had foolishly interpreted some of her instructions, he now obeys blindly the knightly instructions Gornemant had given him. In the midst of an extraordinary scene, which should have evoked his questions about its meaning, Perceval remained stubbornly silent, governing his curiosity and intending to inquire privately the meaning of the bizarre event that occurs. The elements of the scene are mysterious enough: A youth holding a white lance, from the top of which a drop of blood issues, leads a procession. He is followed by two other young men carrying candelabra and a young girl carrying between her hands a grail, so radiant with light that the light from the candles seemed dim by comparison. At the end of the procession is another young girl holding a small silver platter of silver. As Perceval eats and drinks, the procession passes before him several times. The grail, a large and presumably slightly concave vessel, is uncovered. Perceval does not inquire who else is being served nor why the lance is bleeding. On the following morning he finds the door to the great hall locked, his horse saddled, and the drawbridge down. As Perceval leaves, the drawbridge is raised abruptly behind him and no one answers his calls: "Where are you that I do not see you? Come forward and I shall see you and I shall ask you news of one thing that I should like to know." Then, says the narrator, "he talks foolishly, for no one wishes to answer him" (73).

The narrator now distances himself from those who hear the story. There is an element of superiority in this distancing, a hint of mysterious and secret knowledge that is not to be shared. The audience, too, wants to call to the closed door: "Where are you that I do not see you? There are things I want to know." But no explanation is offered, and Perceval's quest becomes the quest of those who initially regarded him as foolish.

After the events in the Grail Castle, Perceval does not hesitate to make necessary inquiries. Just outside the castle, he meets a woman weeping over the body of a slain knight. She identifies the visionary castle as that of the Fisher King, who had been wounded with a javelin through both his hips (the French of the passage clearly suggests genitals). After a probing interrogation, the woman rebukes Perceval mightily for not inquiring the meaning of the mysterious Grail procession. She declares that the king would have been cured of his affliction and would "hold his land" had Perceval asked about the procession. She adds that great trouble will ensue and that his failure was caused by sin against his mother, who had died of grief when he departed from the Waste Forest. Her final prediction is that the sword given Perceval by the Fisher King will betray him in battle. It will "fly into pieces."

In this segment of the story, a second event is related that parallels to a lesser degree the mystery of the Grail Castle. The scene is a snow-covered meadow. Perceval is described as rising early because "he wished to seek and encounter adventure and chivalry." A falcon had wounded a goose in flight, but the fallen bird had been able to fly away, leaving three drops of blood in the snow. Perceval, looking down at the red color on the snow, is reminded of the face of Blancheflor, the maiden whom he had formerly assisted (and abandoned), "for the vermilion seated on the white was on her face just the same as these three drops of blood on the white snow" (89). The memory evoked by the drops pleased Perceval so much that he mused and "used up the whole dawn at it." The squires from Arthur's court see him and believe that a strange knight is sleeping on his charger. Two knights, Sagremor and Keu, approach Perceval in turn, demanding that he come to the court. When Perceval does not answer, he is attacked and recovers enough from his trance to defeat each knight successively, breaking Keu's collarbone in the process. By this action Perceval avenged himself, for Keu had struck the laughing young woman in Arthur's castle who had once predicted Perceval's renown.

Finally, Gawain approaches Perceval courteously, just as the last drop of blood is melting from the snow and Perceval is recovering from his trance. After introductions—Perceval is sure of himself by now and declares his name with certainty—they greet each other with affection and together return to Arthur's court near the meadow. Everyone then returns to Carlion for a celebration in honor of Perceval. From the standpoint of chivalric ambition, Perceval has nothing else to achieve.

But on the third day of festivities, a hideous-looking woman arrived. Singling out Perceval, she rebukes him violently for his failure at the Grail Castle to ask the appropriate questions and to release the Fisher King from his infirmities. "He is very fortunate who sees such beautiful times that none is better fitting, and still waits for fairer to come." She declares further that because of Perceval's decision to remain silent, "Ladies will lose their husband . . . lands will be ravaged . . . and maidens disconsolate, who will remain orphans, and many knights will die for it" (99).

Then to the king she describes a "Chastel Orguelleus" where 566 "knights of renown" live and where anyone can find jousting or battle or chivalry. And, if anyone wants "the esteem of the whole world," there is a besieged damsel available also. Then the hideous woman departs. Immediately, Gawain leaps up with a vow to rescue the damsel. Other knights say that they are determined to go to the castle. Perceval, however, stung by the words addressed to him, vows that he will undertake no other work until he knows of the Grail and who is served with it, until he has found the lance that bleeds and the truth of why it bleeds. Then fifty knights leave, seeking marvels and adventures in "however felonious land it may be."

The storyteller interrupts the story of Perceval at this point to relate the adventures of Gawain, whose honor has been challenged by a fellow knight, Guinganbresil. Lines 4747 to 6216 in the original poem are devoted to Gawain without mention of Perceval. The interlude occupies five years. At line 6217 the story of Perceval resumes. The narrator omits everything that happened to Perceval in the interim between the hideous woman's declaration, Perceval's determination to seek the Grail and the bleeding lance, and the concluding episode of the story. We know only that the Grail and the lance have presumably disappeared into another world, that they are not to be found by any means known to the Arthurian court or to Perceval himself, whose initial determination became transformed into oblivion and despair. In the final Perceval segment, the story is interrupted again with a hint from the narrator of more to come, but not before we hear of Gawain. The remaining segments of the poem concern Gawain only (11.6519–7223).[9]

However incautious it may seem to reach conclusions about the meaning of an unfinished work, any analysis of the Perceval story here is not without precedents. Critical attention has been directed primarily to the Grail procession and its possible symbolic meaning, as well as to the scene with the hideous woman. Here we are concerned about the vision in terms of its function of initiating interior change in Perceval. What kind of revelation accomplished that change?

The most common, although not unchallenged, interpretation of the mysterious bleeding lance in the procession is that it represents the lance of

---

[9]Arguing for the unity of the Perceval-Gawain segments, which I do not dispute, Norris Lacy describes the "dismantling" of the Arthurian chivalric world that shapes the Gawain sequence and functions as a commentary on the Perceval events. See Norris Lacy, "Gawain and the Crisis of Chivalry in the *Contes del Graal*," in *The Sower and His Seed*, ed. Rupert T. Pickens (Lexington KY: French Forum, 1983) 155-64. See also Friedrich Heer, *The Medieval World*, tr. Janet Sondheimer (New York: New American Library, 1961):

> Integration, the ripening of the whole personality, entails the obligation of bringing to equal maturity both poles of a man's nature, the masculine and the feminine. In the romance, Perceval's quest for the Grail thus runs parallel with Gauvain's for the Lance. Gauvain had slain the father of a strange knight, Perceval was bound to expiate the death of his mother. Perceval and Gauvain are mirror images, figures of a single individual reaching his maturity as a human being. (184)

Longinus, and that the drop of blood represents the blood of Christ, paralleling the host or the body that nourished the invisible king in the adjoining chamber. The twelfth century was not without numerous representations of this kind of symbol. The Church was frequently represented by a woman holding a chalice—sometimes even holding it to the side of Christ and receiving the blood of the Crucified. This imagery can be seen, for example, in the Cathedral of Bourges, in one of the stained glass windows, and similarly at Sens, Strasbourg, and Worms.[10] In some of these representations, Longinus is present, piercing the side of Christ and making the wound from which blood flows into the chalice. M. Roques notes the twelfth-century manuscript *Hortus deliciarum*, illustrated by the Abbess Herrode of Landsberg, which includes just such a picture.[11]

He interprets the Grail procession and Perceval's lack of response to it as related to ignorance of Christian dogma in Britain and the need to instruct the Britons of the full implications of Redemption and the New Covenant. It is a revelation that Perceval could bring back to his own world, but does not.[12]

---

[10]M. Roques, "Le Graal de Chrétien et la demoiselle au graal," *Romania* 76 (1955): 1-27.

[11]Ibid., 19:

Thus we could represent to ourselves the Grail procession as a tableau animated, endowed with movement, of the motionless symbols of the Crucifixion, not just a spectacle but rather a demonstration ready to be expressed and developed if the desire to know is born in the spectator. If he simply asks for whom is this service, he will learn that it is a gift to all from God who has died on the Cross, a gift that the Church distributes and administers in fact to all, and which protects them from the snares of the Evil One, from the ills of earth, and from worse ills of the next world, if, at least they have the wisdom to see, the will to know, and the strength to believe [my translation].

[12]See also R. S. Loomis, *The Grail from Celtic Myth to Christian Symbol* (Cardiff, 1963), and *Arthurian Tradition and Chrétien de Troyes* (New York: Columbia University Press, 1949). Loomis considers any religious interpretation of the procession of the Grail unconvincing. Tracing the elements of the scene to Celtic folklore, he identifies the immediate prototype of the Fisher King as "Bran the Blessed," a primitive mythical figure who became king of Britain. The Christian element, according to Loomis, is a blunder caused in part by a mistranslation of the word *cors*, which in Old French (nominative) meant both "horn" and "body." It is difficult to reconcile Loomis's deprecation of the Christian significance of the Grail procession with subsequent Christian elements in the story, such as Perceval's repentance on Good Friday and his reception of the Sacrament on Easter Sunday. There

The lance is clearly associated with blood imagery, which pervades the story of Perceval from the first moment when he kills the red knight and seizes his vermilion armor, to the blood drops on the snow that suggest both violence (the attack of the falcon) and love (Perceval's association of the color with the complexion of Blancheflor). The bleeding lance has similar multiple associations: violence (the crucifixion and piercing of Christ's side), love (the significance of the Blood of Christ for salvation). Perceval's life of chivalry began with the shedding of blood and is characterized by the color of blood. Perceval had become known as the knight with vermilion arms. (The lance's further significance is hinted at in the Gawain fragment when it is predicted that the lance will one day destroy the kingdom of Logres—the Arthurian world.) Perceval must transcend the world of violence and identify himself with love and spiritual life.

The Grail procession and Perceval's response is a turning point in the story of Perceval's conversion. His development had begun with the series of impetuous questions directed to the knights he met in the Waste Forest. His eagerness to know was not a search for wisdom and truth but rather a show of curiosity and ambition. He had begun his life of chivalry with an act of violence: hurling a javelin through the eye of a hostile knight. Only after this incident had he received instruction from Gornemant de Goort in the rules of chivalry. He had made rapid progress, abandoning his cruder speech and blatantly aggressive manner. Success had followed success until the incident at the Grail Castle. Perceval had been knighted and loved, but at the crucial moment he could not respond to the mystery before him. The narrator suggests that something about this experience deepened Perceval's self-understanding, for only afterward could he tentatively identify himself. "He who did not know his name, guesses and says that he had Perceval the Welsh for name, but he does not know if he speaks true or not; but he spoke

---

is no question that Chrétien's story derives in part from Celtic legend, but what has happened is that Celtic legend has been fused with Christian tradition. Even the Byzantine Mass would help to explain the Grail procession. The Introit of the Greek medieval Mass, which influenced the gallican rite, consisted of a similar procession in which a small knife was once carried to represent the lance of Longinus.

For a comment on Loomis, see William A. Nitze, "The Fisher King and the Grail in Retrospect," *Romance Philology* 6-7 (1952–1954): 14-22. There are eight schools of interpretation of the Perceval test. See J. Frappier, "Le Graal et ses feux divergeants," *Romance Philology* 24 (1971): 373-440; and Harry F. Williams, "Interpretations of the *Contes del Graal* and Their Critical Reactions," in Pickens, *The Sower*, 155-64.

true and did not know it" (76). Whatever the mystery, the Grail Castle revealed Perceval to himself—darkly. Failure to comprehend a new experience was succeeded by growth in self-knowledge.

The bleeding lance and the luminous grail sustain several themes in the narrative: violence, love, revelation, the division between spirit and flesh. The Grail Castle is the intersection between two worlds, a moment in time rather than space, a dark revelation, and a call to save. Although the question that Perceval never asked constituted an unspelling and is a familiar theme in Celtic legend, Chrétien's treatment of this theme is not based entirely on its appeal to the preternatural. We have a clear sense of moral failure in Perceval when he is rebuked by the weeping maiden and subsequently by the hideous woman in Arthur's court. By trusting completely in the rules of chivalry and the weapons of violence, he had not been attentive enough to possibility. He had missed both Fortune and Providence. When the hideous woman darkened his sense of achievement by her violent accusation of his failure, the memory of his guilt isolated him from his sense of triumph and from the other knights; it further divided him from himself. This moment is worth reexamination.

On the third day of the Arthurian celebration, the hideous woman had burst into the proceedings as a morose and disastrous presence. She has been identified variously as the woman who carried the Grail and the weeping woman outside the castle, but this transmogrification seems unlikely. She may know the Grail mysteries, but she declares Perceval's failure to be irrevocable. "If you asked it, the rich king who is much dismayed, would have been wholly cured of his wound, and could hold his land in peace which he will never have more. . . . All these evils will come about because of you" (98). Her speech was calculated both to bring Perceval to despair and to disrupt the court. But Perceval's destiny had been curiously foreshadowed by the incident of the defective sword, which the weeping woman had warned him about.

"Now tell me if you know," Perceval had replied then (just after leaving the Grail Castle), "if it came about that it should be broken whether it would ever be remade?" (78). "Yes" had been the answer of the weeping woman, "but there would be great difficulty." She had then instructed Perceval that only Trebuchet, the smith who made the sword, could remake it (78). Perceval was not to abandon the sword as completely useless. It could, after all, be remade. The image of the sword is thus important as the promise of Perceval's own regeneration; and the hideous woman clearly represents the figure of Despair, Perceval's most serious temptation. Both figures—the weeping woman, whose tears and grief and promise of regeneration suggest repentance and mercy—and the hideous woman, who evokes Arthurian ambition and spiritual despair—are aspects of Perceval's own soul, the signs of his own inner division.

At Carlion, Perceval's response to the hideous woman's announcement of possible renown, joustings, and battles distinguished him from Gawain especially but also from the rest of the court. After everyone leapt to the opportunity to seek fame, Perceval said "quite differently" that

> never will he hear news of strange passage without going there to pass, nor of knight who is worth more than any other knight or more than two, without going to combat him, until he knows of the grail whom they serve with it, and until he has found the lance which bleeds, and until the proven truth is told him why it bleeds; never will he leave it for any pain. (99)

And so began the quest of the Grail—a different motive for a knight's life than what Perceval had experienced until then. The other members of the court were remarkably indifferent to the existence of the lance and the Grail. Their motivations were quite different, and Chrétien here distinguishes Perceval from all of them. His search for another identity was initiated. As the others depart, the narrator leaves us with the tormented Perceval, whose determination was fierce enough to suggest that he would succeed in his quest.

But Perceval found neither Grail nor lance, and, plunging yet deeper into a violent life, forgot what he had started out to discover. Five years elapsed between the hideous woman's declaration and Perceval's conversion to another way of life. The knight is described as having "lost his memory." Earlier in the text, it was memory that had impelled him: the memory of his mother's instructions, of Gornemant de Goort's admonitions, of Keu's insults. It was memory that led him from adventure to adventure.

One of the most lyrical moments in the poem is the memory evoked of Blancheflor by the three drops of blood in the snow, a recollection so tender that Perceval— remembering the love of a woman and forgetting warfare—had lapsed into a trance. Only the assaults of various knights had interrupted his dreaming. Perceval in that scene was on the threshold of two kinds of consciousness: inner memories of love and tenderness, outer defenses against attack. As the memories faded in the sunlight, Perceval went with Gawain. When five years had passed and he had forgotten everything but the habit of battle, only the exterior consciousness, imaged by his alliance with Gawain, had remained. The love of a woman, usually the chivalric antidote to the violence of the twelfth century, was not sustained and was inadequate, in any case, to lead Perceval to his destiny.

• Perceval: The Penitent •

In the concluding segment, the young knight has so lost his memory that he no longer remembers God. We are told "that he has entered no church or adored God or his Cross, that he had spent his time seeking chivalry and strange adventures, especially the felonious and harsh ones" (129). He had sent sixty knights to King Arthur as prisoners and was now making his way through a wilderness. It was at this moment that he met the three knights and ten ladies doing penance, who expressed their shock at seeing Perceval armed "on the day JesuChrist died." Perceval inquired, "What day is it then today?" (130). Time (especially sacred time), interiority, God—all have been lost.

The response of the penitents to Perceval's question is a twelfth-century credo, a more specific explanation of Christianity than the vague instructions his mother had once given to pray in churches and in minsters. It includes—besides some anti-Semitism—a resumé of Incarnation, Passion, Crucifixion, Burial, and Resurrection; it is a narrative. When as a child Perceval had asked what a church was, his mother's reply was a fragmented catechism. The church was "a holy house" of "holy bodies and treasures." The body of Jesus Christ had been sacrificed, "the holy prophet, to whom the Jews did many a shame."[13] Besides the unconventional reference to Jesus as "a holy prophet," the instruction had omitted any reference to the future and to the Resurrection. It was a credo about death.

What the penitents offer Perceval is much more complete, and it follows another challenge to Perceval's self-understanding. Upon hearing the account of the death of Christ, Perceval begins to weep. Without much narrative assistance, we are left to interpret what kind of awareness caused Perceval's tears. His subsequent confession to a hermit suggests that Perceval recognizes in the story of the Passion and death of Christ his own destructive past. "It is five years since I knew where I was, nor did I love God nor did I do anything except evil" (131).

The account of the Christ story, the Word as narrative, penetrated his oblivion, stirred him to awareness of his deeds, of his responsibility for them and thus of his own need for mercy. He removed his armor at the

---

[13]For a discussion of the Jewish religious element in the text, see Urban T. Holmes, "A New Interpretation of Chrétien's *Contes del Graal*," *University of North Carolina Studies in Romance Languages and Literature* 8 (Chapel Hill, 1948); Sister M. Amelia Klenke, "Chrétien's Symbolism and Cathedral Art," *PMLA* 70 (1955): 223-43; and Urban T. Holmes and Sister M. Amelia Klenke, *Chrétien, Troyes, and the Grail* (Chapel Hill: University of North Carolina Press, 1959).

entrance to the hermit's cave—the armor that had symbolized the adoption of a whole set of values—descended from his horse, and began his confession. The hermit, upon hearing Perceval's name, declares himself his uncle, brother to Perceval's mother, and says not only that Perceval's mother died from grief, but that Perceval's sin in leaving her had accounted for his failure at the Grail Castle. Only his mother's prayers had saved him from prison and death.

The king who previously is served with the Grail is the hermit's brother, Perceval's other uncle.[14] The old king in the adjacent room survived only with a single host, which was carried to him in the Grail. He has so survived for fifteen years.[15]

Upon completing this explanation, the hermit urged Perceval to a prayerful life, repentance, penitence. Perceval agreed to persevere in the good works assigned to him and to recite a mysterious prayer containing the "names of the Lord" whenever he was in peril. "Thus," concludes the extant Perceval segment of *Li Contes del Graal*, "Perceval recognized that God on Friday received death and was crucified; at Easter Perceval received communion very worthily" (134). It is assumed that the audience invoked by the storyteller approves.

Even if we consider just the Perceval section of *Li Contes del Graal*, it is clear that Chrétien intends Perceval to achieve a degree of acculturation outside the crude innocence and naïveté of the Waste Forest. This acculturation, however, brings with it its own corruption, which Perceval must transcend as he renounces the identity he had achieved in the Arthurian world. He does so by awareness of his inadequacy—pointed out repeatedly by others—by an experience of despair, and finally by a knowledge of the god who died. First it was his own god who died, "the king who made knights." Then it was the god symbolized by the bleeding lance and

---

[14]William Nitze comments that the motif of the sister's son was used widely, and that in Chrétien, the plot of the story turns on it. "Perceval was the sister's son of the Fisher King and . . . his success with his maternal uncle was impaired by his failure to his mother. He himself is so conscious of the wrong he has committed that, as he approaches the Grail Castle, it is uppermost in his mind. He has infringed a (Celtic) tribal taboo for which he must atone" ("The Fisher King and the Grail," 19).

[15]Regarding the possible economic implications of this spiritual good (plenty) symbolized by the host and by the Grail, see especially Marc Shell, "The Blank Check: Accounting for the Grail," *Stanford French Review* 7 (1983): 5-25. The grail, argues Shell, "is a free and infinitely large gift, a blank check, which solves or resolves the quest and the question of the wasteland" (25).

the host. That god could not be found as long as Perceval remained in his armor and lived by violence. The momentum of Perceval's adventures had been interrupted when he encountered at the Grail Castle a world whose values were in inverse proportion to the way of life Perceval had adopted to define himself. But only in the encounter with that world could he begin to name who he was, could his self-knowledge begin. But it was not enough to know his own name, which had been hard enough to discover. He had to name the real source of his life; only that name could save him.

If Perceval recognized that "god" died on Good Friday, the audience recognizes the problem of finding out who god is and the consequences of selecting the wrong world in which to find him. The quest, wrongly conceived, leads out of the Waste Forest but into wilderness and oblivion. To misconceive the past and to reject one's origins is to be ignorant of the source of life and to lose one's identity. Perceval could not enter the future until that identity was recovered.

In *Li Contes del Graal* the romance structure has faltered, partly because it was not adequate to deal with the religious concept of *metanoia*, of a quest beyond the quest for fame, or of a protagonist morally corrupted by his own success. But the artistic concept of character is deepened as identity becomes shaped by the encounter with mystery. Perceval's perception changes only as he discovers that worlds intersect and gods die. And as his perception changes, so does his character. The penitent Perceval recovering from oblivion in the hermit's cave is not the foolish, insensitive youth of the Waste Forest. The story of Perceval is adventure only insofar as that which was to come was less the advent of fortune than the evolution of identity. Not inappropriately has this adventure been considered the beginning of the modern novel.

Per Nykrog speaks of Chrétien de Troyes and his contemporary, Gautier d'Arras, as creators of narrative form, an interpretation based on their introduction of cultural and psychological realism: "Both twelfth-century authors create heroes who are projected into events that form their history . . . by an *interior* conflict that opposes them to *themselves* or to their implicit image of themselves."[16]

The heroes of Gautier's and Chrétien's narratives become aware of personal deficiency or sin. They are not what they had once projected themselves to be, and they fail because of the deficiencies of their own will.

---

[16]Per Nykrog, "Two Creators of Narrative Form in Twelfth-Century France: Gautier d'Arras—Chrétien de Troyes," *Speculum* 48 (1973): 258-76, at 266.

"Perceval," argues Nykrog, "has committed no sin against God, only against his fellow man or against his own deeper self."[17] Self-knowledge, in earlier literature, usually followed the discovery of information, of the truth of events—especially events of the past. Conflict was a debate between impulse and reason (as when Medea considers whether she will kill her children). In Perceval, we see conflict as the tension between self-projection and a realization of moral failure. The preoccupation with this kind of interior conflict was not sustained during the Middle Ages, but it was recovered and developed in the Renaissance. Nykrog notes that Chrétien is actually closer to Stendhal and Tolstoy than to his own contemporaries.

If Perceval falls short of his own self-image, if he fails himself, as well as his God, we see in Chrétien's text the beginning both of a new concept of the self and an awareness of a new connection between self-consciousness and recognition. The god one believes in can be a god projected by an inauthentic self. For worship to be at least minimally authentic, that self-projected god must die again and again, as personal consciousness must change again and again. Perceval begins to change when his self-conception is challenged by the mystery of another world and by the perception of others about him. His self-awareness is altered. His conversion occurs when he finally becomes aware of the "god who died" on Good Friday. Perceval the knight dies on the same day.

Perceval's inner psychology is suggested only in objectified symbols—the hideous woman, the weeping woman, the drops of blood in the snow. Events occur but seem less the consequences of the characters' motivations than the narrator's invention. Relationships between discrete events in the story are tenuous. What is important is the connection between events and their suprahistorical significance. The narrator is to the story as God was perceived to be to the twelfth-century world, Chrétien's world. God is above and events are symbolic of what is not visible. The story of Perceval and Gawain, like the story of the world, contains its own secret meaning, its own luminous symbols to which one must attend. The story of "JesuChrist" is dropped into Chrétien's story from a world outside of it, a world shared by storyteller and audience. But only by means of that story can the audience comprehend Perceval's abandonment of his knightly career and begin to comprehend the mystery of the Grail Castle. The interplay of these two stories sustains what Edwin Williamson has called "the continual interplay between the visible and invisible, external events and hidden meanings, appearances and es-

---

[17]Ibid.

sences that betrays the pervasive . . . determining influence of medieval Platonism on Chrétien's romances."[18]

In that Platonic world, to live was to journey through events; to live successfully was to "pierce the veil" and to be changed by them. "There can no longer be any doubt," observes Friedrich Heer in his history of twelfth-century Europe, "that the theme of the great romantic epics . . . is initiation, dedication, metamorphosis, and absorption into a higher and fuller life, at once more human and more divine."[19] Li Contes del Graal traces that interior development and does so more effectively than the didactic manuals of pedagogy and morals current in the same period. "This is the literature of wisdom," adds Heer, because "danger, temptation, error, sinning, lack of purpose and lack of achievement are all necessary if the inner core of a man's personality is to be truly and effectively unlocked, moulded and ennobled."[20] The poetics of revelation in the romances of Chrétien de Troyes clearly signaled a new adventure in the quest for a religious meaning.

---

[18]Williamson, Half-Way House of Fiction, 11.

[19]Heer, Medieval World, 181.

[20]Ibid., 182.

DON QUIXOTE: THE WORD FROM BELOW

The relationship of the human being to his own corporeality, to the wider sphere of nature and his own ecological environment, is constitutive of our humanity. So human salvation is concerned with this.

—Edward Schillebeeckx, Christ:
The Experience of Jesus as Lord

The twelfth-century Perceval and the seventeenth-century Don Quixote represent two versions of the quest motif. In both stories the central character seeks fame and glory, and in both, the protagonist experiences a radical change of heart, with a corresponding realization of identity. Perceval and Don Quixote discover eventually that valor, for the sake of being proclaimed valorous, is a sterile ambition; both are led to the realization of identity (salvation) only after passing through a period of inner division. Don Quixote and Perceval end their knightly careers in a profoundly religious experience of lucidity. Perceval had to experience a world beyond both his comprehension and his self-understanding and then enter into a death that the narrator describes simply as oblivion. Cervantes narrates Don Quixote's orphic experience (the Cave of Montesinos) more explicitly, and that analysis is important to the understanding of how Don Quixote is saved.

The primary distinction in narrative technique between the two texts is crucial. The story of Perceval is not rooted in history. Its geography is outside any recognizable time and place, and the "story"—however exemplary or symbolic, never touches down. Perceval, unlike Don Quixote, never has to relieve himself. That distinction—between an ideal world and a world with measurable dimensions of time and space, which make claims upon the body—brings us out of the popular literature of chivalric romance and into modern narrative. The clash (and the blend) of these two worlds shapes the tension of *Don Quixote* and becomes, at the same time, an expression of Cervantes's theology of revelation.

In Cervantes's novel what Don Quixote realizes and what the reader recognizes are not the same. His moment of lucidity climaxes a long process of self-doubt about his imitated identity and restores him to an acceptance of the finitude of history, something that he had initially rejected. He returns to being Alonso Quixano, but in his death he has reached a sense of limitation as well as a corresponding sense of his identity that is surer, and—if the word can be permitted here—a holier state than that in which his story begins. Cervantes surrounds his hero's death with the props of religion, and there is no reason not to accept the description of these at face value. Alonso Quixano the Good is a wiser man than Don Quixote ever was and a still-wiser man than the obscure hidalgo who once sallied forth from "a village in La Mancha" with a makeshift visor and an old horse. What the reader recognizes, especially when *Don Quixote* is contrasted with the chivalric romances Cervantes intended to satirize, is the necessity of blending the ideal with the real, the timeless with time if narrative is to be art. Cervantes knew that narrative had to be something more than chronicle or fact and something other than escape. Like all art, it required the transformation of reality. The word must become flesh and the flesh word. Recognition for the reader of *Don Quixote* is awareness of the claims of reality upon the ideal and of the poverty of both word and flesh when they are separated from each other. As Americo Castro has reminded us:

> Such a new conception of life expressed in art led to the liberation of fiction . . . from the narrowness in which it had lain fettered since antiquity. Before Cervantes it had not been possible organically to harmonize the expression of the imaginary or fictitious and the concrete, contemporary experience of the character or author, without falling into moralizations or grotesque farce. The unreal time of the narration and the contemporary time of the writer were irreconcilable.[1]

What Americo Castro calls Cervantes's "new manner of fictional creation" is the reconciliation in narrative of unreal time (and place and event) with history and the human condition. This necessity of incarnating the ideal and of allowing flesh to modify word is the Cervantine gospel. We see the clash and the blend in him of two perspectives, not only in the very texture of language used to recount the story, but especially in the pervasive theme that evokes the narrative initially: the influence of nar-

---

[1]Americo Castro, "Incarnation in *Don Quixote*," in *Cervantes across the Centuries*, ed. Angel Flores and M. J. Benardete (New York: Dryden, 1947) 138.

rative upon reader and, conversely, the creation of new stories or new word-events through the hearer and reader of the word. "For me alone Don Quixote was born," concludes Cervantes in his final paragraph, "and I for him. We two alone are as one."[2] That line was written to ward off spurious imitations and "further adventures" of Don Quixote, a major concern of Cervantes, for whom a writer was one with his word. But the word itself must pass the test of authenticity.

Therein lies an important theme in *Don Quixote:* the problem of discerning the authentic from the impersonated and of converting from the taste for "false and absurd stories" to the tale of "my *true* Don Quixote." For Cervantes, what is "false" and what is "true" constitutes a theology of revelation. That is not "true" which is not somehow accessible through history, even though history itself is mutable, obscure, limited, deceptive, apparently insignificant. The "false" Don Quixote is an imitation, not of life, but of language.

To the post-Tridentine church, as well as to the medievals, divine revelation was a gift from God, mediated through Scripture and the Church, to which one, assisted by an inner light, could assent. Its content was the things of God and the morality appropriate for one to whom the things of God had been revealed. Because the Protestant Reformation had brought with it a theology of the immediate revelation of the Holy Spirit, Roman Church theologians struggled to demonstrate the sufficiency of mediate revelation. They sought to distinguish clearly between inner illumination and the objective presentation of doctrine.[3] Cervantes was not, after all, a theologian. But he has much to say about the problem of individual perception of the objective, about the difficulty of ascertaining some kind of univocal truth, about the inevitability of disagreement, the need for discretion and charity, the claims of earth and body, the ambiguity of language, and the importance of self-doubt. To Cervantes's sectarian contemporaries, the clash of perspectives was bitter indeed, but to him it was the stuff of life itself. Even in his mad misperceptions, Don Quixote could elicit love and fidelity, and evoke possibility; and out of the clash of perspectives, he could consent finally to who he was.

The tension of *Don Quixote* can be summarized by suggesting that Cervantes is an Aristotelian and Don Quixote a Platonist. For Don Quixote there

---

[2]Miguel de Cervantes Saavedra, *Don Quixote of La Mancha,* trans. Walter Starkie (New York: New American, 1964) 1050. All citations are from this edition; page numbers will be indicated in the text.

[3]See Rene Latourelle, *Theology of Revelation* (Staten Island: Alba House, n.d.) 181ff.

was an ideal world, a Golden Age, form distinct from matter. For the narrator, the realist, there was never a Golden Age. Ideas and ideals cannot be separated from the world in which they emerge. Don Quixote's sorrows derive from his denial of the world of time and space; his salvation, conversely, derives from its recovery. To recover that world, he had to know himself and accept the limitations as well as the possibilities of the self. Out of his disillusionment with a false self, he could begin to see. It is that movement we will trace, because in Cervantes vision and self-knowledge correspond, and imagination is distinct from misperception.

"Our gentleman was about fifty years of age" writes Cervantes (ch. 1, bk. 1). "*They say* that his surname was Quixada or Quesada (for on this point the authors who have written on this subject differ), but we may reasonably conjecture that his name was Quixana" (57). This introduction to the character who becomes Don Quixote (temporarily) tells us something about the difficulty of assigning an initial identity to him. When we contrast it with the deathbed statement, "I was once Don Quixote of La Mancha, but I am now . . . Alonso Quixano the Good," we know that whatever happened to this elusive old bachelor has culminated in some degree of sexual affirmation, as well as self-knowledge. After admitting that his sources are muddled on the real name of his hero, the narrator asserts: "We swerve not a jot from the truth." What follows is a thousand pages of multiple perspectives, multiple authors, stories within stories, illusion, disguise, deception, madness, and a final rejection on the part of the hero of romantic literature itself. The *truth* is that access to truth is a struggle with every form of self-deception and illusion. Both Sophocles and Cervantes understood that struggle. But Cervantes added to his protagonist's dilemma not only the illusions that life normally offers, but the illusions that language offers.

The man of La Mancha, whose first name is not revealed immediately, is discovered abandoning, at fifty, the responsibilities of life to live in a literary fantasy. "He had sold many acres of arable land to purchase books of knight errantry." Already, the narrator hints that the exchange was no bargain. Something that could bring forth life has been sacrificed. What did these texts offer such a gentleman that life did not offer? The answer is new identity, sexual differentiation, fame, triumph in conflict—in short, a heightened sense of significance and relief from obscurity and melancholy. Reality for a middle-aged bachelor in an undistinguished Spanish village could be not merely boring but, to all appearances, valueless. It led only to death and oblivion. The way to escape would be to create the kind of reality that could lead to immortality, fame, significance. How else but to enflesh romance? Romance. The one form of literature that could not yield to incarnation.

At last having lost his wits completely, he stumbled upon the oddest fancy that ever entered a madman's brain. He believed that it was necessary, both for his own honor, and for service of the state, that he should become a knight errant, roaming through the world with his horse and armor in quest of adventures and practicing all that had been performed by the knights-errant of whom he had read. He would follow their life, redressing all manner of wrongs and exposing himself to continual dangers, and at last after concluding his enterprise, *he would win everlasting honor and renown.*" (59)

And so he did. Not because he turned literature back into historical event, but because he responded to literature and created a new event. There was, after all, *never* a knight-errant like Don Quixote. As Señor Quixada (Quesada, Quixana, Quixano), his historical reality was so obscure that even his neighbors could not quite identify him: "Take heed, sir, that I am neither Don Rodrigo de Narvaez nor the Marquess of Mantua, but Pedro Alonso, your neighbor, and you are neither Baldwin or Abindaraez, but the honorable gentleman Master *Quixana*" (82). But reality, however obscure, is reality nonetheless, and it asserts its claims. Señor Quixote, after testing his first homemade visor, found it wanting: "To test its strength and see if it was swordproof, he drew his sword and gave it two strokes, the first of which instantly destroyed the result of a week's labor" (59). After remaking the visor, he passed up the opportunity to test it again.

Thus begins a life of illusion: a refusal to test dream against reality, and so the way is opened to all possible deception. Cervantes's novel becomes a plea not only for the claims of reality, but for literature attached to those claims. Don Quixote rejects oblivion, insignificance (which he equates with oblivion), and time—choosing instead fame (apparent significance) and immortality. The choice and the refusal account for his fury at windmills (among other things), those monsters of seventeenth-century technology. Their existence not only suggests that the age of knights-errant has passed, but that he, Don Quixote, lives in time and thus is subject to change, death, oblivion.

Since the story of Don Quixote is one of the supreme accounts of recognition in world literature, a chronology of the stages of his recognition and repentance will demonstrate how he was "saved" and in what salvation for Cervantes consists.

In the first stage Don Quixote, presumably out of disaffection with the consequences of time and change, elects to stabilize himself in an ideal world of the past and to impose that ideal world upon his historical situation. He adopts an abstract, archaic language that corresponds to his self-concept. Writing in his imagination a story about himself, he begins:

> Scarcely had the rubicund Apollo spread over the face of the vast and spacious earth the golden tresses of his beautiful hair, and scarcely had the little painted birds with their tuneful tongues saluted in sweet and melodious harmony the coming of rosy Aurora, who leaving the soft couch of her jealous husband revealed herself to mortals through the gates and balconies of the Manchegan horizon, when . . . (62-63)

To which the narrator adds, "And all the while he rode slowly on while the sun rose with such intense heat that it would have been enough to dissolve his brains, if he had any left" (63).

This fictive presentation of a man's mind contrasting with actuality is an indication of how close to modernity literature was approaching. This bewildered knight, unaware of his confusion, attempts to subvert actuality by applying to it the language of a sentimental and trivialized ideal world. He is separated from the world not by misinformation, naïveté, or unbelief, but by will: the assertion of a subjective reality, first created in him by the written word. We have a character in literature who sees himself as a character in literature and thus effects such intense subjectivity over against the world that the problematic relationship between literature and reality would be forever identified with him. This imagining of oneself as a character playing a part tells us something about the effects of writing and especially of printing on the development of a sense of individuality and interiority in a literate society.[4] Don Quixote's self-image in book 2 is powerfully reinforced by the effects of stories circulated about him and by the effects even of "spurious" stories. Cervantes seized this opportunity offered by an imitation of book 1 to develop another study in appearances: there is a real Don Quixote and an inauthentic Don Quixote; the inauthentic is as far removed from the "real" as Don Quixote-the-"real" is removed from Alonso the Good. Some imaginative structures are truer than others.

Despite Don Quixote's insistence on his idealized world, the existing, substantial world continues to assert itself. Don Quixote's long artificial discourse about the Golden Age is not so controlled that his own subconscious longings are not perceptible:

> The heavy share of the curved plow had not dared to open and expose the compassionate bowels of our first mother, for she without

---

[4]The relationship between interiority and the written word has been analyzed admirably by Walter Ong, S.J. See especially *Orality and Literacy: The Technologizing of the Word* (New York: Methuen, 1982).

compulsion offered through all the parts of her fertile and spacious bosom whatever could nourish, sustain, and delight the children who possessed her. Then did the innocent and beauteous maidens trip from dale to dale and hill to hill with braided locks or flowing tresses wearing just enough clothing to conceal modestly what modesty seeks and has always sought to hide. (118)

The sexual allusions clearly indicate Don Quixote's own unfulfilled desires, and the entire discourse asserts unrecognized (or at least unadmitted) reality. We are consistently reminded of the disparity between Don Quixote's ideal perspective and these claims. The "healing" balsam in chapter 17, for example, works such a purgative effect, especially on Sancho, that the contrast between illusion and reality becomes the major source of humor in book 1. Nevertheless, the smallest confirmation of Don Quixote's perspective reinforces his subjective vision and begins to set the claims of objective and subjective reality against each other. Feeling himself cured and seeing Sancho in agony, Don Quixote observes dispassionately, "I am sure Don Sancho, that all this trouble has befallen you because you haven't been dubbed a knight, for I am sure that this liquor can only do good to those who are professed" (164).

Mambrino's helmet is the *locus classicus* for this display of tension between reality and perception; and schools of criticism can be identified by their interpretation of this scene. Is a basin used as a hat—a helmet? John J. Allen describes the partisans of the helmet interpretation as the "soft" critics; the basin partisans as the "hard" critics; and the basin-helmet advocates as the perspectivist critics.[5] But Don Quixote's insistence that Mambrino's helmet is a basin used as a head covering is not simply a question of perspective. His interpretation is another example of his insistence on seizing opportunities to warp other people's reality into his own by a kind of epistemological synecdoche.

> "What are you laughing at, Sancho?" said Don Quixote
>
> "I laugh," answered the latter, "to think of the great head the pagan owner of this helmet had; it is for all the world like a barber's basin."
>
> "If you want to know my views," replied Don Quixote, "I say this piece of the enchanted helmet must have fallen by some strange accident into someone's hands who did not know its great worth." (200)

---

[5]John J. Allen, *Don Quixote: Hero or Fool* (Gainesville: University Press of Florida, 1979) 39.

The barber himself asserts a reality distinct from Don Quixote's interpretation, and Cervantes is clearly on the side of the barber, as we see in
chapter 45. When Don Quixote's friends conspire in a plan to humor him
and to agree on the helmet interpretation, the barber cries—and one can
scarcely be unsympathetic—"Is it possible that so many honorable gentle-
men should say this is not a basin but a helmet? Sure, this is enough to strike
a whole university dumb with amazement, no matter how wise it be" (457).
Despite the ensuing tumult—for the barber has a few dispassionate witnesses of his own—Don Quixote's will triumphs over the divided testimony
of others. In this will, more than in his imagination, the basin remained a
helmet until, says the narrator calmly, Judgment Day.

When Don Quixote resists the claims of an agreed-upon reality with his
particular kind of fury, he can become, for all practical purposes, not merely
lunatic—as the Mambrino's helmet episode suggests—but dangerous to the
common good. No insistence on a theory, such as freedom of the will, and
no appeal to Cervantes's own experience can justify Don Quixote's releas-
ing of the chain gang of galley slaves who subsequently go about terrorizing
the countryside (ch. 22). An example of the "soft" or idealizing view of Don
Quixote is Waldo Frank's comment in his essay "The Career of the Hero":

> In such episodes as this, we touch the core of the miracle of Don
> Quixote. His nature is ridiculously funny, and is Christlike. The
> freeing of legally judged robbers, the letting of lions out of cages, is
> farce: and yet illumines a justice above laws whose vision is Christ-
> like and whose enactment brings upon the knight a Christlike fate.
> In laughing at Don Quixote we crucify him. Mockery and buffets cre-
> ate the knight of the Sorrowful Figure: our own roars of glee at his
> well earned mishaps hail the ridiculous Christ.[6]

Cervantes, fortunately, helps us to interpret Don Quixote more accu-
rately by including characters who function as norms against which both the
madness of Don Quixote and the chicanery and silliness of others can be
measured.[7] Such a character is Dorotea in the Cardenio-Dorotea-Luscinda-

---

[6]Waldo Frank, "The Career of the Hero," in *Cervantes across the Centuries*, 183-
94, at 191.

[7]For a full discussion of the "norm" against which we observe Don Quixote,
see Oscar Mandel, "The Function of the Norm in *Don Quixote*," *Modern Philology*
55 (1957–1958): 154-63. The question of the value of interpreting Don Quixote's
departure from the norm is whether or not the fictive norm is depraved as in *Gul-
liver's Travels*. I agree with Mandel that the norm in Don Quixote (which includes
many narrative comments) is less interesting than Don Quixote as character, but
it is Don Quixote, nevertheless, who needs to repent.

Fernando sequence. Cardenio responds to the apparent infidelity of Luscinda and the real infidelity of his friend Fernando by retreating into sentimentally induced lunacy. Dorotea responds to her betrayal by Fernando with an active effort to redress the wrong done to her. In her clear-headed commitment to bring Fernando to a sense of responsibility, she rectifies a whole variety of injustices. Her impostures, moreover, are motivated by prudent self-protection and by compassion. Impersonating a princess, she enters Don Quixote's subjective world for the purpose of restoring him to home and family. Her foil is Luscinda, who can only faint when events thwart her desires. Don Quixote's imitation of Cardenio's love-inspired silliness is madness of another order, since Cardenio's madness, like Luscinda's passivity, derives from psychological weakness. Don Quixote's lunacy results from sheer concentration on his self-assigned role: "That is just the point of it; and that is where the subtleness of my plan comes in. A knight errant who goes mad for a good reason deserves no thanks or gratitude; the whole point consists in going crazy without cause, and thereby warn my lady what to expect from me in the wet if this is what I do in the dry" (242).

It can be argued that imitated madness is sanity, that Don Quixote is a "split" personality whose intentions are noble and whose deeds are foolish, but sanity ungoverned by fidelity to any reality outside the self is scarcely normative, however well intentioned.

Another measure against which we judge Don Quixote is Sancho. It is Sancho Panza who often bears the painful effects of Don Quixote's vision. It is he who experiences the drubbings and hunger and thirst and weariness consequent upon his fidelity: "Master . . . is it a good rule of chivalry that we should be wandering up and down through these mountains after a madman who perhaps, when he is found will take it into his hand to finish what he began—not his story, but the breaking of your head and my rib?" (240). It is he who asserts the claims of flesh. His earthy proverbialism balances Don Quixote's archaic idealism. Proverbs are born out of human experience. Don Quixote's imitative language is disembodied. It is Sancho who knows that Dulcinea is Aldonza Lorenzo, a garlic-reeking farm girl, and Sancho who first experiences the disillusionment consequent upon attachment to his own ambition: "I was not born to be a governor, or to defend islands or cities from enemies who wish to attack them. I know more about plowing, digging, pruning, and planting vines than about making laws or defending cities and kingdoms" (book 2, p. 909).

Dorotea, Sancho, Sancho's wife, Don Quixote's niece, and a whole range of soldiers, monks, innkeepers, and whores give us a perspective against which to see Don Quixote's isolation. What illumines is precisely this pervasive earthy reality of the text, the animals, blood, bones and broken teeth, the sweat and human effluvium that are so much a part of the texture of the story. The clearest example of the haplessness of Don Quixote contrasted with Dorotea's grasp of events occurs at the inn when, as all are reconciled, problems are resolved quite without the knight-errant's assistance. He, all the time, is engaged in lunatic combat with a roomful of wineskins, which he systematically destroys, along with the innkeeper's supply of vintage for the season.

But the most important instrument of salvation— and the penultimate stage of his recognition—is the small, almost invisible self-doubt that eventually brings Don Quixote to question his idealized identity. This self-doubt is comparable to what Perceval experienced after his failure at the Grail Castle.

When he first adopted his new role, Don Quixote had refused to put the physical world to too severe a test. At the inn, and after numerous misadventures, he still insisted that the barber's basin was at least an incomplete helmet. The barber had argued, "If this basin is a helmet, then this pack saddle must be a horse's trappings." To which Don Quixote had answered, "To me it looks like a pack saddle." Then he added, "By heaven, . . . so many strange and unaccountable things have befallen me in this castle on the two occasions I have stayed here that I would not dare to make a positive affirmation concerning anything contained in it, for I imagine that everything here works by enchantment" (457).

In book 2 he finally gives himself away. Meeting a traveling group of players who are acting *The Parliament of Death*, Don Quixote says:

> By the faith of a knight errant . . . when I saw the cart, I imagined that some great adventure was at hand, but I do declare that *one must touch with the hand what appears to the eye, if one would be undeceived.* God speed you, good people, and carry on your festival. Remember, if there is anything in which I may be useful to you, I will do it willingly, for from childhood I have always been fond of the masquerade, and in my youth I had a craving for the stage. (600)

We hear an echo of the First Epistle of John, with its eloquent appeal to believe in the testimony of those who witness to what their eyes have seen and their hands have touched, and here Don Quixote adds the luminous foreshadowing—"if one would be undeceived."

Later, when the Duke and Duchess mimic belief in Don Quixote and confirm him in his self-created identity, the narrator remarks: "Don Quixote . . . for the first time . . . felt thoroughly convinced that he was a knight errant in fact and not in imagination, for he saw himself treated in the same way as he had read that such knights were treated in past ages" (745). Howard Mancing classifies this sequence with many of the events in book 2 as "pseudo adventures" because the illusions are arranged by others and are not part of Don Quixote's imagination. The cold conviction Don Quixote expresses is forced and cannot be sustained.[8]

The crucial moment of Don Quixote's actual undeceiving, his *desengaño*, is his underworld experience. Like Odysseus, who tasted the desolation of life after death and returned to the world with a new understanding of the price one pays to be human, Don Quixote enters into his own particular Cave of Darkness. Time and space are dislocated as the knight-errant descends into his own subconscious, exteriorized in the narrative by the labyrinthine Cave of Montesinos. The cave represents, in part, Don Quixote's own sexual desires; chapter 22 begins with the happiness of newlyweds, a discussion of love and marriage, and Don Quixote's observation: "I myself am not married, nor so far, has it even come into my mind to be so." Subsequently, Don Quixote asks to be taken to the Cave of Montesinos, "for he had a great wish to explore it and see with his own eyes if the wonders reported there were true" (680). In front of the cave he prays to Dulcinea: "I am about to plunge, to engulf, and to sink myself into the abyss . . . if thou dost favor me, there is no impossible feat I may not accomplish" (683). And then "finding that it was not possible to let himself down or make an entrance unless by force of arms or by cutting a passage, he drew his sword and began to cut away the brambles at the mouth of the cave." Upon his return—presumably an hour later—Sancho says, "Welcome back, master, we fancied you were staying down there to found a family" (684).

A series of incidents in Don Quixote's dream while in the cavern reveal to him the illusion that had supported his masquerade. His hero Durandarte apparently is dead, but he had asked that his heart be sent to Lady Belerma. The Duke of Montesinos, who is showing Don Quixote around, states that he had been faithful to Durandarte's request, but that it had been necessary to salt the heart a bit to keep it from smelling. This subversion of the romantic illusion is the beginning of Don Quixote's *desengaño*. Montesinos introduces Don Quixote to Durandarte as the possible agent of the latter's "disenchantment." The term suggests here the status of the literature Cervantes is satirizing. Idealistic, dissociated from the claims of time and place, it is dead, enchanted. Don Quixote, in an effort to make the ideal real, is trying to disenchant it. But the dead heart of Durandarte smells. Neither Durandarte nor his supporting characters

---

[8]Howard Mancing, *The Chivalric World of Don Quixote: Style, Structure, and Narrative Technique* (Columbia: University of Missouri Press, 1982) 168.

can withstand the glare of time and place. Montesinos, telling the fate of Durandarte's squire, describes him as having been changed into an underground river. "But when he [river/squire] reached the surface of the earth and saw the sun of another heaven, so great was his sorrow at finding that he was leaving [Durandarte] that he plunged into the bowels of the earth" (689).

The heroes and heroines of Don Quixote's fantasy cannot be revived. The literature they exemplify is dead. "Wherever he (river/squire) goes, he shows his sadness and melancholy and takes no pride in breeding choice and tasty fish, but only coarse and tasteless kinds" (689). Durandarte's squire is no more melancholy than the Knight of the Rueful Figure himself, "who had sacrificed arable land for chivalric romances" and whose whole appearance as well as that of his horse suggested malnutrition. What Don Quixote discovers, although he admits it only later, is that the heroes whom he thought were immortal had always been dead. When Don Quixote had tried to enter the cave, "crows and jackdaws fluttered out so thickly and with such a rush that they knocked Don Quixote down. Had he been as superstitious as he was a good Catholic, he would have taken it for an evil omen and would have refused to bury himself in such a place" (683-84).

Chivalric literature represented for Don Quixote a sublimation of his own sexual frustration. The Cave of Montesinos is the transposition of sexual desire into the lust to revive, to "disenchant," a world. Yet that world cannot be brought to reality. What was always disembodied cannot be revived. Durandarte moans strangley in his tomb, "Patience, and shuffle the cards." Fair damsels walk in a funeral procession, and even Belerma "was not as beautiful as fame had reported" (690). All the life that can be attributed to the enchanted is that "their nails, hair, and beard grow. They do not eat . . . nor do they void excrement" (690). This vision of the kind of life Don Quixote thought he could substitute for his own was to lead him eventually to repentance and self-knowledge.[9]

The most serious problem confronting Don Quixote in the cave is his incapacity to disenchant Dulcinea. He had first enchanted her, with the

---

[9]John G. Weiger, *The Individuated Self: Cervantes and the Emergence of the Individual* (Athens: Ohio University Press, 1979) 68. Weiger sees the *desengaño* of the Cave of Montesinos as the realization that "fame" or the second life is just as limited in duration, just as destined for oblivion as one's first or historical life. "Don Quixote's discovery then is that the attempt to gain a worldly glory also results in ultimate corruption and a second death. He need not display his manliness (literally or figuratively) after all!"

help of Sancho's imagination, by removing her in his fantasy from reality and making her inaccessible. In the cave he recognized her, but "she ran at such a pace," he says later, "that an arrow would not have overtaken her" (693). Yet his account is qualified by Dulcinea's offering her petticoat (as collateral) through the intermediary of an attendant and pleading for disenchantment. Her "disenchantment" would cost Don Quixote six reals. He had only four. The realization of his sexual inadequacy will force Don Quixote eventually to come to terms with his limitations. But he is not yet ready for that. Rather, he vows "to abstain from eating bread off a table-cloth for however long," assuming, or perhaps merely wishing, that such a knightly pledge could substitute for real currency.[10] It cannot. Dulcinea will be forever enchanted, forever inaccessible—and Aldonza forever repulsive, however available. The real, accessible world of change, time, corruption would never become an ideal, accessible world of peerless beauty and incorruptibility. The choice is for one or the other. There may be fair and innocent damsels but none who deliver their favors. The intact Dulcinea would be forever elusive; the less-than-virginal Aldonza would always reek of garlic. Don Quixote's sanity and perhaps his salvation depended upon what he would decide is life.

The meaning of the cave incident was not immediately evident to Don Quixote. What began in his subconscious must be explicitly admitted, and that process required time. Shortly after describing his dream to Sancho, who regarded it all as nonsense, Don Quixote saw an inn as an inn, and Sancho noticed in his master a certain sobriety of judgment. The knight, still puzzling over his vision, inquired of a performing ape (manipulated by the escaped galley slave, Gines de Pasamonte, in disguise) whether his vision had been "true" and then he observes, "The future will tell . . . Time, the discoverer of all things, leaves nothing that it does not drag into the light of the sun, even though it be buried in the bosom of the earth" (711). Several more incidents gradually clarify the sequence of events in Don Quixote's cave vision until, in the final stage of his conversion, he consciously accepts what has been revealed to him—postponing his acceptance, however, as long as possible.

When Don Quixote became naively entranced by a puppet performance, he shouted at the narrator of the play, "Boy, boy, go on straight ahead with your story and don't go off into curves and crossways, for proof after proof is needed if we would establish a truth" (714). His own

---

[10]Ibid., 73. As Weiger observes, this vow is actually a pledge of sexual abstinence.

folly then became apparent, even to him. After slashing the puppet villains to pieces and later realizing that he had done so in madness induced by his uncontrolled imagination, he remarked: "I am willing to condemn myself in costs for my error, though it did not proceed from malice. Let Master Pedro see what he wants for the damaged figures, for I offer to pay him for them in good and current money of Castile" (718). His admission of folly led to self-knowledge, as well as conversion, for Don Quixote later fled in terror when he was outnumbered by a band of villagers, arguing after the event, "Courage not based on prudence is called rashness" (728). This is a different Don Quixote than he who once freed convicts from their chains and fought lions.

One of the last episodes suggesting Don Quixote's madness describes the knight and Sancho being rescued by a group of millers from the possible consequences of Don Quixote's imagining. These men save the knight and squire from drifting in their presumably enchanted boat over a waterfall.

But the definitive repentance and conversion of the knight is delayed by illusions created by others. When, after failure and cowardice, it seemed that Don Quixote could have been brought to terms with his real identity, the Duke and Duchess corroborate his feigned identity, and by manipulation and masquerade they reinforce his madness. At this point, Don Quixote becomes the victim not only of his own illusion, but of the deceit and malevolence of others. Both Cervantes and his public had a taste for practical jokes, but readers, if not all critics, have consistently perceived the aristocratic couple as less than compassionate and often as cruel.[11] The Duke and his wife became, in their own way, the "malicious enchanters" against whom Don Quixote was always struggling. Their kind of enchantment was the final obstacle to Don Quixote's conversion. They had fed Sancho's illusion also by naming him the governor of (something like) an island, but in so doing they hastened his disillusionment. Sancho's fantasies, which he had often resisted up to this point, became so uncontrolled in the presence of the Duke and Duchess that he begged them for the privilege of governing "just a teeny weeny bit of the sky."

But, after his resignation from the governorship, Sancho's disaffection with the dreamed-of joys of being a governor was made explicit by his own comic underworld experience. After falling into a pit along with his ass and being heard above by Don Quixote, he had to be rescued from darkness:

---

[11]See Mandel, "The Norm in *Don Quixote*."

"Here am I, a poor, feckless chickenhearted loon, who am forever fancying that the earth is going to open all of a sudden under my feet. . . . " Such were Sancho's despairing laments as he cautiously groped his way through the vaults, until at last, after going somewhat more than a mile and a half, he saw a glimmering light like that of day, shining through an aperture above, which he looked upon as an entrance to another world. (921)

The long sequence involving the Duke and Duchess's practical jokes on Don Quixote and Sancho represents Cervantes's obvious pleasure in prolonging his story of the woeful knight, but it has the added function of disclosing the senses and language itself as misleading.[12] Initially Don Quixote was the victim of his own subjectivity. Gradually, he became victimized by the disguises of the world. When Sancho and Don Quixote leave the castle, Don Quixote experiences a new freedom. His speech is, in one sense, a simple paean to liberty and perhaps echoes Cervantes's own feelings about freedom. But, in another sense, Don Quixote's relief was the result of his escape (and the reader's) from the oppression of a perpetual masquerade. His growing self-knowledge is further suggested by his remarks upon seeing statues of Saints George, Martin, James, and Paul: "They conquered Heaven by force of arms, because Heaven suffers violence, but up to now I do not know what I conquer by force of my labor . . . who knows but I may direct my steps along a better road than that which I am now following" (937).

Although he had yet to admit completely to his impotence, he consented to divert the responsibility of disenchanting Dulcinea to Sancho, whose assigned "redemptive suffering" of 3,300 lashes was a prank imposed by the household collaborators of the Duke and Duchess. The joke had the psychological advantage of allowing Don Quixote to prolong his dream. If Dulcinea was not to be disenchanted, it would be Sancho's fault. This transfer of guilt and responsibility was Don Quixote's last illusion.

---

[12]Leo Spitzer, "Perspectives in *Don Quixote*," in *Linguistics and Literary History: Essays in Stylistics* (Princeton: Princeton University Press, 1948) 521. Note the author's comment on the deceptive nature of words in Don Quixote: "Words are no longer, as they had been in the Middle Ages, depositories of truths nor, as they had been in the Renaissance, an expansion of life: they are, like the books in which they are contained, sources of hesitation, error, deception—'dreams.' " Spitzer's remarks refer to the disparity between Don Quixote's consciously univocal use of words and the casually ambiguous and deceitful use of words by other characters, a disparity indicative of the tension between the static ideal and the shifting "real" throughout the book.

In the final state before repentance, when Don Quixote, in a last desperate spasm of self-assertion, assumed the task of defending Dulcinea's beauty against all challengers, he was trampled by a herd of bulls. Later, he applied to himself an overheard remark: " . . . you'll never see her in all the days of your life."

But to save his assumed identity for a while, he continued his theater, submitting to the obligation of remaining in his village for a year and agreeing to enter upon a new style of literary madness: playing the shepherd in a pastoral idyll. When his housekeepers, those blessed guardians of the prosaic, described the realities of the pastoral life—the summer's heat, the winter's frost, the howling of the wolves in the open country— Don Quixote decided to go to bed, dying there to his pretenses, dying both as Don Quixote and Alonso Quixano. Self-knowledge brought with it the death of an assumed identity and the acceptance of whatever obscurity was appropriate to Alonso the Good, who had come to terms finally with limitation.

If Cervantes's sole aim was "to arouse men's scorn for the false and absurd stories of knight errantry," much more was accomplished in passing. Popular literature, which had so enchanted Don Quixote, became for readers the medium of disenchantment, in the Cervantine sense of that word. Flesh is seen trying—and failing—to become disembodied word. But there has never been a Don Quixote except as word; and that word of Cervantes is grounded in the limitations of flesh and time and space, its truth measured by its fidelity to those limitations. "We two alone are as one."

Penelope, Sophocles' Electra, Oedipus—none had a taste for illusion. Their goodness (Aristotle's *chrestos*) is based on their resistance to illusion. As hero, Chrétien's Perceval is more difficult to measure, because his access to reality is dependent upon a mythos apart from the text itself. If we already believe in all that Perceval converted to, then we believe that Perceval found the "truth." As in earlier literature, we are given none of the interior debate of Perceval. Only the shedding of his armor and the descent from his horse suggest that he abandoned at last an inauthentic identity. That he is a divided self, that he was transformed, is unique in pre-Renaissance literature and is a transfer from Scripture and hagiography, rather than a development from within literature itself. What Chrétien gives us is the possibility of transformation, or *metanoia*, in a literary character. It can be argued that Achilles changed and Odysseus also—the latter changing, for instance, into a civilized ruler after being a sacker of cities. The alterations of Homeric heroes were usually consequences of maturity or the result of a shifting environment (from war to peace). Transformation in classical literature was possible only in the Ovidian sense: Philemon and Baccus could become trees. Growth in wisdom was the classical ideal, not conversion.

In *Don Quixote* we see transformation, or conversion, measured not in terms of the character's conformity to a credo outside the text that is inserted arbitrarily into the story, but in exact relationship to the character's self-understanding and self-acceptance. Truth is not a proposition outside the character's experience or outside the text, but emerges within experience and is part of his growing consciousness. At the same time, it is not exclusively subjective. Alonso Quixano finally "connects," to use Forster's term, between word and self, and Cervantes, grounding his own imagination in reality, connects: "We two alone are as one." And from that union derives a new literature correspondent in its own way to a new epistemology.

EMMA:
THE ENCLOSED WORLD

How, indeed, is a mind to become conscious of its own bias?
—Bernard Lonergan, Insight

Sancho Panza, without his master, would have lived uneventfully and died unknown. What glorified him was the specter of an ideal who seized his imagination, companioned him, and even rescued him from his own pit of darkness. It was Sancho who, until seized temporarily by Don Quixote's fantasy, knew the limitations of time and space, and spoke no language other than that distilled by his peasant ancestors. Don Quixote's unearthly word changed his dream and journey, and gave him a new identity. It has been argued that the realism we see in Sancho as literary character had begun as early as the twelfth century. As we saw in an earlier chapter, what distinguishes Gautier d'Arras and Chrétien de Troyes from all other *romanciers*, including those of the succeeding generations, is the dissonance their heroes (Eric, Perceval, Lancelot) experience with themselves. "Perceval falls short of what was expected of him in the Castle of the Grail. All of them suffer from the awareness of an imperfection, of a downfall that has demonstrated that they are not what they ought to be."[1]

But the narrative structure of Perceval, especially the Gawain segment, which I did not consider in chapter 3, is rooted in a literary world "that does not pretend to have reference to history or reality, but is clearly marked out, by various signs, as a self-contained world of pure narrative movement."[2] In other words, Chrétien's narrative leads us toward psychological interiority but away from "realism." He calls our attention to

---

[1]Per Nykrog, "Two Creators of Narrative Form in Twelfth-Century France: Gautier d'Arras—Chrétien de Troyes," *Speculum* 48 (1973): 258-76, at 266.

[2]Ibid., 274.

events, but not to a recognizable world in which those events occur. Cervantes was reacting not to Chrétien, but to Chrétien's less artistic successors, who considered neither interiority (psychological realism) nor the world of historical experience (literary realism). Cervantes wanted to root us in both kinds of realism, without limiting us to either. The ideal had to submit to change, language to flesh.

That insistence on an objective ground of reality, against which every vision had to be measured, is the beginning of the realistic novel. We see such insistence in the eighteenth-century English novel and could trace, if we had time and world enough, how writers in this century gradually moved away from objective absolutes, not only from slicing life in the same direction, but from the whole business of life slicing. Here we are concerned with the more immediate post-Cervantine world of perception and discovery.

Two landmarks of the English tradition, *Emma* and *Middlemarch*, lend themselves to a comparative study of how the central character discovers the reality of her situation and thus acknowledges the truth about herself and her fallen world. Both characters are rescued by their authors from the tragic consequences of misperception. What is common to the novelists under discussion is that truths achieved, theories adopted without experience, as well as time and societal engagement are variations of the quixotic: no different than Alonso Quixano sallying forth from his country home, as much like a knight as the sun to rubicund Apollo. Since critical attention has been lavished on both texts, it is not my purpose here to analyze them in detail. What I will explore is how writers representing two distinct literary periods both charge their novels with the tension between knowledge in the abstract (information, theory, fantasy, desire) and knowledge acquired through flesh and time. What is equally important is how this epistemological conviction both reflects and is prophetic to religious thought.

Jane Austen's *Emma* is a snare. The reader who is not alert is caught in the same delusion as Emma herself. Limited for the most part to Emma's perception, the reader glides easily into Emma's prejudices, despite the author's initial warning: "The real evils indeed of Emma's situation were the power of having rather too much her own way, and a disposition to think a little too well of herself."[3] The hidden metaphor of the novel is the charade and its variation, the enigma: one, a parlor-game panto-

---

[3]Jane Austen, *Emma* (Boston: Houghton-Mifflin, 1957) 1. Subsequent citations are from this edition and will be indicated in the text.

mime that requires the participants to guess at meaning as partial information is acted out; the other, a riddle that discloses meaning only through polyvalent language. Emma, who prided herself on her swiftness in interpreting puzzles, never managed to discern to whom the riddles she solved were addressed. Mr. Elton's "courtship" riddle to her with the line, "Thy ready wit will soon the word supply," was quickly solved and handed to her young friend Harriet, "Read it in comfort to yourself. There can be no doubt of its being written for you and to you" (56). Emma's belief that she could effect a proper match between Mr. Elton and Harriet derived from a false sense of power: a serious miscalculation about her rights and the limits of her control. This kind of miscalculation, a fundamental misreading of the charade of her own situation, creates Emma's tragicomedy: her fall from isolated sovereignty, eventual salvation by Mr. Knightley, the redeemer and (to sustain the metaphor) bearer of the true word.

Only in book 3, chapter 5 does Jane Austen separate us clearly from the limitations of Emma's perceptions. The occasion is another parlor game, this one played by Frank Churchill, Jane Fairfax, and Emma—who knows nothing of the secret engagement between Frank and Jane. Only Mr. Knightley, through whose eyes we witness the game, begins to interpret the signal correctly:

> These letters were but the vehicle for gallantry and trick. It was a child's play, chosen to conceal a deeper game on Frank Churchill's part.
>
> With great indignation did he continue to observe him; with great alarm and distrust, to observe also his two blinded companions. (272)

When confronted by Mr. Knightley's suspicions, Emma responded, "Oh, it all meant nothing; a mere joke among ourselves" (273). But the joke was on Emma, and at this point the reader also becomes aware (the reader who has not already decoded Jane Austen's clues) that Emma has misread her situation almost completely. Emma, the riddle solver, the mistress of the charade, has misinterpreted every signal, has been duped by every fragile disguise, has even misappraised Robert Martin, who didn't even attempt a disguise.

Jane Austen is clear about Emma's faults. Her heroine is not stupid. She is not lacking in virtue. She is simply a little too sure, a little too sovereign in her own estimation, a little too autonomous. The novel itself is a parlor game: Jane Austen's enigma for her typical reader, who also is a little too sure (that the narrative perspective is reliable), a little too sovereign (over Emma's world), a little too autonomous (not reflecting that it is the narrator who controls access to the reality of the fictive situation).

If the hidden metaphor of *Emma* is the charade, a major theme of the novel is communication.[4] The difference between the two men Emma considers marrying is their allegiance to the integrity of message. Frank Churchill contrives deception, lives disguised, and Emma is deluded by his every signal. In the same interval, she does not hear Mr. Knightley, whose message is withheld but not disguised. Emma herself notes, "Mr. Knightley does nothing mysteriously" (174). Every conversation in the novel is a study in the capacity of human society to communicate or misrepresent, to code or decode or misconstrue. Intercalated chapters allow us to see Emma struggling to interpret, reflecting on her own interior response to the Highbury communication system. She exemplifies the new "individual" who, according to Lionel Trilling, was a product of the eighteenth century. We see the public and the private Emma in scenes possible only when "individuality" was possible in literature. Trilling writes: "Certain things he did not have to do until he became an individual. He did not have an awareness of what George Gusdorf calls internal space. He did not, as Delany puts it, imagine himself in more than one role, standing outside or above his own personality. . . . It is when he becomes an individual that a man lives more and more in private rooms."[5]

Emma must reflect periodically on her public or social experiences. What is curious in these moments of privacy is that she consistently mis-

---

[4]The presence of this important pattern does not exclude others. See Joel Weinsheimer, "Major Austen Studies, 1970–1975," *Papers on Language and Literature* 12 (Spring 1976): 209-13; Barry Roth and Joel Weinsheimer, *An Annotated Bibliography of Jane Austen Studies, 1952–1972* (Charlottesville: University Press of Virginia, 1973); and Barry Roth, *An Annotated Bibliography of Jane Austen Studies, 1973-1983* (Charlottesville: University Press of Virginia, 1985).

[5]Lionel Trilling, *Sincerity and Authenticity* (Cambridge: Harvard University Press, 1972) 24-25. See also Francis R. Hart, "The Spaces of Privacy: Jane Austen," *Nineteenth Century Fiction* 30 (December 1975): 305-33. Hart's analysis of space in Jane Austen and its relationship to social and personal psychology is illuminating:

It is tempting to apply to the spatial experience and behavior of Austen's characters the categories evolved by recent anthropologists and sociologists of personal space. The general applications are often strikingly suggestive. . . . The problem is how to achieve the true society of intimates and how to effect the necessary restrictions by testing possible intimacies, by adjusting and readjusting social distances, by learning how to live prudently and humanly with those inescapably "nearby" who threaten or violate the privacy of that society. (312)

interprets what she has experienced. She is misled by her own subjectivity, not—like Don Quixote—by her book-induced fantasies. She never finishes a book. Emma's reflections are invariably inaccurate readings of what she has experienced. As Paul Fry has noted, "Fact and fiction are both epistemological mysteries for Emma."[6]

Sending and receiving messages occurs between characters (with more or less success), but also between narrator and reader, with the latter receiving a different set of signals—assuming, of course, that we know to whom the message is being sent and from whom: "Pray, Miss Woodhouse, take care, ours is rather a dark staircase—rather darker and narrower than one could wish" (185). We have been warned.

On the parabolic level, the real plot of *Emma* is the question of whether or not the sender of the true message will be recognized. A mirror image of this structure is the endless debate among the characters about who sent the pianoforte to Jane Fairfax. If the plot is about the identity of the sender of the message, Mr. Knightley, not Emma, is the protagonist of the story; Emma, the object of his quest; and Frank Churchill, the opponent. For Emma, Mr. Knightley's message constitutes a "reticent text." But Knightley's message—not Frank's—is the good tidings, an expression Jane Austen uses occasionally as a reminder of the radical plot. Knightley is the one who sees (usually) and saves; Emma is the loving but partially blinded Edenic exile who will be saved when she discerns who is sending the *good* news.

The scene providing her first important moment of perception is the Crown Inn ball (bk. 3, ch. 2). All the fundamental movements and signals of the ball are a choreographed miniature of the entire narrative, beginning with Frank Churchill's manipulation of the guests and ending with Emma's joining Knightley in the final dance. In this chapter Harriet is the victim left outside society by Mr. Elton's deliberate refusal to engage her for a dance. Emma, already with a partner and seeing Harriet's humiliation, finally concedes Mr. Elton's selfishness. When Harriet is rescued by Mr. Knightley, saved from societal exclusion by his invitation to join the dance, Emma recognizes in her faithful and chivalrous neighbor all that she fundamentally admires. She admits to him later: "I do own my-

---

[6]Paul H. Fry, "Georgic Comedy: The Fictive Territory of Jane Austen's *Emma*," *Studies in the Novel* 11:3 (Fall 1979): 129-45, at 135. "Emma's 'imaginism' should be understood . . . as proceeding from an empirical vacuum; her mind soars without obstacle in a fine empyrean where intelligence without insight is perfectly possible—as it is never possible for the merely fatuous tribe of literary victims of bad literature" (135).

self to have been completely mistaken in Mr. Elton. There is a littleness about him which you discovered, and which I did not; and I was fully convinced of his being in love with Harriet. It was through a series of strange blunders" (258).

Then, called to join again in the dancing by Mr. Weston's appeal, "Come, Emma, set your companions the example. Everybody is lazy! Everybody is asleep!" Emma replies, "I am ready whenever I am wanted." Having reached some degree of self-knowledge, she is ready to move into human society.

Her renunciation of power and implied submission to Mr. Knightley is confirmed subsequently when she resists the temptation to create, even imaginatively, a possible romantic link between Frank Churchill and Harriet after Frank had rescued Harriet from a band of gypsies. However romantic the occasion, Emma restrains her conjectures: "Everything was to take its natural course . . . neither impelled or assisted. She would not stir a step, nor drop a hint. No, she had had enough of interference" (262).[7]

The episode at Box Hill (bk. 3, ch. 7), generally considered to be the turning point of the novel, needs closer examination, for it functions as a model of revelatory experience in the Jane Austen mode.

The cast of characters gathers at Box Hill for an outing. Initially, nothing is right emotionally, as the party fragments into separate groups. But as they sit down together, Emma perceives that Frank is making her the center of attention. Her own soul is divided; she is flattered but not attracted to Frank. She imagines herself as a character in the gossip and letters of the members of the group. Hence, she proves capable of seeing herself from the outside, as someone written about, however inaccurately. Her reflection is a curious fictionalization of her actions, one that she herself would recognize as only partially true. But Frank's noisome flirtation and manipulation of the group leads Emma past the boundaries of charity she normally observed. She allows herself to mock the foolish Miss Bates and, unaware of the pain she has inflicted, permits Frank to sustain the false gaiety. She accepts Mr. Weston's flattery and even agrees to pick out and educate a wife for Frank, whose mock suggestion touches her at the vestiges of delusion. Throughout the scene we observe Emma out of her own control, capable of some self-observation, but not recognizing all that is really occurring. She has missed the mockery and deceit of Frank's performance, his manipulation of her even as he persuades her

---

[7]There is a clear rejection in this passage of the romantic conception of storytelling. What happens in a novel must happen within the range of plausible human experience.

that she is in control. She is an inaccurate and deluded reader of Frank's text. She has missed observing Mr. Knightley's misgivings about her behavior. But she is sensitive enough to know that the party was somehow wrong, the guests "ill assorted," the pleasures strained. Standing alone afterward and looking forward to the prospect of a quiet drive home "which was to close the questionable enjoyments of this day," she is confronted by Mr. Knightley, who bluntly criticizes her for her insensitivity and cruelty.

> Emma recollected, blushed, was sorry, but tried to laugh it off.
> Nay, how could I help saying what I did?—Nobody could have helped it. It was not so very bad. I dare say she did not understand me.
> I assure you she did. She felt your full meaning. (293)

A violation of human relations, an offense against human dignity is not enigmatic; even the stupid understand and feel. Knightley would not let Emma delude herself.

As he assisted Emma into the carriage, she turned her face away, and he is described as not interpreting correctly her silence. Only the reader is told of her recognition of "the truth of his representation," her tears, and her subsequent depression. Frank's excessive flattery and banter had discomposed her. Mr. Knightley's candid assessment had cut through to the source of self-knowledge that she had never reached in her solitude. Chrétien never gives us such a solitary moment of introspection and self-knowledge in his depiction of Perceval. The carriage in *Emma* encloses the solitary individual in space. The carriage ride imitates the passage of time during which a full experience of self-knowledge is possible.

Emma's response to Mr. Knightley's accusation was complete surrender to his judgment, and a serious and determined effort to reconcile with Miss Bates. With this newfound sense of her limitation, she is in a position to correct other extravagant suppositions and open herself to hear what else Knightley would have to say.

The Box Hill incident, so crucial to the denouement of the novel, is typical Jane Austen microculture, but its implications for a theology of revelation are pointed. Self-knowledge and moral apprehension are commensurate with each other.

The narrator's communication to the reader is no less reticent initially than Knightley's messages to Emma. The truth has not been disguised, merely withheld, until we become alerted to the necessity of overhearing—not unlike Emma at the Westons' Christmas Eve dinner party (ch. 14), who heard only snatches of conversation at the other end of the table. What she had wanted to know was just slightly out of hearing, especially since Mr. Elton, close to her ear, demanded her attention. Those who want to hear the truth must deal with competing messages. She had to wait until after dinner to receive the other information intact. This postponement of cognitive gratification is a persistent commentary on the problem of communication in *Emma*. The narrative voice was silent about Jane Fairfax, not for the purpose of deceiving (although we are deceived), but rather to encourage us to overhear better and wait for the integral message.

And wait we must. The Highbury world is continually waiting. They wait for Frank Churchill to arrive; they wait for the Eltons to arrive; and they wait for the Sucklings to arrive. They wait for the mail. In the meantime they speculate on why people are not arriving and what the news will be when they or it does arrive. In the absence of people and news, they reread letters, scrutinize penmanship, repair their glasses, and fantasize. As Miss Bates says, "Everyone needs two pairs of glasses." When Frank Churchill finally informs his parents of his engagement to Jane Fairfax, Emma—despite her protests—had to walk to the neighboring estate to receive the information from Frank's stepmother, even though Mr. Weston, walking at her side, knew perfectly well what the news was going to be.

"Have you indeed no idea?" said Mrs. Weston, in a trembling voice. "Cannot you my dear Emma—cannot you form a guess as to what you are about to hear?" Emma had formed many guesses, all of them wrong, before she settled herself to wait for the information. She had given no credence to Knightley's earlier suggestion of a collusion between Frank Churchill and Jane Fairfax.

Knightley is always the sender of messages to Emma. She, preferring her own interior dialogue and the voice of fancy, always begins by resisting them. In the crucial scene in the garden (bk. 3, ch. 1) when Knightley is trying to express his love, she is still so far deceived that she thinks he is talking about his love for Harriet. Assuming that his news is scarcely "good tidings," she argues, " . . . don't speak it, don't speak it. . . . Take a little time, consider, do not commit yourself" (336). The irony is complete. At thirty-eight, Knightley had taken plenty of time, waiting not only until Emma grew up but until she had lived through a few flirtations and more than one confused set of signals. His ploy then is to praise her for sustaining her friendship with him when other words of his had been difficult to hear: "You hear nothing but truth from me—I have blamed you and lectured you, and you have borne it as no other woman in England would have borne it. —Bear with the truth I tell you now" (337). Knightley's quest is achieved when his declaration of love is finally heard and accepted. Consenting to marry Mr. Knightley— wanting, in fact, to marry him—Emma admits her incompleteness, her limitations. Her faults are atoned for, and in this Austenite world, she can look forward to a modest earthly paradise regained.

But there is yet another obstacle, a miniscule anticlimax. Emma's father—that guardian of every fear and every fantasy and thus, however amiable and silly, the folkloric tyrant—must needs be informed. Only his fears of housebreaking, gratuitously evoked by the news of turkey pilfering in the neighborhood, impel him to admit Mr. Knightley to Hartfield as husband to Emma and protector of the house. A new ruler succeeds to the Hartfield universe, saving the little kingdom, if not from fancy, at least from its destructive effects.

The microscopic dimension of the human situation Jane Austen has created should not mislead us to undervalue the author's moral purpose. Her characters are not Aristotle's *phauloi* for whom life is trivial. Jane Austen's world is quintessentially serious. But for all her insistence on sober reality, her fiction is not quintessentially realistic. What is foreshortened in this parable of societal interaction is the sense of historical time and space. Except for an allusion to London's being sixteen miles away, the historical-geographical world of Jane Austen's *Emma* is opaque, the text no more transparent to history than the story of Perceval. London, Scotland, and Ireland are all offstage, as are Mr. Perry, the Dixons, the Campbells, and the Churchills: those elusive people whom everybody in the novel talks about and we never see. Space is limited. We need only recall the anxiety about the size of the ballroom at Crown Inn. Would there be room enough to dance? We must measure it again. And again. Equally compressed is time. Beginning in the fall and ending in the following October, the novel is shaped in the best Thomsonian sense around the seasons. But it could have been any fall or any October in the century. The temporal backdrop is as nonsuggestive as the geographical backdrop. Highbury alone is the stage. There is no other time and place, no hint of history other than those sociological changes and tensions that bear upon an otherwise enclosed human community.

The final scene is a tableau. We have the narrator's good tidings that society can be integrated, that truth is finally available, if we but admit its initial partiality. As if it were necessary for readers to have all the information, Knightley's own story is told in the final chapters—breathlessly. We are not allowed to surmise his jealousy of Frank Churchill; we must be told explicitly. At this stage of the novel, the parlor game is over. No more guessing. Here are the missing pieces. The conundrum is solved.

Ultimately, the values Jane Austen asserts are candor, openness, truth in its completeness, which must always be desired. Secrecy is an evil, which is why Jane Fairfax and Frank are "expelled" from Highbury at the end of the novel. Subjective impositions on facts are deleterious, which is why Emma must repent. By rejecting historical romance, Jane Austen argues that sober reality is as interesting as escapist storytelling and, what is more important, reality is both available and salvific.

George Eliot, in another period, would be more attentive to the socio-temporal dimensions of human knowing. The Victorian Eliot would do so only because the late-Renaissance and neoclassic novelists had offered such psychological density in their probing of intimate human interaction and reflection that an awareness based on an expanded consciousness of time and space could begin.

MIDDLEMARCH:
THE CURVE OF HISTORY

Spirit apprehends itself. . . . .

—G. W. F. Hegel, <u>Philosophy of Spirit</u>

When Dorothea Brooke learned that her dead husband had previously added a codicil to his will designed to declare his suspicions about another man and to threaten her freedom, her entire view of her marriage and her past collapsed. Although her awareness of Casaubon's limitations—and her own—had been growing and would have culminated eventually in full consciousness, this information brought her to swift and total awareness of her original error. The recognition occurs in book 4, chapter 50, and effectively begins the last third of George Eliot's *Middlemarch:*

> Dorothea . . . now threw herself back helplessly in her chair. She might have compared her experience at that moment to the vague, alarmed consciousness that life was taking on a new form, that she was undergoing a metamorphosis in which memory would not adjust itself to the stirring of new organs. Everything was changing its aspect: her husband's conduct, her own duteous feeling towards him, every struggle between them—and yet more: her own whole relation to Will Ladislaw. Her world was in a state of convulsive change: the only thing she could say distinctly to herself was, that she must wait and think anew. One thing terrified her as if it had been a sin; it was a violent shock of repulsion from her departed husband, who had had hidden thoughts, perhaps perverting everything she did. Then again she was conscious of another change which also made her tremulous; it was a sudden strange yearning of heart towards Will Ladislaw.[1]

---

[1]George Eliot, *Middlemarch* (New York: Norton, 1977) 340. All quotations are from the Norton Critical Edition, ed. Bert G. Hornbach. Subsequent references will be indicated in the text.

That her sister Celia is caring for her own baby during this calculated annunciation to Dorothea and interspersing her comments about the dead Casaubon with others about the wonders of infancy is not without relevance to what is happening to Dorothea, who was "undergoing a metamorphosis." Past and future were being rearranged as she admitted the avalanche of another's perception into her vision. She was not Oedipus learning that something had occurred. She was learning of something another suspected had occurred or could occur and how that other perspective now altered her own reality. Dorothea Brooke's recognition experience also differed from the discoveries of Perceval, Don Quixote, and Emma Woodhouse. Of Perceval's inner search, we know almost nothing. Five years of "oblivion" are summarized in a sentence. Perceval hears the explanation of Good Friday, seeks out a hermit, and repents. Neither time nor space bears upon his decision. Don Quixote's self-discovery is achieved alone in a dream sequence scarcely distinguishable from his own self-consciousness. An intimate friend had revealed Emma to herself, and she had wept alone in an enclosed carriage. (Neoclassic repentance is scarcely the *metanoia* of Perceval, but in the absence of a mythic landscape, Emma's tears will do.)

George Eliot's Dorothea Brooke is a new heroine. The advent of greater consciousness, the entrance into self-knowledge is characterized by the author's different understanding of both the relationship of the individual to society and the very shape of knowledge itself. That Dorothea is innocent, at least of any moral failure that her husband imagined to be possible, and that she was a victim of her narrowness of conception is part of her tragic recognition. But if she was innocent, she was not entirely without responsibility. She was the victim not only of her husband's misperception, but of her own, a misperception that had led her originally into an ill-conceived marriage.

Fifty years separated the publication of *Middlemarch* from *Emma.* In that interim, England had suffered a sea change, and George Eliot was as aware of the new intellectual currents as anyone in England. The intimacy of the neoclassical personal world, the miniatures and cameos of that world, had yielded to landscapes. George Eliot's epistemology is not definable without an analysis of how she regarded the individual not so much in the context of a few intimates, but within the network of village and country and the larger web of the world. Individuals could neither know nor be known apart from their social matrices in all the particularities of daily existence.

The historic depth perspective in *Middlemarch*, the peripheral vision in Eliot's narrative, corresponds to a new understanding of consciousness. Erich Kahler has pointed out that the "inward turn of the mind" corresponds to an expanded view of the world, that awareness of the subjective or personal intensifies as knowledge of the universe around the individual extends:

> In fact, man himself has developed by means of the perpetual interaction between consciousness and reality, between his interior world and his exterior world. As a result of the growth of consciousness man's outer world expands and changes. The reality in which man moves and which he must manipulate changes in extent and character. And his experiencing a changed reality in turn propels consciousness onward.[2]

George Eliot gives us a wide, deep, historical, social world in which her characters perceive and choose. If the landscape is primarily a provincial village, that village lives within earshot of London lawmaking, German philosophy, and Italian art. The historical allusions in *Middlemarch* are pervasive and constant, and their significance is deeply embedded in the structure of the novel.[3] The political, social, and scientific history of the years 1829–1832 is not mere backdrop to give a feeling for historical reality in the narrative. Her characters can only *be* within their history and as part of their history. They cannot live out their lives exempt from social forces outside their immediate world.[4] There is no mythical landscape, no "descending symbolism,"[5] no waiting for supernatural messages to be delivered from someone or someplace beyond *Middlemarch* itself. What is to be known is *there*, like Heidegger's god within the temple, sur-

---

[2]Erich Kahler, *The Inward Turn of Narrative*, trans. Richard Winston and Clara Winston (Princeton: Princeton University Press, 1973) 4.

[3]See Jerome Beaty, "History by Indirection: The Era of Reform in *Middlemarch*," *Victorian Studies* 1 (1957–1958): 173-79; rpt. in Norton Critical Edition.

[4]The "pinched narrowness" we observe in *Middlemarch* exists because its inhabitants were so often unaware of the implications of the historical and scientific events they hear about. The narrator consistently reminds the reader of those events lest Middlemarch, like Highbury, seem to be the world. The reader always has more peripheral vision than Dorothea's fellow burghers.

[5]The term is Kahler's. He distinguishes between the hieratic or mythic symbolism of antiquity whose significance is drawn from preexistent reality— as in Dante's world—and modern, wholly psychological symbolism, which, he argues, begins with Don Quixote. "The new symbolism is 'ascending' because it rises from below, from a purely human natural world, from individual characters and events which . . . have been invented by the artist" (Kahler, *Inward Turn of Narrative*, 57).

rounded by the temple, hidden by the temple, but not accessible apart from the temple.[6]

> I am reading the Agricultural Chemistry [says Sir James Chettam during a dinner conversation related in chapter 2] because I am going to take one of the farms into my own hands, and see if something cannot be done in setting a good pattern of farming among my tenants. Do you approve of that, Miss Brooke?

As the theme of reform continues, each character emerges clearly against the horizon of the scientific world and its impact on provincial life:

> "A great mistake, Chettam," interposed Mr. Brooke. . . .
> "Surely," said Dorothea, "it is better to spend money in finding out how men can make the most of the land which supports them all, than in keeping dogs and horses only to gallop over it."

In a succeeding conversation, Casaubon's view of cottage reform is peculiarly revelatory:

> Mr. Casaubon apparently did not care about building cottages, and diverted the talk to the extremely narrow accommodations which was to be had in the dwellings of the ancient Egyptians, as if to check a too high standard. After he was gone, Dorothea dwelt with some agitation on this indifference of his. (21)

Dorothea's error lay in not dwelling enough on her agitation and in not recognizing the vacuity of using the quarters of ancient Egyptians as a norm against which to measure the living space of nineteenth-century Britons. Casaubon's deficient sense of time, his lack of awareness of what kind of changes occur in history, begins to define him. His utter unconsciousness is all the more visible against the historical contours of the

---

[6]See Martin Heidegger, *l'Origine de l'oeuvre d'art* (Frankfort: Vittorio Klostermann, 1950) 31. Also cited in F. J. J. Buytendijk, *Phénomenologie de la rencontre* (Paris: Désclée, 1953) 37.

A building, a Greek temple, copies nothing. It simply stands there in the middle of a steep and rocky valley. The building surrounds the figure of the god, and as it encloses it allows it at the same time—because of the open colonnade—to stand outside and within the sacred enclosure. By the Temple, the god is present in the Temple. This presence of the god is, in itself, an extension and a delimitation of the enclosure. . . . However, the Temple and what is enclosed do not float into definiteness. [author's translation]

The passage in which Heidegger is discussing phenomenology in art lends itself to an analogy of how God, or the "Holy," is present in experience both personal and collective (history).

novel. Eliot, according to Michael York Mason, chose the time 1829–1832 not only because it corresponded in some ways to the period during which the novel was written (the late 1860s), but especially because so much was begun during the Reform era that was visible to Eliot's compatriots:

> The forward dimension in time comes from a sense of what is prophetic or germinal in the selective features of the novel's period. In this way George Eliot has contrived, paradoxically, a result both static and dynamic. The Nazarene group of painters in Rome carries with it the overtones of the movement that was to transform English painting in a few years. The implied power of German scholarship in Ladislaw's sketchy allusions is meant to entail its convulsive effect on Victorian religious thought from the forties onward.[7]

Dorothea's central awareness in her moment of recognition is that the world she knew, or thought she knew, had changed. Her understanding of the past was subverted, her sense of the present was still in motion. Her sensibilities were shifting. All of her relationships were changing ground. Self-knowledge was correspondent to her sudden awareness of her husband's real attitude toward her, her revulsion for him, and her yearning for Will Ladislaw.

If recognition is, as I am urging, a model of religious experience, which includes both illumination and conversion, in what sense does Dorothea change? Perceval had altered his way of life by shedding the habiliments of war. Don Quixote had returned eventually to La Mancha and renounced his fictive identity. Emma wept, became conspicuously more compassionate, and married Mr. Knightley (renouncing solitary autonomy). Dorothea's reform is expressed in her eventual marriage to Will Ladislaw. But the significance of that decision needs elucidation, since the marriage implied a whole restructuring of her way of knowing and living among the Middlemarchers of this world. But first, the pattern of revelation of which the recognition scene is the culmination.

After a dinner-table conversation with a certain Mr. Casaubon, whom the Brookes meet upon their arrival in Middlemarch, Celia observes bluntly: "How very ugly Mr. Casaubon is!" But Dorothea compares him to the portrait of Locke and argues that Casaubon is "distinguished looking," that his face has a "great soul." Celia's direct vision is more accurate. It is she who sees Casaubon's "two white moles with hairs on them."

---

[7]Michael York Mason, "*Middlemarch* and History," *Nineteenth Century Fiction* 25 (March 1971): 417-31, at 420.

Since, however, Casaubon's eye sockets resemble Locke's, according to Dorothea's memory of Locke's portrait, Casaubon's appearance is not to be measured by Celia's taste in men or her superficial view of what makes them worthy. (That it is Locke whom Dorothea sees in Casaubon is part of George Eliot's luxuriant irony in this scene: Locke, who insisted on the merits of sense perception in the acquisition of truth.) We are shown immediately how minimal is Dorothea's capacity to see what is concretely in front of her. Imposing a memory of Locke's portrait over Casaubon's physiognomy was enough to evoke in her a wave of happy speculation. With Casaubon, she was to discover that week, she could discuss "the secondary importance of ecclesiastical forms and articles of beliefs compared with that spiritual religion, that submergence of self in communion with Divine perfections which seemed to her to be expressed in the best Christian books of widely distant ages"(14).

No one could persuade Dorothea of the infelicity of her decision to accept Casaubon's offer of marriage. Celia's observations about his disagreeable way of eating soup and his irrelevant blinking, and Mr. Brooke's hesitant reminder that Casaubon is twenty-seven years older than Dorothea were not, after all, formidable objections. Dorothea had her own views, which were not to be contradicted. Mrs. Cadwallader, the village matchmaker, observes with Middlemarch good sense, occasionally indistinguishable from oracular genius, that "these charitable people never know vinegar from wine till they have swallowed it and got the colic" (38).

Only after the marriage ceremony does Dorothea begin to see. First, Casaubon mentions that if Celia were along on the honeymoon trip to Rome, he "should feel more at liberty." Dorothea notes with annoyance that her services to her husband-scholar were supererogatory. There are clear suggestions that Casaubon is impotent. In Rome, we see her confused, unhappy, and weeping:

> . . . for that new real future which was replacing the imaginary drew its material from the endless minutiae by which her view . . . of Mr. Casaubon and her wifely relations, now that she was married to him, was gradually changing with the secret motion of a watch hand from what it had been in her maiden dream. It was too early yet for her fully to recognize or at least admit the change. (135)

Clinging to her original view of what her relationship to Casaubon would be, Dorothea urged him to let her assist in his writing so that his vast unfinished research could be published. But finishing work was not Casaubon's particular genius. Dorothea's persistent urging only reminded him of his own vaguely perceived incapacities. Because her insistence reflected "superficial" judgment, discussion only led to mutual incomprehension and anger.

When Will Ladislaw, Casaubon's nephew, alerted Dorothea to the possibility that her husband's research was futile and outdated, she gradually began to accept the actual situation. But correspondent to her growth in awareness was a deepening of her sympathy:

> Dorothea was strangely quiet—not immediately indignant, as she had been on a like occasion in Rome. And the cause lay deep. She was no longer struggling against the perception of facts, but adjusting herself to their clearest perception; and now when she looked steadily at her husband's failure, still more at his possible consciousness of failure, she seemed to be looking along the one track where duty became tenderness. (252)

Dorothea was to learn subsequently that neither fidelity to duty, nor tenderness, nor pity could save her from the kind of destruction that another's egoism could accomplish. It was Casaubon's fears, not Dorothea's moral principles, that controlled the marriage relationship—fears that were exacerbated, in fact, by Dorothea's moral candor. Her expectations of him became a mirror of his failure, intensifying his own self-awareness. Without that mirror in his presence, he could suspect that he was not unadorable. A less perceptive Dorothea, a less morally principled Dorothea, would have been comforting indeed. A more Sartrean hell for the two of them cannot be imagined.

Diminished perception alone would not have caused Dorothea's tragedy, for she was morally adequate to the task of readjusting her motives for love and fidelity. Her growing knowledge of another did not lead her to alter the direction of her life. Despite misgivings, despite the inexorable accumulation of direct experience with Casaubon's limitations and her deepening awareness that she had walked into a tomb, mistaking it for Minerva's palace, Dorothea sustained her commitment to Casaubon and to Casaubon's wishes. "She saw clearly enough the whole situation, yet she was fettered; she could not smite the stricken soul that entreated hers" (334).

Dorothea intended to sacrifice herself for Casaubon, basing her decision on the same ideas that had motivated her to marry—"that submergence of self in communion with divine perfections." In this sense of moral purpose and moral vision, she had not changed. Her agony would be caused by the discovery of Casaubon's perception of her and his manipulation of her capacity for self-sacrifice. Her blindness lay in her failure to see that others were not guided by her principles. Arguing rightly that Ladislaw had more of a claim to her husband's money than she had, and urging that the will be altered, Dorothea was too innocent to realize what suspicions her sense of justice was evoking in Casaubon's murkier consciousness.

Dorothea needed to test her moral vision against a world that included other human beings. She needed to see apart from the filter of her own self. "The characters move," writes Quentin Anderson, "in a landscape of opinion, but those who concern us have an inner life; they can look within as well as without, and measure their sense of themselves against the world's demands and expectations."[8] Dorothea had to measure herself against her husband's demands and expectations and then act. How was that to happen?

The Dorothea we first meet is an unusually attractive but temporarily dislocated young woman whose dignity Eliot compares to a biblical quotation "in a paragraph of today's newspaper" (11). She knew many passages from Pascal and Jeremy Taylor by heart, we are told, and was "likely to seek martyrdom." Eliot, however critical of Dorothea's appetite for lofty conceptions and self-submergence, is sympathetic. Celia had more common sense. But the implication of the text is that Celia would never have anything but common sense. Dorothea had something else: a vigorous mind and moral intensity—qualities that raised questions about her marriageability.

> And how should Dorothea not marry?—a girl so handsome and with such prospects? Nothing could hinder it but her love of extremes, and her insistence on regulating life according to notions which might cause a wary man to hesitate before he made her an offer, or even might lead her at last to refuse all offers. A young lady of some birth and fortune, who knelt suddenly down on a brick floor by the side of a sick labourer and prayed fervidly as if she thought herself living in the time of the Apostles—who had strange whims of fasting like a Papist, and of sitting up at night to read old theological books! Such a wife might awaken you some fine morning with a new scheme for the application of her income which would interfere with political economy and the keeping of saddle horses; a man would naturally think twice before he risked himself in such a fellowship. Women were expected to have weak opinions; but the great safeguard of society and of domestic life was, that opinions were not acted upon. (3)

But Dorothea was not one merely to entertain opinions. The test of her experience of recognition would lie in how her decisions would be

<hr>

[8]Quentin Anderson, "George Eliot in *Middlemarch*." In *George Eliot: A Collection of Critical Essays,* ed. George R. Creeger (Englewood Cliffs NJ: Prentice-Hall, 1970) 141-60, at 148.

effected. According to Eliot, the moral question was twofold: one must act. But on what understanding of human society, and on what terms? Dorothea's initial tragedy consisted in choosing to act on the basis of an abstract sense of the world and on her voluntaristic preference for abstractions. Even when knowledge was specific, her ideals sustained her in commitment to a self-denying principle, rather than to self-affirming relationships; and that obstinacy, according to Eliot, had to be cracked. Dorothea's realization of the extent to which her husband's suspicion and tyranny led him urged her finally to the assertion of her own individuality and away from self-submergence. She would not comply. She would not commit herself to finishing *his* work. The question was to do her own. Dorothea's conversion begins at the moment she refuses fidelity to a tyrannical—though deceased—husband and claims an individual destiny.

George Eliot is sometimes considered a post-Christian novelist—"post-Christian" indicating those histories that refer to Christian faith not as the spiritual goal or fulfillment of an individual's life, but as a phase through which an individual develops and beyond which the true modern hero progresses.[9] *Middlemarch* has been interpreted as an example of such a study. The question could be raised as to whether the kind of Christianity Dorothea "goes beyond" is really Christianity at all. If she read Jeremy Taylor and Pascal and was willfully abstracted from social reality as a consequence, the fault is hardly Christianity's. Her defective vision, described as a physical limitation in the early chapters, is not a consequence of her reading habits or her understanding of the supernatural, but of an idealistic cast of mind, in combination with sheer inexperience. Her moral challenge will be the clash between ideals in the abstract and limitations imposed on her desire to act on them. In analyzing the "post-Christianity" of George Eliot, Sara M. Putzell-Korab describes the conventional distinction between the Christian and the post-Christian protagonist:

> Thus if the conventional Christian heroine follows what she knows to be right and is rewarded by a love that is right for her, the Eliot heroine transcends her sense of self as an isolated locus of ethical truth and relinquishes any claim to special rights. The typical Eliot protagonist finds, indeed, that his or her claims are frustrated by a world of other individuals with similar claims; from his suffering

---

[9]Sara M. Putzell-Korab, *The Evolving Consciousness of George Eliot.* Institut für Anglistik und Amerikanistik (Universität Salzburg, 1982) 2. See also, in this context, Brian Davies, O.P., "George Eliot and Christianity," *Downside Review* 100 (1982): 47-61, who argues that "the practice of Christianity is not necessarily a matter for censure and destruction on the part of George Eliot" (57).

and frustration, he learns to imagine their feelings and then devotes himself to their happiness. Whereas the Christian hero(ine) moves through inner struggle to assurance of his personal salvation, the Eliot hero(ine) moves from egoism to sympathy.[10]

The correspondence between conventional and authentic Christianity collapses under theological scrutiny, as any comparison with such Christianity and biblical ethic would determine. For Eliot, Dorothea Brooke may have been post-Christian not because Christianity is limited, but because the conventional understanding of it is limited. Eliot herself had a deep enough moral vision to recognize that orthopraxis is impossible apart from active sympathy with human persons, whatever constraints those persons may impose on one's own sense of the "oughtness" of things. The structure of Dorothea's conversion, therefore, is not Christian in the Victorian conventional sense, but it may well be Christian in a more radical, unthematized sense. Just as revelation was not possible for her prior to the kind of personal experience that could enable her to believe, conversion from egoism to sympathy was not possible for the same reason. She could not believe Celia's pronouncement about Casaubon until she had married him and discovered that he had other flaws, in addition to the hair on his moles. The pattern of her evolving consciousness is not a paradigm of instruction and submission, but of disillusionment with her theories and change—that is, knowledge by accretion of experience and conversion by growth in understanding better the concretely real human beings with whom she interacts. Action on the basis of such understanding would be more fruitful, even if the motives for such action necessitated some negotiated compromise with the ideal.

The influences on George Eliot's thinking are multiple, and she was genius enough to discern and to select what aspects of the thought of another she would admit to her own. We see in her not only Matthew Arnold, Feuerbach, George Henry Lewes but also, by 1850, the influence of G. W. F. Hegel. A comparison of Eliot's novels with Hegel's *Phenomenology of Spirit* and *Philosophy of Mind* undertaken by Sara M. Putzell-Korab gives us a basis on which to study the pattern of conversion in *Middlemarch*.[11]

For Hegel, consciousness becomes self-consciousness when the self is acknowledged, but knowledge of the self must be fulfilled in action, for

---

[10]Putzell-Korab, *Evolving Consciousness of George Eliot*, 3.

[11]Note that Sara Putzell-Korab does not insist on the direct influence of Hegel's texts, only that Eliot's thought is Hegelian. I am following Putzell-Korab's analysis here.

only in action is such knowledge thematized. Because of Dorothea's presence, Casaubon becomes aware of his limitations. Dorothea, in turn, recognizes her own initial naïveté as well as the inadequacy of ideals abstracted from experience with the human community. Hegel lists three modes of consciousness through which growth to maturity is accomplished: (1) Lordship and Bondage (or the Servant-Master relationship in more recent translations), by which he means self-understanding through others' perception; (2) the Unhappy Consciousness, which sees the ideal world as the only world worth living in; (3) Rational Consciousness, by which we (historically and collectively, as well as personally) recognize that 'reality' is actual, not ideal existence.

The third mode of consciousness is in turn subdivided into three phases: (1) a pleasure-seeking phase in which individuals see the world as a self-extension rather than as a set of relations; (2) a romantic phase in which individuals try to reform the world in terms of their own moral principles; (3) the virtuous search for an external rule of right that "leads at last to an awareness that moral action is inseparable from individual perception and cultural situation."[12]

Dorothea's growth in self-consciousness and her subsequent praxis correspond closely to Hegel's analysis of "the evolving consciousness." In fact, it can be argued that she effectively experiences and passes through all three phases of consciousness outlined by Hegel in *Phenomenology of Spirit*. For decades, readers have debated the implications of Dorothea's abandonment of her inheritance and her marriage to Will Ladislaw, arguing that Will is not worthy of her (he isn't); that the novel ends on a peculiarly minor key (it does); and that Dorothea has simply failed her ideals. But Dorothea hasn't failed her ideals; she has outgrown them. Dorothea's marriage to Will, her having a baby, Will's entrance into the practical politics of reform all suggest that Dorothea has achieved, in Eliot's terms, some degree of moral maturity. She has, in Hegel's terms, relinquished abstraction for 'actuality,' for a concrete achievement of something, however modest, as an alternative to incapacitated desire.

Putzell-Korab analyzes Dorothea Brooke in terms also of Hegel's *Philosophy of Mind*, pointing out that Dorothea begins with what Hegel calls Theoretical Mind (Reason), and at the lowest level, in fact, of Theoretical Mind. In other words, she confuses her aspirations with the intentions of others (witness her conversation in the opening chapters with Sir James Chettam). She does not perceive her separation. She then passes through

---

[12]Putzell-Korab, *Evolving Consciousness of George Eliot*, 23.

a confusion of her self with the world while gaining gradual awareness of the separateness of the world from her ego; she represents "objective" reality to herself in memory and imagination, and finally admits that this newly achieved spectator relationship to the world will not do. Her actions must connect to the "observed" world. This maturation of her Theoretical Mind, or Reason, corresponds to a concurrent maturation of her Practical Mind, or Will. Thus, beginning her life with the assumption that the world should correspond to her idea of it, a decision that must inevitably confront certain obstacles, Dorothea moves to the final phases of the Practical Mind, or Will, by experiencing, strangely enough, a new freedom. Her freedom consists in a willingness to choose to act as an individual *participant* in a larger life, as distinguished from an individual unaware of a larger life or an individual confronting a larger life.

According to the codicil attached to Casaubon's will, Dorothea must relinquish her inheritance if she chooses to marry Will Ladislaw. When she so decides, her break with Casaubon is final. Will, in the course of the novel, has experienced his own phases of maturation, but Dorothea has few illusions about her second husband. She seeks neither father, nor mentor, nor spiritual director. That Will engages himself in the politics of reform and that she is present to give him "wifely help" is enough for her. Eliot editorializes on the constraints society imposed on the talented woman of the nineteenth century, but those constraints also had to be factored into consciousness and decisions:

> Many who knew her thought it a pity that so substantive and rare a creature should have been absorbed into the life of another, and be only known in a certain circle as a wife and mother. But no one stated exactly what else that was in her power she ought rather to have done—not even Sir James Chettam, who went no further than the negative prescription that she ought not to have married Will Ladislaw. (576)

Even Celia objects to the marriage, but Dorothea's argument is formidable: when Celia wants to know "how it came about," Dorothea answers, "You would have to feel with me, else you would never know" (563).

This is no longer the Dorothea of earlier moral pronouncements and self-projection, but one who is aware that knowledge must shape itself to history and experience, and that action must correspond to the dialectic between the self and others. "For there is no creature," writes Eliot, "whose inward being is so strong that it is not greatly determined by what lies outside it" (577).

According to Hegel's theory of evolving consciousness, then, Perceval's conversion was less than complete, since it exemplified merely the Unhappy Consciousness, not the consciousness of an individual aware of his or her participation in the world—the *conversio ad mundum* of some spiritual writers. Sophocles' Electra, by the same norms, represents the individual confronting the world, the Practical Reason struggling to impose a subjective ideal upon actuality and indifferent to the futility and destructiveness of action motivated solely by abstract principles. Don Quixote represents a cultural moment when abstraction and actuality begin interpenetration. Don Quixote's is a fuller conversion than Perceval's since he renounces the abstract or the un-actual, but his conversion is incomplete because the author forces him out of the world before Quixote can begin the arduous business of reconnecting with society. In Don Quixote's world, however ardent the skirmish, the ultimate resolution of idea and actuality is never achieved. Sancho Panza and Don Quixote remain two separate persons; and one of them must die.

Emma Woodhouse's conversion is limited to a private world. She scarcely emerges from her own ego long enough to acknowledge the existence of a world beyond Highbury. In fact, the conclusion of the novel finds her remaining in Highbury with her husband. Jane Austen suggests that her charity to the poor had always been a little too condescending, a little too imposed. We are to conclude, apparently, that her attitude shifts to something more humble. But the poor of Emma's world are considerably detached from the great social forces that bred poverty in early nineteenth-century England. Emma lives in a socially intimate world, detached from a London sixteen mythical miles away. By contrast, Dorothea's Middlemarch is struck by the scientific, social, and political forces of the century. The England of 1829–1832 is not offstage; it is the stage. If Dorothea's consciousness is enlarged, it is because it has been invaded by the world she tried to reform. At the end of the novel, just before she moves away from Middlemarch—and that movement is an important contrasting motif to Emma's remaining at Highbury—she is almost inconspicuous. The dialogue assigned to her is minimal and her presence is muted. Her quiet answer to Celia, "You would have to feel with me, else you would never know," suggests the interiority caused by an expanded consciousness of the world and a consequent rejection of knowledge not touched by that consciousness.

Eliot's epistemology, her understanding of how interior and exterior worlds correspond in depth to one another and eventually resolve into one another, contrasts with Jane Austen's more distinctly separate public and private worlds where the heroine retreats to the private world to analyze her public experience. Our last view of the Austen heroine is in public ceremony ("The wedding was very much like other weddings"). Our last view of the Eliot heroine is scarcely a view at all; for, says the narrator, "The growing good of the world is partly dependent on unhistoric acts, and that things are not so ill with you and me as they might have been is half owing to the number who lived faithfully a hidden life, and rest in unvisited tombs" (578).

Since Dorothea has disappeared, the narrator looks to the reader, urging her anonymous hearer—for "you and me" imitates the speech-event—to be aware: what is important is hidden, incalculable. The assault on external and public significance in the world is clear. But the exaltation of the invisible has its own consequences. The external world, as a public, agreed-upon reality, will be seen as more and more irrelevant to the problem of knowing and, more especially, of judging what is important to know.

Which brings us to Walker Percy, Kierkegaard's quarrel with Hegel, and the loss of self that typifies much modern and postmodern literature. If Kahler is correct, the universe and history have expanded to quasi-infinite proportions, and the self, in turn, has become an abyss: too deep for human vision, more and more impossible to find. How, then, in such vastness does one discover a horizon, identify the limits that define the self?

WALKER PERCY:
THE VISION OF A MOVIEGOER

This, the first of his signs, Jesus did in Cana in Galilee.

—*John 2:11*

"The only difficulty was that though the universe had been disposed of, I myself was left over."[1]

Binx Bolling, Percy's existential man in search of a meaning, had described himself as reading only "fundamental" books such as *War and Peace*, Schroeder's *What Is Life?*, and Einstein's *The Universe as I See It.* "Certainly it did not matter to me where I was when I read such a book as *The Expanding Universe*," and so he finds himself a moviegoer—or rather does not find himself—because no theory accounted for *him*. A moviegoer is a spectator in darkness who waits for a sequence of events to offer significance. For Binx, there was no significance, only form; and his dilemma is his consciousness of his situation. Reading *Arabia Deserta* in his office, he enclosed it in a Standard and Poor binder—"a telling action," observes Lewis Lawson, "for he is the outwardly successful businessman who really conceives of himself as a ghost wandering a deserted space."[2] The problem of most people, according to Binx, is that they are unaware of how deserted their space is. Whatever grace they discover, or think they discover, whatever illumination they claim, has not passed through *their* time and space, *their* consciousness, *their* individuality.

At the end of *Middlemarch*, George Eliot's Dorothea Brooke had achieved a realization of how inadequate a religious spirit was when cultivated in isolation and abstracted from any sympathy with a human commu-

---

[1]Walker Percy, *The Moviegoer* (New York: Knopf, 1961) 70. Subsequent references will be indicated in the text.

[2]Lewis Lawson, "Moviegoing in *The Moviegoer*," in *Walker Percy: Art and Ethics*, ed. Jac Thorpe (Jackson: University Press of Mississippi, 1980) 29.

nity. Eliot had no illusions about the pinched dimensions of that human community and the constraints it imposed on personal genius, but spiritual growth was possible only in the context of society, in awareness of the dialectic between the individual and society. Dorothea could grow only when she became aware of how illusory ideas are when abstracted from that tension. Her consciousness enlarged as she wrestled with the perceptions of others, entered into their consciousnesses (sympathetically), and saw herself as an individual participant within a human community.

Walker Percy's Binx Bolling finds that everyone's consciousness is so engulfed by everyone else's consciousness that an individual perspective is rarely achieved, and the struggle to meet grace is the struggle to get out from under the weight of a worldview that is no one's world and no one's view. His argument against the salvific power of depersonalized knowledge is in part Kierkegaard's argument against Hegelian ethic and the Hegelian state.[3]

If the medieval understanding of salvation was an other-worldly view (Perceval's final illumination coming from above), Eliot's view of salvation was this-worldly (Dorothea's illumination coming from experience with this world and history). Walker Percy's Binx, neither this-worldly nor other-worldly, finds a means to salvation in an inner world, in the eyes of another lost self in whom he recognizes (finally) his own self and so can begin to love.

> At last I spy Kate; her stiff little Plymouth comes nosing into my bus stop. There she sits like a bomber pilot, resting on her wheel and looking sideways at the children and not seeing, and she could be I myself, sooty eyed and nowhere.
>
> Is it possible that—For a long time I have secretly hoped for the end of the world and believed with Kate and my aunt and Sam Yerger and many other people that only after the end could the few who survive creep out of their holes and discover themselves to be themselves and live as merrily as children among the viny ruins. Is it possible that—it is not too late? (231)

Binx, realizing that in his aloneness he is not alone, that Kate has accepted dependence upon him, begins to hope. The suggestion of *metanoia* is muted but sure:

> "What do you plan to do?" [Kate]

---

[3]See Søren Kierkegaard, *Fear and Trembling,* trans. Walter Lowrie (Princeton: Princeton University Press, 1941).

I shrug. "There is only one thing I can do. Listen to people, see how they stick themselves into the world, hand them along a ways in their dark journey and be handed along, and for good and selfish reasons." (233)

What has led to this conversion, and what precisely does Binx recognize that he did not perceive before?

The world of Binx Bolling is a caricature of Hegel's ethical state. It is a Kierkegaardian malaise, a society neither fearful nor trembling, a world sick unto death. In this kind of world, all virtues are inherited or borrowed or imitated; all experience is measured against the Ideal and secretly found wanting; clichés are perceived as the distillation of Spirit; and the religious seeker is as isolated as a castaway on an island.

Percy's argument is that most people live in the malaise because they do not trust their experience. They seek "certification" of its value, secretly suspecting that nothing they experience has meaning unless it is confirmed by the group or the group's representatives. (A psychiatrist must certify that a symptom is interesting and significant; an anthropologist, that a tourist's experience is appropriately folk cultural; companions on a camping trip, that "we really are having a good time.") Movies are significant. Life is not. Movies filmed in one's own city can certify that the city is significant. The universe is significant. This time and place are not. History is significant. Yesterday's events are not. Religion is significant. My religious agony is not. In one sense, we are all castaways, but few recognize their predicament. For the others, what message about the means of rescue can reach them?

To avoid the despair that follows the denial of significance to this time, this place, this city, this self, we seize upon a self, any self at all, a self constructed from tradition, from society, from professional identity, from popular values and borrowed creeds. Here, according to Percy, is where most of us are. This behavior makes us inhabitants of the malaise—true "malaisians." If the borrowing of a self does not give the sense of significant existence, pain can be avoided by rotating pleasures (in the absence of absolutely new ones, like those an amnesia victim would experience), or we can construct artificial plotlines in life that seem to eliminate dead time between significant events:

> The moments of rotation or repetition are of such peculiar interest to the contemporary alienated consciousness because they represent the two obvious alternatives or deliverances from alienation. . . . The fugitive in the English thriller who catches the next available train from Waterloo station and who, thinking himself on a routine journey, suddenly catches sight of a landmark which strikes

to the heart and who with every turn of the wheel comes that much closer to the answer to who am I?—this one has stumbled into pure repetition (as when Captain Ryder alighted from his blacked-out train to find himself—back in Brideshead).[4]

Dead time between repetitions is "everydayness." The usual method of redeeming everydayness is to adopt a form and lower it over one's life, thus giving existence an impression of significance. Like Auden's Unknown Citizen, Binx Bolling could be theoretically identified only by what information is available about him: "I am a model tenant and a model citizen and take pleasure in doing all that is expected of me. My wallet is full of identity cards, library cards, credit cards. . . . It is a pleasure to carry out the duties of a citizen and to receive in return a receipt or a neat styrene card with one's name on it certifying so to speak one's right to exist" (6-7).

Binx's Aunt Emily, Southern grande dame and stoic, incarnates form minus substance. She says to Binx in the moment of her greatest disappointment in him: "I did my best for you, son. I gave you all I had. More than anything I wanted to pass on to you the one heritage of the men of our family, a certain quality of spirit, a gaiety, a sense of duty, a nobility worn lightly, a sweetness, a gentleness with women, the only good things the South ever had and the only things that really matter in this life" (224).

Uncle Jules finds meaning in reliving the triumphs of the 1932 Tulane football team and dreaming of reviving them. In the meantime, he lives in everydayness, not knowing that he has emptied time of meaning and is thus a victim of the malaise. To relive any event is to cancel the sense of empty time between and thus to pretend that, as in the movies, there is no empty time. Binx had discovered once—when he was in a foxhole in Korea—that time could have newness and urgency, be dense with significance, that it could be redeemed. When a comparable experience of contingency recurred, his search began. He came, as he said, "onto something."

> . . . this morning when I got up I dressed as usual and began as usual to put my belongings into my pockets. . . . They looked both unfamiliar and at the same time full of clues. I stood in the center of the room and gazed at the little pile, sighting through a hole made by thumb and forefinger. What was unfamiliar about them was that I could see them. They might have belonged to someone else. (11)

---

[4]Walker Percy, "The Man on the Train," in *The Message in the Bottle* (1954; New York: Farrar, Straus, Giroux, 1982) 87.

With this glimpse of himself as stranger, Binx would begin to discover himself. Part of his search was the exploration of what he had inherited: the uncertain memory of his father, killed in a war, who was only happy in crisis; the stoic tradition of his Aunt Emily, who wanted to mold him into familial culture and is disappointed by his apparent lack of ambition. For Binx, Emily's stoicism, her rootedness in class, was simply another dead form against which he had been unconsciously revolting most of his life. Dead forms emptied existence of meaning. In the midst of Aunt Emily's most furious tirade against his untraditional behavior, he had heard the chimney sweep outside: "R.r.ramonez la cheminée du haut en bas." But before he emptied his life of form, he had attempted every kind of escape from the pain of everydayness. When neither repetition nor rotation enabled him to escape the pain, he could only hope that the world would come to an end, that perhaps a few survivors gathered together could find innocence and newness and community.

To Percy, salvation is the recognition that the authentic self is already certified; it exists with or without the confirmation of the group (preferably without); it creates value rather than inheriting it; *this* time, *this* place, is the locus of significance. This castaway on this island will be alert and hungry for messages appropriate to this specific predicament. Rescue for an islander does not consist in imagining oneself on the mainland or on a more populated island noted on tourist maps. In "The Message in the Bottle," Percy distinguishes the message from "news" and insists on the relevance of the message to the predicament of the castaway. But he goes beyond Kierkegaard's quarrel with Hegel:

> Kierkegaard, of all people, overlooked a major canon of significance of the news from across the seas . . . the most Kierkegaardian canon. One canon has to do with the news and the newsbearer, the nature of the news, and the credentials of the newsbearer. But the other canon has to do with the hearer of the news. Who is the hearer when all is said and done? . . . The hearer is the castaway, . . . the man who finds himself cast into the world.[5]

The Moviegoer concentrates not on the problem of the news and the newsbearer, but on the hearer of the news, the castaway who is conscious of his situation. It is consciousness that isolates, that tells us we are lost. It is that consciousness, heightened now to the point of pain, that must be addressed.

---

[5] See the title essay in *Message in the Bottle*, 147-48.

Given the Kierkegaardian world where most of us, according to Percy, are lost because we cannot locate ourselves on any map of the universe, where subjectivity has been exchanged for external form, the only illumination possible is the recognition that one is not alone in one's longing to be; indeed, two or three together, admitting their aloneness, can become a world. Touching on the redemptive aspects of such a community, Percy writes in "The Man on the Train":

> The modern literature of alienation is in reality the triumphant reversal of alienation through its re-presenting. It is not an existential solution such as Holderlin's Homecoming, or Heidegger's openness to being, but is an aesthetic victory of comradeliness, a recognition of plight in common. Its motto is not "I despair and do not know that I despair" but "At least we know that we are lost to ourselves" which is very great knowledge indeed.[6]

Percy did not want to write the classic novel of alienation, filled with rotations and repetitions, as resolution of the dilemma. His are not characters with gestural perfection, the Clint Eastwoods, Gary Coopers, and Rory Calhouns of the movies, or even the Charles Ryders and the Frederick Henrys of literature. His Binx Bolling fails miserably at both seduction and copulation. His eventual marriage to Kate is the union of two fallen people who know their vulnerabilities and their limitations, and who cast their lot with one another. No gestural perfection is required, no amnesia or artistically arranged coincidence throws them together. What will draw them to one another and possibly effect their salvation is their mutual recognition and knowledge that the world around both of them is dying—sick, in fact, unto death. It cannot save. Thus, Percy's account of the moviegoer who finally discovers how to be rescued from the movies is threaded with images of sulfurous dying and ashes and soot from old fires. Before Binx sees Kate drive up in her Plymouth, he looks at the deserted playground: "A watery sunlight breaks through the smoke of the Chef and turns the sky yellow. Elysian Fields, glistens like a vat of sulfur: the playground looks as if it alone had survived the end of the world" (182).

The death experience had to be accomplished, moreover, within Binx's own personality. Aunt Emily's withering attack against him for his apparent betrayal of her values, by what had looked like a seduction of Kate, was the final trial. Binx collapses into despair, seeing himself like Kafka's Gregor Samsa—the archetypal dung beetle of human society:

---

[6]Percy, "Man on the Train," 93.

Now in the thirty-first year of my dark pilgrimage on this earth and knowing less than I ever knew before, having learned only to recognize *merde* when I see it, having inherited no more from my father than a good nose for *merde*, for every species of shit that flies— my only talent, smelling *merde* from every quarter, living, in fact, in the very century of *merde* the great shithouse of scientific humanism where needs are satisfied, everyone becomes an anyone, a warm and creative person, and prospers like a dung beetle, and one hundred percent of people are humanists and ninety-eight percent believe in God, and men are dead, dead, dead; and the malaise has settled like a fall-out and what people really fear is not that the bomb will fall but that the bomb will not fall—on this my thirtieth birthday, I know nothing and there is nothing to do but fall prey to desire. (228)

Only when Kate comes to him, triumphing in her own way over Aunt Emily's titanic disapproval, could Binx begin to hope. When Kate realizes that Binx understands her own malaise and her self-destructive response to it, she turns to him, and he recognizes the way out (possibly) for both of them. It is Ash Wednesday, the day of repentance and conversion and remembrance of dying. There is soot on the foreheads of churchgoers. Reviewing the risks of his commitment to her, he takes her hand and kisses blood from a small self-inflicted injury. "But you must try not to hurt yourself so much" (234). The gesture is both self-offering and union. Promising to take care of Kate, whose mental illness will require patience and constant attentiveness, Binx in the final chapter offers her a flower, watches her, and hears finally "my brothers and sisters call out behind me" (242). He has given himself to Kate, to family, and to the business of loving.

The postrecognition experience is resurrection. *The Moviegoer* begins with death and ends with death and resurrection. When Binx's older brother Scott dies in chapter one, Aunt Emily informed Binx that he must act "like a soldier." And thus Binx had been thrown into the world of the malaise, acting like a soldier in good stoic fashion. But Binx had never been quite satisfied with acting like a soldier or a doctor or a Southern gentleman or anything else. However, he did manage to act enough like a stockbroker to make money, and he tried to act like Gregory Peck and Rory Calhoun when he was on one of his rotating pleasure trips. When, in the final chapter, Lonnie dies, Binx is in the interesting position of notifying Lonnie's brothers and sisters. He has already ceased acting himself and does not impose a role on anyone else.

"Is he going to die?" Therese asks in her canny smart girl way.

"Yes . . . but he wouldn't want you to be sad. He told me to give you a kiss and tell you that he loved you." They are not sad. This is a very serious and out-of-the-way business. Their eyes search out mine and they cast about for ways of prolonging the conversation, this game of serious talk and serious listening. . . . Donice casts about. "Binx," he says and then appears to forget. "When Our Lord raises us up on the Last Day, will Lonnie still be in a wheelchair or will he be like us?"

"He'll be like you."

"You mean he'll be able to ski?" The children cock their heads and listen like old men.

"Yes."[7] (240)

Binx has now become the message bearer, the one who brings news from across the seas and announces it "in perfect sobriety and in good faith."[8] With the hint of Lonnie's resurrection, we observe the birth of authentic self in Binx Bolling. If the moment seems scarcely observable, its relative invisibility is consistent with Percy's theme: that in the search for significance, we must include the invisible moments of loving where grace is offered, the self is acknowledged, and everydayness is redeemed.

Walker Percy's *The Moviegoer* inverts the Aristotelian theory of recognition. In Aristotle, recognition occurs as part of the plot. In Greek drama, the discovery of relationship is crucial: that Jocasta is Oedipus's mother, that the traveler is Clytemnestra's son and Electra's brother, that Pentheus is Agave's son. Such realizations, before or after a possible death or killing, will determine whether we have a fatal or fortunate plot. Penelope, in Greek narrative, must discern whether the stranger in her house is Odysseus. Binx Bolling begins farther back. He must discover that he is someone who can recognize. The problem raised is not who Kate is or Aunt Emily or Lonnie, but who he (Binx) is, if anyone. No information is offered in his Gentilly neighborhood or family universe that helps him to recognize the stranger within. If Odysseus is an unknown guest in his own house, Binx does not even have a house. He rents a basement in someone else's house, an alien to himself as well as to others. Kierkegaard's observations about inauthentic persons never inhabiting their

[7]Percy admitted to John Carr that this dialogue is a gloss on the end of *The Brothers Karamazov*. See John Carr, "Rotation and Repetition," in *Kite-Flying and Other Irrational Acts: Conversations with Twelve Southern Writers* (Baton Rouge: Louisiana State University Press, 1972) 49.

[8]Percy, "Man on the Train," 93.

houses but always living in the basements of their own personalities are clearly pertinent here.[9]

In Greek drama, according to Aristotle's theorizing, the artistic problem was to construct a causal sequence of events and then to create a character (out of an agent) whose motivating power can charge or impel forward the events to be enacted. In Percy's fiction, the sequence of events is less important than the emergence of character. First, one must recognize the self. And at that point, the novel is almost over, since self-acknowledgment is such a major achievement in a self-denying society. Illumination is correspondent to the discovery of self, for knowledge in the abstract is not experienced truth, is not "message."

But there is change also—conversion—in *The Moviegoer*. The sharp tonal shift in the final chapter effectively reveals Binx's new perception. If he was "onto something" earlier, he had begun to apprehend at the end what that "something" was about. Binx's love for Kate will make particular demands of him not comparable to his attraction to interchangeable secretaries (Marcia, Linda, Sharon). It is Kate's lostness that draws Binx to her, and their mutual recognition initiates what *peripeteia* occurs in *The Moviegoer*.

The only other hint of such mutual discovery in the novel is that between Binx and Lonnie, and that experience functions as a catalyst in the final commitment of Binx to Kate. Binx had recognized in Lonnie someone who was confident of the religious meaning of his life and who could resist the values of less persuaded people. It was Binx who accepted Lonnie's stubborn rejection of mere ethics. When Lonnie wanted to fast in his illness because of his own sense of sin and despite every human and reasonable objection—his own version of Kierkegaard's "teleological suspension of the ethical"—Binx did not argue except on Lonnie's terms, which were religious. Binx, hostile to the traditional ethic he had been exposed to from Aunt Emily and equally suspicious of the apparent shallowness of his mother's religion, could comprehend Lonnie's authenticity. The scene at the Moonlite Drive-In when Lonnie, Sharon, and Binx watch *Fort Dobbs* functions almost as a covenant ceremony between Lonnie and his half-brother. "A good night: Lonnie happy (he looks around at me with the liveliest sense of the secret between us; . . .) the secret is that Sharon is not and never will be onto the little touches we see in the movie" (143).

Both Lonnie and Binx thrill to gestural perfection and self-assurance and know that neither is possible in life. They are both in on the secret:

---

[9]Søren Kierkegaard, *Sickness unto Death*, trans. Walter Lowrie (Princeton: Princeton University Press, 1941) 176.

there are no cowboy heroes in the Western desert. The communion between Lonnie and Binx prepares the latter for communion with Kate, for Lonnie in parabolic fashion had testified to the possibility of health in a world sick unto death. Binx, aware of Lonnie's faith and later of Kate's willingness to risk life with him, enters into both self-discovery and communion, committed to those few at least who know they are on a "dark journey."

Walker Percy's Binx bears comparison with the character types we shall see in the Fourth Gospel: the "believers." In that text, only those whose fundamental attitude was "searching" or who were open to *metanoia* came to believe in the hidden Presence in their midst. Only the believers accepted that Presence who could reconcile the transcendent with the historically particular. "Unbelievers" are nonsearchers who live in a world of darkness and resist any light, which exposes their vulnerability. The world of *The Moviegoer* is populated by nonsearchers who move in darkness. But it is a darkness where lights are always blinking, as if to hint at the possibility of vision in however brief a moment or a space.

Only in the chapter introducing Lonnie do we have an excess of light: "I cannot believe my eyes. It is difficult to understand . . . there is the camp ablaze like the Titanic. The Smiths are home" (136). Yet the image of the Titanic suggests the kind of world Binx visualizes his family inhabiting. Their cottage was "a cone of light" amid "the blackness of night over water." But inside, Lonnie, who wanted a "Trans-World" radio, informed Binx:

> "I am still offering my communion for you," and then . . .
> "Do you love me?"
> "Yes."
> "How much?"
> "Quite a bit." (165)

The small resonances with John's Gospel (see John 21) are persistent and curious. It is during the interval at the cottage that Lonnie is described as offering his suffering to the "pierced heart of Jesus Christ" (137). (When Lonnie speaks in outworn religious vocabulary, it recovers its meaning because he is at home in the language he speaks.) Binx, allowing his laconic mask to drop when he is with Lonnie, converses honestly with him, and while with his family in that interval of honesty, he begins his search in earnest, writing notes to himself in the dark about the signs of God.[10]

---

[10]See Gary Ciuba's commentary on this scene in "*The Moviegoer:* Signs of the Divine Eiron," *Notes on Contemporary Literature* 17 (November 1987): 10-13. "But

In the final moment of conversion with Kate in the car, Binx looked at the Ash Wednesday visitors to church, soot on their foreheads, and wondered about the complexity of motives that may have impelled the well-dressed black he saw in the rearview mirror to come to the services: "Is it part and parcel of the complex business of coming up in the world? Or is it because he believes that God himself is present here at the corner of Elysian Fields and Bons Enfants? Or is he here for both reasons: through some dim dazzling trick of grace, coming for the one and receiving the other as God's own importunate bonus?" (235). Binx's angle of vision in this scene suggests the analogy between him and the stranger. How does God find his way to us if not in history, at those intersections where old worlds die and the self is born?

The invisibility of God, the gratuitous gift, the ambiguity of existence, the occasional believer, the final mystery: Percy leaves us in a world open to possibility, where seekers find one another in the darkness and grace touches down on street corners. If the historical world seems to have spun out of the world of the novel, it is only that we may focus on the world of the individual and his or her struggle to find the boundary between two abysses.

Recognition in *The Moviegoer* does not hint at final answers, totality of significance, or a blissful future for the loving couple. Darkness is not unrelieved, but neither is it dissipated. What is hidden can be revealed (briefly) only if one knows that "if the proofs were proved and God presented himself, nothing would be changed" (146). For change is possible not because "truth" has been announced, but because a hearer, knowing that s/he is lost, has recognized the relevance of a message "from beyond the seas" to a particular broken, fragmented, and apparently insignificant moment in history. Understanding that message brings a spectator out of the darkness of theatre. Consenting to less plotted, particularized human existence will have its problems, but illusion will not be one of them.

---

for Percy the answer to the castaway's situation originates not in himself but beyond the sea. . . . Binx's apathy toward the traditional proofs enables him to be open to the newsbearer who does not offer arguments but embodies faith amid his own terrible predicament." Lonnie is such a news bearer.

PINTER'S <u>NO MAN'S LAND</u>: THE LIMITS OF LANGUAGE

Secrets, in short, are at odds with sequence, which is considered as an aspect of propriety; and a passion for sequence may result in the suppression of the secret.
—Frank Kermode, <u>The Art of Telling</u>

The loss of illusion is at the heart of contemporary literature. This is somewhat of an ironic turn, certainly, since literature seemed always to be itself an illusion of some kind. But the loss we are considering here is the assumption that literature should promise meaning within the text. Not every critic looks for meaning, and not every novelist or playwright acknowledges that a story should make what we like to call "sense." In such texts, neither recognition nor self-discovery seems possible. We cannot trace here all the directions to which the loss of this last illusion has taken contemporary writers. Part of the purpose of this book has been to suggest that the epistemological issue (how do we know anything that we know?) is not new, but that the assumptions on which the argument has been conducted have shifted. The issue has become intensified because premises have been displaced. Much of contemporary literature assumes the disappearance of a language world that narrator and reader once shared. That world has been cut adrift from its traditional moorings in both intentionality and reference. Even if we know what we know, how can we say it? and to whom? If Binx Bolling was Walker Percy's castaway on an island, we could raise the question of the problematic existence of an island, since the possibility of an accurate map is arguable. Given the questions being raised, it is not surprising that the literary enterprise is more engaged in the mystifications of maps than in the predicament of castaways. If this attentiveness seems misplaced, we have to admit anew that a map is not itself a rescue operation, yet it may be all that we have to employ. It will not hurt us to know its limits. And that— knowing the limits of language—is the critical task.

A Harold Pinter play is generally about limits: the limits of life, of time, of space, of love, and of the language we use to talk about these things. It is more about the silences between words than words themselves, or about the space on a page where little black marks act like people speaking. To hear and watch a Pinter play is to be aware of the white space on a printed page, or perhaps *not* to be aware of it and so misread. As few other playwrights do, he shows us how much space there is and how small are our words. Although it may seem eccentric and disorderly, in a book that has proceeded chronologically, to compare Pinter and the Bible—a sacred text antecedent to modern drama by 1900 years—the Gospels raise questions not unlike contemporary narratives. To look at Pinter's *No Man's Land,* for example, and then at Mark's gospel (in the next part of this book) can remind us of how much is at stake when we think we know to what scale our language map is drawn and what the configuration is about. To study this gospel requires a critical effort comparable to that required by postmodern fiction—and I use Pinter's *No Man's Land* as an exemplum of that genre—for possible meaning in the Gospels, especially Mark's, lies very much in the space around the words. We approach that meaning not exclusively by examining what is outlined, but by considering what has been deflected by the outline, what we perceive as being absent.

When Harold Pinter's characters in the modern drama of the absurd arrive on stage, we are not prepared to comprehend, we are not enlightened about their motivations. They speak, and we hear but do not understand. We listen, but the dialogue does not explain the dramatic situation we are witnessing. At least, the dialogue does not explain it to our satisfaction. But more. The dialogue is not merely unenlightening; it is mystifying. Language absorbs us, but opens to us at the same time the ambiguity and darkness of our relationship to one another.

Such a narrative can suggest that there is no ultimate meaning, or that meaning is inaccessible, or simply that any claim—especially on the part of a playwright—that we can know a human situation is pretentious. Since we have no access to another's mind and motivations beyond those which are declared to us, or what we can infer, a playwright or novelist is justified in leaving characters similarly inexplicable. We have been disciplined to anticipate the disclosure of meaning in a text. But texts may also express an experience of nonmeaning. Pinter's dramas "state"—and that word surely can be subverted—that preconceived understanding of who another is, or will be, how he or she will talk, what dialogue will be "about" are all foreign to our actual experience. Drama that translates our lack of knowledge, or habitual misperceptions, and our cognitive discomfort is faithful to reality. "After all," urges Martin Esslin, "the opaqueness, the impenetrability of other people's lives, their feelings, their true motivations, is precisely an essential feature of the true quality of the world and of our own experience of it."[1]

Clearly, what distinguishes a Pinter dialogue from unstaged conversations is its structure, intensity, tempo, silences—its capacity, in short, to compel our attention, to draw us into the mystery of human interaction. Ruth and Lenny in *The Homecoming* "converse":

LENNY
Excuse me, shall I take this ashtray out of your way?

RUTH
It's not in my way.

LENNY
It seems to be in the way of your glass. The glass was about to fall. Or the ashtray.[2]

(Act 1)

This is heightened, rhythmic, antiphonal discourse, dense with conflictual energy. We are not hearing a random conversation, but an agon. Within a few lines, we hear an allusion to the limitations of space and a struggle between Lenny and Ruth about the wisdom of rearranging an object. Can Lenny and Ruth occupy contiguous space without one or the other falling? The fact that we do not understand what Lenny and Ruth are really talking about at this moment in the play only intensifies the sense of struggle—theirs and ours. What kind of recognition is possible when the audience struggles throughout a play with consistently enigmatic dialogue? Are we to suppose that the characters know more about each other than the audience does, or does the audience know (presumably) more than the characters? What is the cathartic effect of an audience confounded? We must assume the struggle with nonmeaning has its revelatory dimension and that Pinter darkly implies just that.

No Man's Land represents a struggle to resist death, only to fall back and consent to entombment, to be "no man." It is a character in past time faced with the opportunity of being "present and active," but acknowledging finally that the past can be fixed, however arbitrarily, and the present never admitted. This paralysis in fantasized memories and hopelessness constitutes the resolution, for the tempo and tension of the play

[1]Martin Esslin, *Pinter: A Study of His Plays* (New York: W. W. Norton, 1976) 42-43.

[2]Harold Pinter, *The Homecoming* (New York: Grove Press, 1975) 33.

is mere desperate twitching, the choked attempt of a few people to save themselves. We watch the effort:

> HIRST (pouring whiskey)
>
> As it is?

> SPOONER
>
> As it is, yes, please, absolutely, as it is.[3]

And their final words in the second act suggest that nothing has happened because of their interaction—or ever will.

> SPOONER
>
> No. You are in no man's land. Which never moves, which never changes, which never grows older, but which remains forever, icy and silent.
>
> *Silence*

> HIRST
>
> I'll drink to that.
>
> *He drinks.*
>
> *Slow fade.*   (95)

Between these two moments of chilled discourse we observe the taut interaction of four characters in something resembling a struggle. It is not clear for what. According to Pinter, it does not have to be. We can speculate, however, as critics and audiences are wont to do, desiring to know why we have consented for an hour or so to watch these four actors gesticulate (minimally) and speak their appointed lines.

Martin Esslin argues that Spooner is a broken-down poet who wants a more secure position as companion and "Chevalier" to the wealthy poet-essayist Hirst, and that Hirst's "secretary" (Foster) and "butler" (Briggs), who already provide such a service, exclude the overeager Spooner, thus relegating him to a life of absolute loneliness.[4]

Hirst, consenting to the bonds already tightening around him and controlled by Briggs and Foster, rejects the possibility of change. Hirst and Spooner, then, are both condemned to live in a "no man's land," both unfree, both without a future. Esslin argues that *No Man's Land* "has a

---

[3]Harold Pinter, *No Man's Land* (New York: Grove Press, 1975) 15. All subsequent citations are taken from this edition and page numbers will be indicated in the text.

[4]Esslin, *Pinter*, 200.

very powerful statement to make—and, as so often with Pinter, on more than one level."[5] He describes the play as a study of the fear of old age: "Throughout a man's life there remains at least the possibility of choice while some of youth's flexibility is preserved. But there comes a point, the onset of old age, when that possibility reaches zero. Then life congeals into the immutable winter of the no man's land between life and death."[6]

Another interpretation is that Spooner is death itself, arriving in Hirst's room like a morality play summoner to whom Hirst says at one moment in the conversation, "Is there a big fly in there? I hear buzzing."[7] But such a reading, if pressed too far, does not account for Spooner's pleading and for what appears to be his rejection by Hirst, who simply says after Spooner's long description of his own admirable qualities as a possible amanuensis:

> Let us change the subject.
>
> *Pause.*
>
> For the last time.   (91)

This certainly sounds like a rejection of Spooner. (He will not be Hirst's secretary.) At the end of act 2, Hirst, still twitching, still realizing that the possibility of some kind of change has been offered him, says of a dream he had: "I was walking towards a lake. Someone was following me, through the trees. I lose him, easily. I see a body in the water. I say to myself, I saw a body drowning. But I am mistaken. There is nothing there" (95).

After the usual Pinter silence, Spooner says, "No. You are in no man's land." His reply is acknowledgment. Whatever recognition occurs within the play is in the silence preceding this comment. Spooner realizes that he is defeated and will be forever drowned. If, as is common in Pinter's dramas,[8] Spooner and Hirst are one divided personality, they are both drowning. Hirst, having resisted the possibility of change, will remain forever unmoved, fixed in his unfreedom. It is possible that an audience

---

[5]Ibid., 191.

[6]Ibid., 200.

[7]See Thomas Adler, "From Flux to Fixity: Art and Death in Pinter's *No Man's Land*," *Arizona Quarterly* 35 (1979): 197-203, at 200.

[8]See Ruth Milberg, "1 + 1 = 1: Dialogue and Character Splitting in Harold Pinter," *Die neueren sprachen* 3 (June 1974): 225-33.

may experience here a kind of low-grade pity and fear. If Hirst seems un-perturbed, we, at least, are not. We are reminded, although less sensa-tionally, of Evelyn Waugh's *A Handful of Dust* when Tony Last's final opportunity for freedom passes and we know he will be reading Dickens forever to his psychotic captor in the South American jungle.

What Pinter is dramatizing—that is, making dramatically experiential—is the inverse of all we customarily expect of drama. For plot, he gives us inaction; for character, enigma; for diction, incomprehensibility; for spec-tacle, perpetual drinking—emblematic of a will to oblivion— and darkness. There is no reversal and no articulation of discovery, only a silence by which we surmise that something has been recognized, and *that* something is that nothing in the initial situation has changed or ever will. Pinter's ability to take all that is nondramatic (silence, darkness, inaction, nonrevelatory dia-logue) and make it dramatic is a tribute to his poetic power. He makes us experience what we are, in fact, trying to get away from by our presence in the theatre. It is still an open question as to whether he has succeeded in pleasing us as well as arresting our attention.

Pinter gives us three paradigms in *No Man's Land*, which evoke a sense of nonaction, nonvision, and nondirection. The first is Hirst's photo-graph album, which represents his fixed memories. In tension with the photograph album and all it signifies to Hirst is Spooner's calculated ef-fort to rearrange Hirst's memories, to create new memories, to question the past, and to introduce a future. First, he contradicts Hirst's own memories (or fantasies) of his happy marriage: "Was she ever here? Was she ever there, in your cottage? It is my duty to tell you that you have failed to convince" (act 1, p. 31).

When Spooner urges his friendship upon Hirst ("You need a friend. You have a long hike, my lad, up which, presently you slog un-friended"), Hirst resists: "No man's land . . . does not move . . . or change . . . or grow old . . . remains . . . forever . . . icy . . . silent" (34).

At the end of their first conversation, Hirst collapses and crawls out of the room, leaving Spooner alone. Upon his return and after Spooner's initial conversation with Briggs and Foster, Hirst suggests that he does not know and has never met Spooner. He has added nothing, in other words, to his memory:

HIRST
Who is this man? Do I know him?

FOSTER
He says he's a friend of yours.

HIRST
My true friends look out at me from my album. (45)

He denies his own identity. With no personal continuum, he need not recognize anything or anyone. That he persistently renames every character in the play at this point as a way of renouncing both their identities and his own is consistent with the nonself Pinter has created. Hirst's present is as arbitrary as his past, because he will not permit his past— problematic, in any case—to extend into it. If Hirst does not want to lose control of his past, his two servants resist losing their control over the present. They have no intention of being threatened by Spooner's intrusion into their arrangement, such as it is, with Hirst. A paradigm of controlled space occurs at the end of act 1 when, in a foreshadowing of what will be Spooner's own destiny, Foster locks him in the parlor overnight and turns the lights off:

> Listen. You know what it's like when you're in a room with the light on and then suddenly the light goes out? I'll show you. It's like this:
>
> *He turns the light out.*
>
> *Blackout.*
>
> (End of Act One)   (53)

The moment functions as an appropriate spatial/temporal center of the drama.

The final paradigm of space/time imprisonment is the monologue in the second act in which Briggs describes how he gave directions to Foster to get to Bolsover Street. If the audience finds the verbal labyrinth amusing, it is their own acknowledgment that Kafkaesque mapping parodied to absurdity can be a grotesquely comic image of our lostness. The sense of directionless space that this image sustains functions in turn as a metaphor for the undiscovered and uncertain self. "All he's got to do," says Briggs in the middle of the long incoherent passage, "is to reverse into the underground car park, change gear, go straight on, and he'll find himself in Bolsover Street with no trouble at all. I did warn him, though, that he'll still be faced with the problem, having found Bolsover Street, of losing it. I told him I knew one or two people who'd been wandering up and down Bolsover Street for years" (62). The elusiveness of memory, moreover, blurs even this narrative, which begins and ends with Briggs's observation: "I should tell you he'll deny this account. His story will be different" (63).

The tension of the play is Spooner's invasion of frozen time and limited space and how that invasion is resisted. He describes himself in act 1 as interested "in where I am eternally present and active," as if he were

a personified verb. Time is Hirst's territory: "There are places in my heart
. . . where no living man . . . has . . . or can ever . . . trespass" (84).
Place is Foster and Briggs's territory:

                              HIRST
The light . . . out there . . . is gloomy . . . hardly day-
light at all. It is falling, rapidly. Distasteful. Let us close
the curtain. Put the lamps on.   (86)

                              FOSTER
Hey, scout, I think there's been some kind of misunder-
standing. You're not in some shithouse down by the
docks. You're in the home of a man of means, of a man
of achievement. Do you understand me?   (48)

Spooner tries to enter both Hirst's time and his servants' guarded
space. But neither the time nor the space that Spooner attempts to enter
has any reference to reality. We suspect that Hirst's memories are fantasies and the Foster-Briggs travel accounts surreal: "Do you know what
I saw once in the desert, in the Australian desert? A man walking along
carrying two umbrellas. Two umbrellas. In the outback" (52).

In this time/space artifice, Spooner is treated as the alien, the Other,
whose presence is threatening because he crosses thresholds. He tries to
rearrange. He tries to impose meaning. "Was it raining?" he inquires of
Foster after hearing his account of the man with two umbrellas. In his final monologue, Spooner offers his services once again—planning a new
existence for the aging Hirst, proposing to bring the author's written
words to life again by public readings: "You would be there in body and
creating a new audience. It would bring you to the young, the young to
you" (90). But recreated life is impossible for Hirst. His text has been written, fixed, its meaning closed, because his words will be forever inaccessible.

                              HIRST
Let us change the subject.
Pause.
For the last time.   (91)

Hirst is entombed in a "last time," and Spooner, his reader, his interpreter—and thus his present, his future, his possibility of life—perishes.
Hirst's servants keep him in existence with food and drink, and possibly
sex, but they do not meet their employer in discourse at any other level,
a fact that makes Spooner's appeal "Let me live with you and be your secretary" peculiarly poignant. The death of both passion and poetry are im-

plied in the Marlovian resonance. Spooner's offer is inadequate. He asks to "exhume" Hirst and is refused, because of the overpowering presence of the two brute forces in control of Hirst. "All we have left," Spooner had said in act 1, "is the English language. Can it be salvaged?" Hirst, in reply, had described Spooner as its "salvation" (19). But Hirst (language, text, paralyzed impotent) cannot deliver himself to re-cognition, and hence the divided self (Hirst-Spooner/text-reader) dies.

If we cannot form conclusions at the end of such a play, we can at least observe our own response to it. Pinter is not troubled by audience perplexity; indeed, he courts it. At the end of *No Man's Land*, we experience what Denis Donoghue once called "epistemological erosion," which, he argues, parallels the undermining of *person* that has been going on in the theater for several decades.[9] We have come a long way from Odysseus, who could not endure to be "no man" for very long, and Electra, whose destiny required that Orestes be surely identified. In Greek drama, the audience is never in doubt about the identity of anyone. But postmodern dramatic consciousness disengaged from the shifting particularities of time and space is not merely epistemological erosion, but subjective disintegration. As audience, our discomfort is a reasonably appropriate response to what the text has offered. And Pinter does not apologize for dramatizing what is possible in a world populated by frightened, lonely, aggressive, and unpredictable people who interact with other frightened, lonely, and aggressive people. The lack of clarity and significance that is our normal lot is intensified and made palpable in this kind of theater.

It has been suggested that Pinter has distorted human experience, that we do not recognize in his theater the lucidity we occasionally experience: the human joys, love, fidelity, achievement—those moments that rescue us now and then from pain and darkness and bewilderment. But Pinter (or any other playwright) is under no artistic obligation to say everything that can be said. He has elected to dramatize our darker experiences: the violent urges, the hostile game playing, the unspoken terror, and ultimately, our apparent loss of identity and language.

What are we to do with this strangely refracted mirror of human action? Pinter illustrates in a particularly intense way fairly simple realities that we probably should not ignore. People (not just women) are unknowable. Some of them are threatening. Most of them are lonely. Life

---

[9]Denis Donoghue, "The Human Image in Modern Drama," *Lugano Review* 1:3-4 (Summer 1965): 155-68, at 161. Donoghue's comments are still relevant.

seems directionless, a prison-house, a closed room. There is no exit and sometimes no love: Spooner: "Have you? Ever? Been loved?" (26) Language is indecipherable. We skirmish for place and for power. We perish. What Pinter offers us is the mimesis of human existence without apparent hope, contracted in space, denied both the memory of the past and the vision of a future. What is left to us is language, and that also is in danger.

·PART III·

RECOGNITION IN CHRISTIAN LITERATURE

*C*hronology is an organizing strategy that allows us to examine change, and the argument of this book has proceeded on the assumption that our understanding of <u>how we know</u> has been explicated differently in different literary classics. In this century the notion of narrative time itself has dissolved as artists challenge and defy the expectations of their audiences, the expectations that lure us to narrative, dramatic or otherwise, with the promise of significance. But narrative, however shaped, is yet the favored mode of expressing imagined life. The classics of literature return us to everydayness with a sense of what David Tracy has described as ''intensification.'' We ''recognize,'' he argues, that the paradigmatic is somehow real.

> When anyone of us is caught unawares by a genuine work of art, we find ourselves in the grip of an event, a happening, a disclosure, a claim to truth which we cannot deny and can only eliminate by our later controlled reflection: it was only play, merely the private expression of a private self, a new quality, an illusion, magic, unreal. But in the experience of art we lose our usual self-consciousness and finally encounter a rooted self—a self transformed into both new possibility

and the actuality of rootedness by its willingness to play and be played by that transforming disclosure.[1]

We return to the classics of literature over and over again because we know their transforming power. We know that whatever the narrative strategy, the artist has ventured into the imaginative possibilities of human existence with the kind of courage and vision we ourselves may lack, and we need to draw from that courage and give ourselves to the vision. So unremitting is our longing for story that it is impossible to conceive even of idle conversation without its narrative dimension.

For this reason, I urged earlier in this book that the classics of Judeo-Christian Scripture are "grounded" in narrative. This is not to deny the numerous other forms of disclosure that are part of the biblical texts: hymns, canticles, apothegms, laws, prayers, proclamations. But I submit (along with David Tracy) that our prejudice is for narrative and that the disclosures of narrative are ultimately more compelling, more transforming than the disclosures of isolated announcements. It is narrative that turns announcement into a message.

Each composer of narrative offers a singular vision, but the response to the visions of great writers is like the response of the first-century audience to the Pentecostal preachers: "How does it happen that each of us hears them in his own native language?"[2] As each generation returns to the stories written in the past, we hear—each in our own language—what has been seen and expressed by others. In that sense, literature has no chronology. Odysseus is as present to us as Leopold Bloom and Godot, but he is present in a way that is different from his presence to Homer's audience.

If the classics of "profane" literature invite each generation to participate in their vision, what are we to say of those classics of religious literature that we continue to hear and hear proclaimed?[3] Do they not also invite rereading?

---

[1]David Tracy, *The Analogical Imagination: Christian Theology and the Culture of Pluralism* (New York: Crossroad, 1981) 114-15.

[2]Acts 2:8-9.

[3]In this study, I have focused on the response to what other writers, such as Rudolf Bultmann, describe as *manifestation*, as distinguished from *proclamation*. I

And if our consciousness is understood in new ways and affected by the stories we have already read, it follows that each generation brings to the classics of religious literature new questions, new ways of understanding story. We need to read scriptural narratives with the same degree of probing inquiry that we bring to literature not specifically identified as "sacred." What is even more important, we must bring to sacred literature a sense of its connectedness to all else that we have read and seen, its connectedness to what we can describe as our own mythos, our own history. Further, the texts we know to be "religious classics" claim to be revelatory in a fuller sense than other classics. They claim to be disclosures of the "whole," from the whole, in David Tracy's words. And in that sense, "belief" or "faith" as a response to them is both recognition and discovery: achievement and gift.[4]

My concern in this book has been with one aspect of plotted narrative: the experience of recognition. I have noted that the strategy of storytelling changes, especially as our understanding of time and epistemology changes. If we bring present understanding of time and consciousness to a rereading of the scriptural narratives, we will hear them "in our own native language." For that reason, my analysis of recognition in the Gospels follows my discussion of recognition in other Western texts. The experience of recognition is so fundamental to their telling and their hearing that an examination of that strategy alone can assist us in understanding their disclosive power. It is not unlike the disclosive power of Oedipus at Colonus, but the Gospel narratives exert a different kind of claim, at least on those in the communities of

would argue that the two concepts are distinguishable, but not necessarily exclusive. The Christian narratives call for proclamation. Those who "hear the Word" are moved to *proclaim* it, but the task of proclaiming requires an understanding of the *recognitive* event that the preacher is attempting (or should attempt) to invoke. In this context, see Mary Catherine Hilkert, "Naming Grace: A Theology of Proclamation," *Worship* 60 (September 1986): 434-49.

[4]Tracy, *Analogical Imagination*, 163. See my discussion in ch. 2 of the sleep of Odysseus and the relationship between achievement and gift. The faith response to a religious classic involves a kind of surrender suggested by Odysseus's sleep just before he recognizes his "native shore."

belief nourished by the Gospels. By examining how it is that in reading them we know <u>again</u>, we can better understand that claim.

THE GOSPEL OF MARK:
THE LIMITS OF VISION

I neither know nor understand what you are saying.

—Mark 14:68

Mark's story is almost as bleak as a Pinter play. He pictures a world in which the innocent hero is recognized by demons, unrecognized by friends, betrayed by his intimates and dies, uttering what is described only as "a loud cry"—a wordless shout, with no signified meaning. In this, the most grim of the four accounts of the Christ story, we are told of the almost total nonperception of the hero's followers and, even more, their equally vast and bewildering failure. The end of the Gospel simply reinforces our view of the ineptitude and blindness of those to whom mystery was being disclosed: "And the women came out and ran away from the tomb because they were frightened out of their wits; and they said nothing to a soul, for they were afraid" (16:19). For inconclusiveness, this sacred chapter can hardly be surpassed.

Apart from our awareness that Mark's Gospel is a confessional text of a believing community and Pinter's an enigmatic text of a bewildered but aesthetically engaged community, the projected worlds of the two writers are not easily distinguishable. In both narratives, naive optimism is crushed, especially naive optimism about meaning, about what will happen; life is described as movement toward suffering and death. Recognition in each case is that the human condition and human understanding are radically finite. And to make the point more demonstrably, in each case the audience is left to its own uncertainty.

To determine why Mark's text is generally considered a proclamation of hope and Pinter's almost unrelieved despair, we can examine the depiction of time in both works, for only those who look to a future can experience either hope or despair. It is time that makes hope possible and knowledge finite.

In Pinter's plays, we are bound to the present. There is no other reality. His characters are stripped of a past and hence stripped of identity.

We know nothing of them but their names. Because the action of the play confines characters to the present, the dramatic effect is scarcely cathartic. We are neither freed nor purged nor purified—suffocated, even cognitively terrorized perhaps, but denied the luxury of pity. We are given a situation to fear but characters who scarcely recognize the situation and who are morally incapable, in any case, of delivering themselves from it.

In Mark's Gospel, we are immediately aware that time is passing; we are not immobilized; decisions must be made. The first spoken word in the text is *erchetai*—"comes" with its powerful implication of an immediate future event: "Comes the one stronger than I," in the Greek structure. Not only is the announcement a firm declaration of what will happen, but it implies radical awareness of a self who makes that declaration. In the next paragraph the text begins, "And it happened [it came to pass that] *came* Jesus from Nazareth." What is future will be. It is. It was. The many occurrences of *kai euthus* ("immediately") in the Markan text need not be dismissed as limited authorial control over transitional devices. They punctuate the narrative like a rapid pulse signaling the passage of time, the significance of the moment, the haste and determination of Jesus:

> And going on a little farther, he saw James the son of Zebedee and John his brother, who were in their boat mending the nets.
>   And *immediately* he called them; and they left their father Zebedee in the boat with the hired servants, and followed him. (Mark 1:19-20, RSV)

Descriptions of the rapid passage of time keep the memory of past events vivid and they suggest also that the future is always on the edge of invading and subverting the present. Expectation is as possible as memory.

Both memory and expectation are components of Markan epistemology. What is disclosed in the present can be comprehended if memory is alive and expectation is transformed into hope. The primary impediment to comprehension in Mark is not fixity in time, as in Pinter, but fixity of expectation. Characters resist recognition when their expectations are confounded. Mark's task is to narrate events so that the expectation of the audience is transformed into hope. Their response to the events narrated must be different from that of the disciples. The evangelist does this by demonstrating the tragic incapacity of the secondary characters to effect that transformation. The audience, given knowledge that the characters do not have, is in a position to measure and to pity their blindness. But at the same time, the audience cannot be so distanced from the characters that their own expectations about the identity of the hero are also fixed. Mark's Gospel is parabolic, and a parable always turns on itself.[1]

Appropriate questions about the epistemology of recognition relate, therefore, to the kind of knowledge given as well as denied. One kind of knowledge offered the reader (and denied to the characters) is initial access to the identity of the protagonist. Mark, more than any other evangelist, involves the reader in the feelings and sufferings of Jesus. If Aristotle described Euripides as the most tragic of Greek dramatists, Mark is surely—for similar reasons—the most tragic of Evangelists, partly because we are so deeply involved in the sufferings of his hero.

In the first chapter, we are given an exposition by John the Baptist ("Comes the one . . .") and immediately are brought close to the point of view of Jesus himself: ". . . he saw the heavens opened . . . and there came a voice, saying, 'You are my beloved Son' " (1:10-11).

We are not told that anyone else heard the voice at this moment, nor in the succeeding encounter with an unclean Spirit who also identified him ("We know who you are—the Holy One of Israel" [1:24]). Nothing in the narrative suggests that anyone in the crowd heard this cry. Jesus alone hears himself identified. By this fact, the audience is now dramatically engaged in the narrative, for we know what James and John, as well as all the other characters, have not yet been told. We—and not they— are the insiders.[2]

From this point on, the pain begins. When Pinter strips his characters of a past and denies us a point of view, we are also denied any reason to care much about what happens. They suffer. They perish. But who are they and why should it matter? In the Gospel text, even though the first-century writers did not have the psychological or literary capability of dramatizing the *interior* self, we know what it is that these characters are not comprehending—what most of them cannot seem to comprehend within the narrative continuum. Unlike Jane Austen in *Emma*, Mark has admitted us to the secret, and we seem to be in control. But the reader who believes he or she understands because the situation has presum-

---

[1]Herbert N. Schneidau, "For Interpretation," *Missouri Review* 1 (1978): 85; cited in Werner Kelber, *The Oral and Written Gospel* (Philadelphia: Fortress Press, 1983) 125.

[2]See Frank Kermode's discussion of insiders/outsiders in *The Genesis of Secrecy: On the Interpretation of Narrative* (Cambridge: Harvard University Press, 1979); Kelber, *Oral and Written Gospel*, esp. ch. 3; and Robert C. Tannehill, "The Disciples in Mark: The Function of a Narrative Role," *Journal of Religion* 57 (1977): 386-405, esp. n. 16.

ably been explained in the text may be no more enlightened than the characters whose incomprehension is pitied: quite simply, more than factual information is required to comprehend the narrative sequence of events.

• Recognizing Presence •

The traditional example of this difficulty of understanding is the triple prediction of the Passion in Mark's chapter 10. After each declaration that "the Son of Man shall be delivered unto the chief priests and the scribes and they will condemn him to death . . . and they will mock him . . . and spit upon him, and scourge him . . . and kill him, and after three days he will rise" (10:33), the hearers indicate by their subsequent squabbling over power and prestige that they have not comprehended. The reader—who lives in the future of this text—may comprehend, but the partiality of reader understanding reflects the total incomprehension of the characters in the narrative because the announcement is more than information. If Jane Austen's *Emma* had been informed that Jane Fairfax and Frank were engaged, the meaning of events would be clear and life would go on with its customary neoclassic lucidity. The disciples in Mark's chapter 10 are told what will happen and so are the readers, the primary hearers of this announcement, but information is not enough because the weight of the message goes beyond cognitive enlightenment. To comprehend the message in its fullness requires an experience that the characters at this point in the narrative do not have and, for that matter, the readers may not have either. Mark's Gospel is about the difficulty of understanding, not the difficulty of getting the right information. The message is frequently subjectively incomprehensible at the time it is uttered. The fullness of truth is present to the characters in Mark's narrative only as promise. It is not difficult to wonder why the content of such a message was not grasped: experience had not caught up to message.

What is to be "recognized" in the Markan Gospel is—as in all the Gospels—the real identity of the hero. The "Son of Man" was to suffer. Could he then be the "Son of God"? As John Donahue has noted: " 'Son of Man' gives the proper interpretation to Son of God. . . . In the important middle section of the Gospel (8:27-10:52), the three Son of Man sayings show in what sense Jesus is the beloved and Chosen Son; that is, as one who follows God's pre-ordained will to the way of the cross."[3]

---

[3]John R. Donahue, "Jesus as the Parable of God in the Gospel of Mark," *Interpretation* 32:4 (October 1978): 369-86, at 378.

In Mark, then, it is the Son of God as one who suffers, one who gives his life as a "ransom for many" that is the problematic. The issue is whether or not a Son of God can, or would, or could be *expected* to submit to aggressive human power in history. That expectation had never been entertained. The Suffering Servant of Isaiah was one person; the "Messiah" was quite another. The primary obstacle to recognition in Mark is the incapacity of the message hearers to assimilate the discrete elements of the message. "Son of God" is not consonant with powerlessness, humiliation, and execution. That consonance must be experienced before it can be believed, before any identification between Son of God and crucified Jesus can be made. That experience would eventually constitute a "memory," which shows up in the appendix, and the memory would transform expectations, but the transformation experience lies outside the earliest narrative account.

In the meantime, the protagonist announced early in the narrative— at least to the reader—as "Son of God" must suffer and die at the hands of human beings. At such a moment only is salvific recognition possible. Before Jesus' death, recognition is like the vision of the partially cured blind man (taken *outside* the village) who says, "I see men but they look like trees walking" (8:24), or like Peter, who says in the middle of the narrative, "You are the Christ," and clearly suggests by his subsequent behavior that, although he knows who Jesus is, he does not know who the Christ is. But a centurion present at the Crucifixion announces at the moment of death, "Truly this man was the Son of God" (15:39). The absurdity of the situation seems patent. The only character to recognize the protagonist is one of his presumed enemies, engaged for the moment in the business of executing him or, at least, supervising the execution. There is no suggestion that this random character had even heard of Jesus of Nazareth prior to his day's assignment. The manner of the victim's dying had strangely testified to his power. Upon hearing the "loud cry," the centurion perceived what all other characters in the Gospel had not comprehended—not even Peter at Caesarea, who could not identify messianic faith with messianic suffering and death.

In contrast to the unprepared centurion, the disciples of Jesus had been warned. The turn of events, nevertheless, clearly took them by surprise. They stood at a distance (*apo makrothen*—"a long way off"). Most of them had fled. Those who "stand at a distance" from the dying of Jesus are not those who recognize him.

In Mark, we have a protagonist who is a text to be read, understood, and proclaimed, but whose readers fail to comprehend. In the Gospel narrative, the text is the Other: fascinating, bewildering, even apparently absurd. The characters mirror the audience in the presence of an unexpected word. Only one character in the story, apart from demons, managed to read and understand; and he was the most unlikely reader of all. He succeeded because he brought to the story no preconceived idea of its meaning, no expectations to be superimposed on the word before him.

The other characters in the story had their own script—fixed, as they supposed, in its meaning, subject to no new understanding or subversion of the old. But, if all words are born(e) in time, they cannot be fixed in it. The Word presented in the Markan narrative is scarcely an exception.

Paul Achtemeier has pointed out the preconceptions about *Jesus* that most of his disciples entertained along with the preconceptions they had about themselves. They had clearly misread their own characters and their own future and, in so doing, blinded themselves to the situation before them. The question "Is it I, Lord?" (14:19), in response to Jesus' declaration that one of them would betray him, calls in Greek for a negative response ("It isn't I, is it?").[4]

Thus, both recognition and nonrecognition in the narrative are consequences of a totally unexpected occurrence. It is this quality of unexpectedness that shapes the responses of the main characters who, like Euripides' Electra, consistently resist what they are not logically prepared to understand, and their resistance is predicated in large part on their lack of self-knowledge. The events after the Crucifixion sustain the pattern. On the first day of the week, women disciples go to the sepulchre expecting it to be sealed. It was not. Like the future, it was now open. They expected to see a corpse and to anoint it. But that had already been done proleptically (14:8) and had not been understood. Instead of a dead body, they saw "a young man" who explained that Jesus was "risen," "not here," and that they should "tell his disciples and Peter: 'he goes before you into Galilee; there you *will see* him, *as he told you*' " (16:7).

If the disciples were unprepared for Jesus' arrest and execution, they were even less prepared for this extraordinary development. The original Gospel of Mark ends here. The ultimate failure was the refusal to tell the story, to do as they were told. The reader, who has been admitted to the secret of Jesus' identity and his destiny because, as Joel Marcus writes, "somehow the news leaked out,"[5] experiences a certain superiority to

---

[4]Paul Achtemeier, "Mark as the Interpreter of the Jesus Traditions," *Interpretation* 32:4 (October 1978): 339-52, at 349.

[5]Joel Marcus, "Mark 4:10-12 and Marcan Epistemology," *Journal of Biblical Literature* 103:4 (December 1984): 557-74, at 574.

these characters. But aesthetic distance is trimmed by the narrator's inclusion of the reader in the mystery. For the disciples, there are no "appearances" of Jesus to confirm the message of the young man. Nor, can we add, have there been many for the average reader. "You will see," these women were told. Did they? The appendix (16:9-20) tells us that they did. And that assertion is to be an assurance.

Despite the appendix, the problem of recognition for the reader is essentially the same as it was for the disciples.[6] The promise not only transcends reasonable expectations, but the implications for believing it are daunting in the extreme. The characters model the twofold obstacle to comprehension: impoverished expectation and fear of suffering. We see the secondary characters confronted with events for which they *could* not be prepared:

> And a great storm of wind arose, and the waves beat into the boat, so that the boat was already filling. But he was in the stern asleep on the cushion; and they woke him and said to him, "Teacher, do you not care if we perish?" And he awoke and rebuked the wind, and said to the sea, "Peace! Be still." And the wind ceased, and there was a great calm. He said to them, "Why are you afraid?" (4:37-40)

> And his disciples answered him, "How can one feed these men with bread here in the desert?" (8:4)

> And they ate and were satisfied. (8:8)

And we see them confronted with events for which they *do not want* to be prepared:

> And he began to teach them that the Son of Man must suffer many things. . . . And he said this plainly. And Peter took him and began to rebuke him. (8:31-32)

But the writer attempts to counteract one of the impediments to belief by providing a pattern of promise or warning, followed by fulfillment of promise:

> Go into the village opposite you, and immediately as you enter it you will find a colt tied. . . . (11:2)
>   And they went away and found a colt tied. (11:4)

---

[6]Robert C. Tannehill has persuasively assessed the reader-discipleship relationship in Mark. Like the disciples, the reader initially feels like an "insider." But "insiders" are depicted as uncomprehending. A sensitive reader, sympathetic to those admitted to the secret, cannot be distanced completely from the incomprehension of these same characters. See "Disciples in Mark."

And he said to it [a fig tree], "May no one ever eat fruit from you again." (11:14)
And as they passed by in the morning, they saw the fig tree withered away to its roots. (11:20)

Truly I say to you one of you will betray me. (14:17)
And immediately while he was speaking, Judas came, one of the twelve, and with him a crowd with swords and clubs. (14:43)

The fear of suffering is scarcely alleviated. What we are given is another promise: that suffering will open into vision and life:

Do not be amazed. You seek Jesus of Nazareth, who was crucified. He is risen, he is not here; see the place where they laid him. But go, tell his disciples that he is going before you to Galilee; there you will see him, as he told you. (16:6)

If the initial response of the women disciples is true to character, why should they respond any differently to this extraordinary promise than they did to all the others? The reader, however, has been given enough of a pattern to sense that the disciples are just as incapacitated here as elsewhere. The lag time between revelation—or the disclosed coherence of events—and recognition is, as usual, considerable.

The realization of the truth of the messenger's words is the moment of recognition for these characters, but it is denied to us in the original text—promised to them as to the reader, who must also deal with the subversion of expectation and the blank space after the last sentence of the chapter. Mark 16:9-19, the appendix to this story, is a laconic affirmation of the promise, a summary of the experiences of all the people in the tradition to whom the now-renamed "Lord Jesus" appeared. The first three people—Mary Magdalene and two unnamed travelers—tell their story and (predictably) are not believed. Finally, the narrator tells us, in a description of messianic irritability, that Jesus appeared "to the eleven themselves as they sat at table; and he upbraided them for their unbelief" (16:14). Then, according to the announcement, if people heard *their* story and would not believe, judgment would follow.

In the appendix we see the conversion experience, the changes effected by recognition: "And they went forth and preached everywhere." The story is retold, the photographs updated. The denouement consists of one sentence that must support the entire narrative weight of disbelief and incomprehension, for most of the Markan text is about the darkness of the present: the sense of menace, collective fear, constricted movement, incomprehensible promises. To a modern reader, it is all very familiar. The argument of the narrative is that, however persuasive this experience of human existence, a promise has been uttered within history and can transform it. The darker forces of history were personified in the opening scene when the hero heard the words, "We know who you are" (1:24). The movement of the narrative is to bring the other characters to this same acknowledgment. It takes the execution and death of Jesus before anyone concedes. First, the evil one had declared Jesus' identity; then Peter, in a half-blind way, had declared him to be the Christ (8:30), but he was unwilling to concede the parabolic implications of that confession. The scene is an appropriate midpoint of the story, for recognition is not yet complete.

In the transfiguration scene, which follows Peter's confession (9:2-8), Peter, James, and John were direct witnesses to a luminous vision of Jesus whom they heard described as "my beloved Son," but nothing in the text suggests that they had any understanding of the event. They could not, according to the writer, until after the Resurrection. They model the essential problem of recognition: revelation can exceed the experiential capacity to comprehend.

Joel Marcus relates the confusion of the disciples at the transfiguration scene to their comparable incapacity in the Garden of Gethsemane (14:40). In both passages, the disciples are described as "not knowing": "not knowing" what to make of the divine announcement, "not knowing" what to answer when the "Son of Man" discovered them sleeping. His disciples comprehend "neither his glory nor the significance of his suffering."[7] Finally, the centurion brings us to full acknowledgment. But the announcement of the "young man" at the empty tomb does not persuade the remaining characters that a promise has been kept and that words have both possibility and power. They are left enigmatically in a state of "numinous fear."[8]

To the contemporary reader, the promise offered by those who themselves were once upbraided for their unbelief is equally mysterious. Given the continued darkness of history, the promise "You will see" (16:7) does not correspond to reasonable expectations; for as Kelber notes, "Mark's Gospel in its entirety points beyond itself to the mystery of the Kingdom of God."[9] Because language frequently resists interpretation, recognition by means of language often hinges on whether, like Electra, we can relinquish logic, or like Don Quixote, we can give up our illusions and rec-

---

[7]Marcus, "Mark 4:10-12," 569.

[8]Donahue, "Jesus as the Parable of God," 381.

[9]Kelber, *Oral and Written Gospel*, 124.

ognize ourselves,[10] or whether we can read a message, knowing that it is neither irrelevant information nor vain promise. Recognition for the modern reader of the Second Gospel is to acknowledge the consonance of suffering and salvation in the Christ-event, and the subversion of the present by the future. It is to be aware of the space between words and experience, to relinquish expectation and consent to hope. In Mark, history is the space between the revelation of Christ and the fulfillment of his promises. The hero in Mark's Gospel, unlike the paralyzed Hirst who resists interpretation, seeks re-cognition: knowing and knowing again. Mark's narrative is the confession of the centurion turned into a new story and a new text. The hidden metaphor of that text is not a closed room nor even an enigma, but a half-blind reader.

• Understanding Absence •

One of the most difficult verses to interpret in the entire Gospel of Mark is the ultimate assertion: "He is risen, he is not here" (16:6). Supposing that at least one purpose of the text is to transform failed expectation into hope and partial blindness into vision, how does the concept of recognition apply to a presence that is not a presence? The disciples were told simply: "He is not here" and "see the place where they laid him."

Since the last the audience really sees of the women is their flight from an empty tomb, we need to examine this place that they have left us. Has the writer prepared either them or the reader for this empty space, this interval before the Galilean vision? Can we recognize in the empty space the culmination of any pattern—one more piece that can reveal the design even if other pieces are still missing?

In chapter 2, after three references to the crowds surrounding Jesus and several hostile interrogations, Jesus is described as saying, "The days will come when the bridegroom is taken away from them" (2:20). This ominous remark is the first of several preparatory lessons and prefigurations of the meaning of his absence and how his friends are to respond. Here they are reminded that "they will fast in that day." Later in the process of further instruction, he tells the twelve privately, " . . . there is nothing hid except to be made manifest" (4:22). The force of the comment is that hiddenness is part of a necessary sequence. What is hidden is hidden *so*

---

[10]Tannehill speaks of "the negation of one's past self" ("Disciples in Mark," 305 n. 2).

that it can be manifest later.[11] As part of the context of this remark, the author gives us the first of several important parables of the kingdom, all of which exemplify the hiddenness, the invisibility of the kingdom for an undesignated period of time. The kingdom is like seed that a man scatters on the ground. He sleeps and rises "night and day," and the seed sprouts and grows, "he knows not how" (4:26). Here the parable exemplifies the hidden power in the seed, a power that the farmer does not understand although he knows the seed will grow, bringing ripeness and fruition.

Paralleling this story of the hidden seed and its secret immanent power is the narrative of the sleeping Jesus in the boat, his power latent, apparently inoperative as the storm rises. His disciples, terrified, turn to him in anger, "Do you not care if we perish?" And, says the narrator, "He awoke and rebuked the wind and the sea" (4:39). This is not the first time in the narrative that Jesus' friends reprimand him for not putting in some kind of appearance sooner. It recalls a very early moment (1:36) when Jesus is described as having gone "to a lonely place" to pray. No sooner is he out of their presence when the disciples track him down (*katediozen auton*) with the impatient statement, "Everyone is searching for you!" They seem unhappy, even indignant, when he fails to be where they want him.

But is the physical body of Jesus absolutely necessary for his power to be active? In the fifth chapter we read the curious story of the hemorrhaging woman who, forbidden to touch the body of Jesus, touches the tassel of his cloak instead. Power does go out from him, Mark tells us, from the body that she did not, could not touch.

Chapter 6 gives us another dramatic demonstration of power, but power made visible after suffering has been experienced. Mark, assuming his prerogative as narrator, describes this scene from the point of view of Jesus himself, telling us the intentions of his protagonist. It is evening and Jesus is separated from his friends. They are on a boat on the sea; he is "alone on the land." In this narrative, Mark tells us that *Jesus saw* that "they were making headway painfully" (6:45), the wind against them. The next sequence suggests that hours passed before he came to them,

---

[11]See J. R. Kirkland, "The Earliest Understanding of Jesus' Use of Parables; Mark IV 10-12 in Context," *Novum Testamentum* 19 (1977): 12-13; cited in Augustine Stock, *Call to Discipleship: A Literary Study of Mark's Gospel* (Wilmington DE: Michael Glazier, 1982): "The textual evidence indicates that the future tense is not implied in verse 22 at all; rather are the secondary clauses to be read as ginal (purposive). The point of the saying is that what is hidden is meant to be manifested *by the act of hiding it* [emphasis in text]. . . . Nothing is hidden except *in order that* [*hina*] it may thereby be revealed" (100-101).

"walking on the sea." It was "about the fourth watch of the night," that is, between three and six in the morning. His friends in the boat had been rowing since the previous evening. Only when dawn was near did he come to them. "They all saw him," writes Mark, but they did not believe that what they saw was Jesus himself. The vision could only be a phantasm, a ghost. But immediately (*Kai euthus*) he spoke to them, uttering the theophanic word of peace, "Take heart. It is I; have no fear" (6:50). This description of a night of suffering, a dawn of appearance and nonrecognition, and then power and presence is followed by the puzzling explanation: "They were astounded, for they did not understand about the loaves, for their hearts were hardened" (6:51).

What was it they did not understand about the loaves? There is no way to interpret this passage apart from the relationship of the writer to his audience (then and now).[12] The loaves—referring to the multiplication of loaves and fishes that had just occurred the day before, and contextually in the preceding passage (6:37)—prefigured the Eucharist. The Eucharist, to Mark's audience, is the sign of the absence of Jesus. It is what believers turn to when the Bridegroom is taken away, when they cannot touch his body, when they are tempted to believe he is only a ghost. Not to understand about the loaves is not to recognize that the power of Jesus is invisible in human history, like the life-giving seed that is hidden beneath the earth. The empty tomb, the vanished body, the promise of vision and power have been prefigured in the text. The audience to the final scene should be prepared for the darkness of the struggle, the hiddenness of power, the imperative to wait.

It has been argued that Mark's Gospel is a creation out of absence,[13] that it stilled the oral tradition ("they said nothing to anyone") and confirms, by reason of its particular textuality, the death of Jesus.[14] It is interesting in the context of this argument to reflect on the wordlessness of the final cry, the shout that transformed the centurion into a christological witness. It is only at the death of Jesus that a human being, and not

---

[12]See Donald Senior, *The Passion of Jesus in the Gospel of Mark* (Wilmington DE: Michael Glazier, 1984) 54-59; idem, "The Eucharist in Mark: Mission, Reconciliation, Hope," *Biblical Theological Bulletin* 12 (1982): 67-72; and N. Beck, "Reclaiming a Biblical Test: The Mark 8:14-21 Discussion about Bread in the Boat," *Catholic Biblical Quarterly* 43 (1981): 57-75.

[13]John Dominic Crossan, "A Form for Absence: The Markan Creation of Gospel," *Semeia* 12 (1978): 41-55.

[14]Kelber, *Oral and Written Gospel*, 130.

a demon, proclaims him "Son of God." Nor is it by narrative chance that this same human being is asked to testify to his death (15:45). The recognition is twofold: he was Son of God; he is dead.

Mark's Gospel as a "counterform" to the living voice of Jesus and the oral tradition proclaims the death of Jesus,[15] his silence and, one could add, his invisibility. Werner Kelber asserts that the Gospel proclaims also the death of his disciples, at least in terms of their influence and credibility, and the death of the Temple.[16] To the extent that Mark does not admit any kind of presence in history of the living Jesus, his Gospel needed to be corrected by Christians whose theology was different. That correction was supplied in subsequent Gospels. We think of Matthew's insistence that Jesus is "God-with-us" and his own character's final "I will be with you all days even to the end of the world" (Matt. 28:16); or Luke's dramatic account of the descent of the Spirit; or John's tender, "I will not leave you desolate" (John 14:18), and "I desire that they also whom you have given me, may be with me where I am" (John 17:24).

But there is a sense in which Mark is radically realistic, one is tempted to say existential. He knew that what his audience was experiencing at the time of his composition was the destruction of everything they valued: Jerusalem, the Temple, the culture, their own lives. To that audience he described a hidden power, a secret presence, a promise of life and vision, eschatological triumph. An audience with a comparable experience of desolation would recognize the darkness and (possibly) admit that what is hidden is hidden *so that* it can be made manifest. For this reason, the Gospel of the absence of Jesus is also the Gospel of power and promise in the darkness. Words testify to absence, but absence is felt only when we are aware of the reality we wait for. Language may not give us presence, but like the Eucharist, like the multiplied loaves given to a hungry people, it can sustain us in our waiting.

The question is who and what it is we wait for and how we will know (again) of his coming.

---

[15]Ibid., 207.

[16]Ibid., 186.

THE GOSPEL OF JOHN:
THE LIMITS OF DARKNESS

Religion is not concerned with a message that has to be be-
lieved but with an experience of faith which is presented as a
message. On the one hand the religious message is an expres-
sion of this collective experience, and on the other its procla-
mation is the presupposition for the possibility of its being
experienced by others.

—*Edward Schillebeeckx,*
in <u>Christ: The Experience of Jesus as Lord</u>

The Gospels, especially the Fourth Gospel, re-create the classic theme that we first saw in the homecoming of Odysseus: the crisis caused by the arrival of the disguised king. We see the motif of the presence of the hidden God throughout ancient literature. In Genesis 19, Lot welcomes three strangers whom the townspeople subsequently seek to treat violently. As Lot struggles to save his guests (if not his daughters) from the brutality of the Sodomites, the strangers reveal themselves as "angels" (in Hebrew thought, extensions of the person and presence of Yahweh). The narrative reversal occurs when Lot and his family are saved and Sodom is destroyed by the righteous deity who will not brook the kind of wickedness Sodom represented—or at least represented within the oral tradition of the Hebrews and the religion of the Yahwist narrator. Ovid gives us another version of the same motif. In *Metamorphoses* 8, Philemon and Baucis entertain Jupiter and Mercury in disguise. The poor couple used the last of their kindling to heat the cottage and, despite their impoverished circumstances, lavished on their unknown guests every kind of hospitality possible. Because the two gods had been refused kindness "at a thousand houses," they rewarded Philemon and Baucis with salvation from a flood and with transformed life.

We are gods, you know: this wicked neighborhood
Will pay as it deserves to; do not worry,
You will not be hurt.[1]

The most conspicuous example of this motif in Christian literature before John occurs in Matthew's climactic chapter 25:

"Come, you whom my Father has blessed, take for your heritage the kingdom prepared for you since the foundation of the world. For I was hungry and you gave me food; I was thirsty and you gave me drink; I was a stranger and you made me welcome; naked and you clothed me, sick and you visited me, in prison and you came to see me." Then the virtuous will say to him in reply, "Lord when did we see you hungry and feed you; or thirsty and give you drink? When did we see you a stranger and make you welcome; naked and clothe you, sick or in prison and go to see you?" And the King will answer, "I tell you solemnly, in so far as you did this to one of the least of these brothers of mine, you did it to me." (25:34-41)

The entire Gospel of John can be considered as a commentary on the question, "When did we see you?" For the author(s) of the text—whom we call John—Jesus is the hidden deity in history, the self-disclosing god, the light in darkness. He is revelation; and the problem of apprehending revelation is essentially the problem of determining the identity of Jesus. To know Jesus is to know the revelation of the Father, for Jesus is the content of that revelation. To believe in him is not a matter of receiving information about God, and of assenting, but of recognizing in Jesus the fullness of truth (in history) and abiding with that truth. To believe or not to believe in Jesus is for John a matter of life and death. It is *crisis* in the literary and religious sense of that word. The crisis can be considered first on the level of the Gospel narrative itself: that is, the characters of the story, how they come to belief or refuse to believe, and the textual configurations that describe their discovery of Jesus; or conversely, the configurations, the patterns that express resistance to belief.

The second locus of recognition is extratextual, the recognition experienced by the reader or hearer of the Gospel narrative. The Gospel story was not written simply to describe the fate of the characters— and thus to engage and please us—but to change the destiny of the hearer of the story: " . . . but these are written that you may believe that Jesus is the Christ, the son of God, and that believing you may have life in his name" (John 20:31).

---

[1]Ovid, *Metamorphoses*, trans. Rolfe Humphries (Bloomington: Indiana University Press, 1955) 203.

Within the story itself there are two aspects of revelation: testimony and response. Jesus testifies to himself by word and work, and especially by those works that John calls "signs." The "signs" testify to the Sign (Jesus) of the Father. These signs reveal the power and presence of one sent by the Father. To recognize Jesus is to discover his origins, to know that he is both within history and from his Father in heaven.

The emphasis here will be not on what Jesus said and did, his own journey and return, but how he was heard and received. What is at stake in the narrative is not the fate of Jesus. The prologue has already told us, "He came to his own home and his own people received him not." What is crucial is how to recognize him. "He lived among us," says the text, "and we saw his glory." And then, "No one has ever seen God; it is the only Son . . . who has made him known."

Who are those who heard the words of this "only Son," saw his works and believed? Who did not? And how does the Evangelist account for the difference? For the hearer or reader of the narrative, which includes both John's immediate audience as well as the whole historical community of possible believers, the words will have to be transposed and the signs perceived against a new horizon.

On the level of narrative, the first moment of dialogue in the Fourth Gospel raises the question of identity: John the Baptist's, initially. "Who are you?" is the question, and it is repeated. The answer: "I am not the Christ." When Jesus enters the story, John says twice: "I myself did not know him." He recognized Jesus only because he who had sent John to baptize disclosed the Spirit upon Jesus. It is the voice from Heaven then who testified to John and revealed to him something about the identity of Jesus. John, in turn, directed two of his own disciples to the one whom he described as the Lamb of God. In the beginning of the Gospel, therefore, before Jesus begins testifying to himself, his Father testifies to him. John the Baptist comes to belief because of his own relationship to God. The two disciples begin their belief experience on the human testimony of this John whom they trusted. When they report their discovery of Jesus, after having personally experienced his presence, they do so by appealing to Jewish expectation: "We have found the Messiah" (1:41).

We need to examine the experience of these two disciples who have now entered the story, because their experience is paradigmatic of the whole theology of belief that structures the narrative. First, the disciples are described as "following" this Jesus whom they have never met. But Jesus— as he will so often do in the story—initiates the conversation: "What do you seek?" (1:38) No other line of dialogue so clearly describes the attitude, the spiritual posture of those who come eventually to recognize Jesus. In some manuscripts, the question is "Whom do you seek?"[2] but the precision of the interrogative does not really alter its theological meaning. In the sapiential tradition, "to seek" is the traditional spiritual attitude of the lover of wisdom. The verb is used thirty-four times in the Fourth Gospel and describes the subjective disposition of those who come to belief, as well as the dispositions of the Father and of Jesus himself, who seeks out his own. The search is mutual, as the knowing and loving will be mutual.

Jesus' response to the disciples is an invitation to recognition: "Come and see." And they stayed, we are told, the rest of the day. The staying is important. Seeing Jesus means abiding with him, and knowing where he abides is to know that he is with his Father.[3]

The chain of human testimony continues. When Andrew tells his brother Peter that they have found "the Messiah," and Peter arrives, Jesus is again described as speaking first. He not only looks at Peter and identifies him, but renames him. The pattern is repeated at John 1:43ff. Jesus calls Philip, and Philip calls Nathanael by appealing to the testimony of Scripture: "We have found him of whom Moses in the law and also the prophets spoke, Jesus of Nazareth, the son of Joseph" (1:45). Jesus informs Nathanael that he is already known. "Before Philip called you, when you were under the fig tree, I saw you" (1:48). Nathanael responds to this recognition by declaring Jesus the Son of God and the King of Israel. Since Jesus had referred to Nathanael as a "true Israelite," the title Nathanael attributes to Jesus is particularly important. It is clear from the entire passage (1:35-51) that "belief" implies a relationship with Jesus that the disciples have entered into but still do not fully comprehend. The final verb is future tense: "You will see" (1:51).

Among the ideas important to an understanding of this passage is the role of human testimony in coming to belief. This testimony is an integral part of the narrative. It is clear, however, that belief is not based on human testimony alone, but follows from the personal experience of the disciples who have been led to Jesus by another. This pattern is seen again in John 4:42: "Now we no longer believe because of what you told us. We have heard him ourselves." But the townspeople in this passage had begun their belief experience "on the strength of the woman's testimony" (4:39-40). Although belief is a personal commitment, the importance in

---

[2]Raymond F. Collins, "The Search for Jesus: Reflections on the Fourth Gospel," *Laval Théologique et Philosophique* 34 (January 1978): 27-48, at 28.

[3]Ibid., 31.

John of human testimony, in human words, cannot be minimized. The concluding chapters of the Gospel will stress precisely this impetus to belief: "This is the evidence of one who saw it" (19:35). Language, especially narrative, is the medium of disclosure.

But not everyone believes the testimony of another about Jesus, or even the testimony of Jesus himself. Parts of John's Gospel suggest that those who come to belief are those to whom the Father testifies, those whom the Father has given to Jesus. John the Baptist's recognition experience seems to depend upon just such testimony. We could consider also John 6:44, "No one can come to me unless he is drawn by the Father who sent me," or 17:2, 6, 12, and 24—all of which suggest a kind of selection process engaged in by the Father.

We cannot conclude from these lines, however, that those who do not believe are simply not the recipients of "special enlightenment." This is not what John is saying. The text does not suggest the irrelevance of human responsibility and human choice in the moment of crisis occasioned by the presence of Jesus. "The testimony of the Father" or the direct revelation of the Father mentioned in the context of the John the Baptist passage should not be considered too primitively as a kind of private locution or as an Inner Light not made available to another. Any interior revelation in John needs to be seen against the background of the character's entire listening attitude. In the Fourth Gospel the Father calls, enlightens, draws all to the Son, and without the Father's call, no one could come to Jesus. The Father's call is the other side of the Father's sending. But this does not mean that the call is audible to everyone or the light accessible to every darkness. Those who are blind cannot conclude that there is no sun.

What can we say about the dispositions of those who respond to testimony? Four patterns can be traced in the Fourth Gospel: (1) those who recognize Jesus are those who search for wisdom; (2) those who recognize Jesus are those who perceive in his flesh—and despite his flesh—his origins from the Father; (3) those who recognize Jesus are already known and sought out by him, recognized by him because he knows "his own"; (4) those who recognize Jesus have studied the Scriptures and have seen in Scripture the testimony of their human experience of Jesus. Each of these patterns of light has in the Gospel a corresponding pattern of darkness. There are those who search for death and not wisdom; those to whom the flesh is an obstacle to belief; those who are not recognized by Jesus because they have left the truth of their own beings; and those who cannot relate Scripture to history or personal experience.

• The Search for Wisdom •

The question that Jesus addresses to the first disciples—"What do you seek?"—is the question directed to every reader of the Gospel.[4] It begins one of the major themes of the Gospel: seek and you shall find; seek wisdom and you shall live. (Compare Amos 5:4-5; Jer. 29:13-14; Isa. 65:6-7.) Boismard suggests that John 1:35-42 is modeled after Wisdom 6:12-16.[5]

> *Wisdom is bright and does not grow dim.*
> *By those who love her she is readily seen,*
>   *and found by those who look for her.*
> *Quick to anticipate those who desire her,*
>   *she makes herself known to them.*
> *Watch for her early and you will have no trouble;*
> *You will find her sitting at your gates.*
> *Even to think about her is understanding fully grown;*
>   *be on the alert for her and anxiety will quickly leave you.*
> *She herself walks about looking*
>   *for those who are worthy of her*
> *And graciously shows herself to them as they go,*
>   *in every thought of theirs coming to meet them.*
>
> (JB)

Thus, in the scene that describes the calling of the first disciples, it is appropriate that their testimony is reported as "We have found."

Similarly, in John 6:24, just before the Bread of Life discourse, the crowd is described as distressed at the absence of Jesus. They got into boats, crossed the sea of Tiberias *to look for* Jesus. When they *found* him, they said, "When did you come here?" This is the kind of multivalent question that probes time, place and, by implication, the origins of Jesus. The search for Jesus with which John introduces the Bread of Life discourse is the motif of the search for wisdom.[6]

But the search is mutual, as the wisdom passages from the Hebrew Scriptures tell us and as John also reminds us: " . . . such the Father *seeks* to worship him," declares Jesus to the Samaritan woman with whom he had initiated a dialogue. And later when Jesus hears about the harass-

---

[4]Ibid., 28. Collins cites both M.-J. Lagrange and R. Bultmann on this point.

[5]Ibid., citing M. E. Boismard, "Du Baptême à Cana," *Lectio Divina* 18 (1956): 78-80. See also Douglas K. Clark, "Signs in Wisdom and John," *Catholic Biblical Quarterly* 45 (April 1983): 201-209.

[6]Ibid., 37.

ment of one whom he had cured, he *found* him and said, "Do you be-lieve?" (John 9:35-36). Further, in John 20:11-18, Mary Magdalene, weeping, does not recognize the Risen Jesus. He questions her, "Who are you looking for?" And he calls to her, "Mary!" Only after his calling, naming her, does she see: "She knew him then."

Because she was looking for him, however limited her faith, Mary Magdalene was the first to discover the Risen Christ. She would have been consoled by the presence of his dead body, but her hope was rewarded beyond all her expectations. The fact that she was seeking, even in her despair, is the key to her vision of the Christ who finally called to her. John generally denotes fundamental attitudes and dispositions by verbs rather than nouns. For him, the verb "to seek" denotes the "finality-governed dynamism of a person's life."[7] Thus, Jesus *seeks* the glory of the one who sent him (John 7:18). " 'To believe' denotes a fundamental disposition of openness to the truth which makes the person capable of seeing the glory of God whenever and wherever it is revealed."[8] Such is the disposition, for example, of the man born blind:

Do you believe in the Son of Man?
Who is he, sir, that I may believe in him? (9:36)

The opposite of this openness to reality is another kind of seeking, the kind we perceive in the debate with the unbelieving populace on the Feast of Tabernacles and in the Gethsemane scene when the cohort arrives to arrest Jesus. Chapters 7 and 8 develop the theme of unbelief in terms of seeking. Jesus initiates the dialogue in chapter 7. "Why do you seek to kill me?" After the ensuing debate among the crowd about the origins of Jesus, the Pharisees send the Temple police to arrest him, but Jesus announces that he will return to the one who sent him. "You will seek me," he states, "and will not find me. Where I am, you cannot come" (7:34-35).

The debate continues. Jesus' identity is concealed within human language. He asks his listeners to discover the "I am" in his language and to believe. He invites them to come to him, resorting to the classic language of the search for wisdom: "If any man is thirsty, let him come to me! Let the man come and drink who believes in me!" (7:38). The appeal echoes Deutero-Isaiah:

---

[7]Sandra Schneiders, "Reflections on Commitment in the Gospel according to John," *Biblical Theology Bulletin* 8 (January 1978): 40-48.

[8]Ibid., 44.

Oh, come to the water all you who are thirsty;
    though you have no money, come! (55:1)

The dialogue represents Jesus' awareness that his disclosure of his identity is not perceived. Neither in his language nor his flesh, which was the language of the One who sent him, could they see. And the response of Jesus to their unbelief is the response of wisdom:

> *Wisdom calls aloud in the streets,*
>   *she raises her voice in the public squares;*
> *she calls out at the street corners,*
>   *she delivers her message at the city gates*
> *"You ignorant people, how much longer*
>   *will you cling to your ignorance?*   (Prov. 1:20-23)

> *"When calamity bears down on you like a storm*
>   *and your distress like a whirlwind*
> *when disaster and anguish bear down on you.*
> *Then they shall call to me, but I will not answer,*
>   *they shall seek me eagerly and shall not find me.*
> *They despised knowledge,*
>   *they had no love for the fear of Yahweh"*
>
> ....
>
> *The errors of the ignorant lead to their death.* (Prov. 1:27-33)

"I am going away," says Jesus, "you will look for me, and you will die in your sin" (8:21). After this declaration, the Jewish leaders debate with Jesus about his identity: "Who are you?" They insist that their own identity, their descent from Abraham will save them. Jesus' reply is: "Before Abraham was, I am" (8:58). Jesus no longer conceals his identity; unbelief hardens into hostility; and they pick up stones to throw at him. We read then that "he hid himself and left the Temple" (8:59).

This scene represents the clearest dialectic on belief and unbelief in the Gospel. And the irony of the dialogue is Jesus' declaration that these very people would seek and not find him. Jesus had cried out, had invited people to know him, to drink from living water. But the moment of decision would not be prolonged. Recognizing the unbelief of his enemies, Jesus could declare that when he would be revealed clearly in his ascent to the Father, it would then be too late: the very unbelief of these people would be the cause of his death and, by implication, their own. The passage ends with an appropriate reference to the departure of glory from the Temple—the glory that had so awed Solomon centuries before, who in his prayer at the consecration of the Temple had asked, "Can God dwell in this place?" (1 Kings 8:27, JB)[9] ("Yet will God really live with men on the earth?" RSV).

Collins reminds us, in this context, of Trito-Isaiah's lament, "For you hid your face from us and gave us up to the power of our sins" (64:6-7), and subsequently the complaint of Yahweh, "I was ready to be approached by those who did not consult me, ready to be found by those who did not seek me. I said, 'I am here, I am here,' to a nation that did not invoke my name" (64:1). The hiddenness of Jesus is the objectification of the blindness of his audience, who in the presence of new light and living water at the Feast of Tabernacles continued to say, "Who are you claiming to be?" (8:54).

The climax of this debate occurs at the arrest and trial of Jesus. As usual, his is the initiating question:

"Whom do you seek?"
"Jesus the Nazarene."
"I am he." (18:4-5)

John's description of the soldiers' falling back to the ground is a declaration of the power of the divinity in the midst of darkness, a power that would yield in that hour to the purposes of unbelievers. The question "Whom do you seek?" is repeated, and then Jesus intercedes for his disciples, who are allowed to go free.

Trying to analyze the apparent incapacity of many of the religious leaders to believe in Jesus, Louis Walter has argued that the refusal to believe has a prehistory.[10] He uses John 3:21 as his matrix ("Everyone who does wrong hates the light and avoids it for fear his actions should be exposed") and states that those whose religion was perverse became Jesus' adversaries because their evil choices were being exposed. Those whose religion was authentic were capable of belief. To the perverse, light was an unwelcome intervention because their works had to be accomplished in darkness. So when Judas left to call the cohort for the arrest, "It was night." "Unbelief," says Sandra Schneiders, "is a deep perversion of the spirit which makes a person incapable of accepting the truth because of an idolatrous commitment to something other than God."[11]

---

[9]Jerusalem Bible translation.

[10]Louis Walter, "Lecture d'évangile: Jean III, 1-21, selon la foi et l'incrédulité," *Esprit et Vie* 28 (14 July 1977): 385-90. This predisposition reminds us of Electra's intuition in the plays of both Aeschylus and Euripides. It is not evidence as such that draws anyone to belief.

[11]Schneiders, "Reflections on Commitment," 44.

Belief is "the fundamental openness of heart, the basic readiness to see and hear what is really there, the devotion to being which refuses to tamper with reality, no matter how frightening or costly it appears to be, in order to preserve the situation with which one is familiar."[12] "Preserving the situation with which one is familiar" is perhaps too modest a factor to account for the hostility-unto-death of those who resisted belief in Jesus. True enough, they wanted to preserve a situation, but not merely because it was familiar. The "new situation," the reality that Jesus declared, subverted the values on which lives around him were based, therefore threatening the very identity of those living such lives. To root oneself in a value system by which, and only by which, one is defined is to preclude the possibility of change and thus to deny both life and mystery. It is this lust for certainty and self-definition that John describes as "seeking one's own glory." It is the opposite of the search for wisdom, a search that implies that reality is beyond the self and can make claims upon it.[13] Attachment to security, then, was not compatible with the search for wisdom or the discovery of Jesus. When Jesus asks, "What do you seek?" within that question is all the dynamism of the Father's search and the Father's sending, as well as all the possible darkness that can envelop those to whom the words are addressed.

• The Origins of the Word •

If seekers after wisdom are those who "recognize" Jesus, what is it that they see in him? Throughout the Gospel of John, Jesus is described as "one sent by the Father." The controlling image is given at the end of chapter 1. He is the ladder between heaven and earth, on whom the angels of God ascend and descend. To discover Jesus is to discover his origins and to

---

[12]Ibid.

[13]See Hans Küng, *On Being a Christian*, trans. Edward Quinn (New York: Doubleday, 1974).

The more banal the truth ("truism," "platitude"), the greater the certainty. The more significant the truth (for instance, aesthetic, moral, and religious truth by comparison with arithmetical), the slighter the certainty. For the "deeper" the truth is for me, the more must I first lay myself open to it, inwardly prepare myself, attune myself to it intellectually, willingly, emotionally, in order to reach that genuine "certainty," which is somewhat different from assured "security." A *deep* truth for me outwardly uncertain, threatened by doubts, which presupposes a generous commitment on my part, can possess more cognitive value than a certain—or even an "absolutely certain"—*banal* truth. (74-75)

know that he has descended to earth and will ascend to his Father. To know his origins is not a matter of assenting to a myth, but to see in the flesh, in the world, in time, and in place that Jesus is from above. He is the intersection between heaven and earth. The obstacle to, as well as the medium of, belief is the flesh of Jesus. Those who refuse the possibility of Incarnation refuse the possibility of a god who discloses himself in history, as part of history, indeed as indistinguishable from it. The mystery of belief is the mystery of Jesus' origins. Where did you come from? How did you get here? How can you be from the Father, since we see you in the flesh?

This theme is introduced in chapter 1. "We have found," says Philip, "the one Moses wrote about in the Law, the one about whom the prophets wrote: He is Jesus, son of Joseph from Nazareth." "From Nazareth?" said Nathanael. "Can anything good come from that place?" (1:47).

And "that place" means not only and specifically a village in Galilee, but the world and the flesh in which Jesus is rooted—the very obscurity in which he is to be discovered. An interesting parallel to the problem of origins occurs in the Cana scene (2:1-12), when the steward tasting the replenished wine is described as "having no idea where it came from." He has experienced the first sign of Jesus, has delighted in the taste, but is not capable of interpreting the experience. The disciples are brought to belief because they know the origins of the wine. He let his glory be seen, we are told, in Cana. To appreciate the implications of this Johannine observation, we have to remind ourselves of the obscurity of this village.

The dialogue with Nicodemus offers another consideration of origins. The believer himself must be "born from above." If not, he cannot, will not, see. The dialogue, which drifts into expository poetry, has Jesus declaring that "God sent his Son into the world" (3:17). Over and over again in debate and monologue, Jesus describes himself as one sent. He has been sent. He originates with the Father. To know his origins is to have recognized that only the one sent by the Father performs the works he does. Thus, in chapter 9:30, we read the marvelously ironic question posed by the man cured of blindness to those who were persecuting him: "Now here is an astonishing thing! He has opened my eyes, and you don't know where he comes from."

But there are characters who do know where Jesus has come from— in the flesh—and that knowledge impedes belief. The tension is most clearly expressed in 6:4-43:

> Meanwhile the Jews were complaining to each other about him, because he had said, "I am the bread that came down from heaven." "Surely this is Jesus, son of Joseph," they said, "We know

his father and mother. How can he now say, 'I have come down
from heaven?' "

We recall the problem of Oedipus. He had enough information about
his origins to be completely wrong about his identity and not enough to
save him from disaster: "Polybus was my father, King of Corinth, and
Merope, the Dorian, my mother" (*Oedipus the King*, 1.775). "Surely this
is Jesus, son of Joseph." And they were correct, but not correct enough.
"He taught this doctrine at Capernaum, in the synagogue," says the
writer, quietly invoking once again the crisis, the intersection of heaven and
earth, which both conceals and illuminates.

"We all know where he comes from," says the crowd in Jerusalem,
"but when the Christ appears no one will know where he comes from."
Such a preconception is significant. Those who question whether Jesus is
"the Christ" assume either that history cannot contain the anointed of
God—that the Christ will never emerge in time or place—or that this Jesus
is not really testified to by Scripture: "Does not Scripture say that the Christ
must be descended from David and come from the town of Bethlehem?"
(7:42-43). In both instances conviction about Jesus' human origins precludes belief. Those in the crowd who believed, however, did so because
they dismissed the theoretical issue as well as the presumed facts about
Jesus' human origins, and were open to the reality before them: "When
the Christ comes, will he give more signs than this man?" (7:31).

If the human origins of Jesus are an obstacle to belief, so are the human origins of his listeners, when those origins are seen as salvific. Thus,
unbelievers argue in John 8:33 and 39: "We are descended from Abraham"; "our father is Abraham"; "we were not born of prostitution." The
commentary on this scene has already been given in John 3:3: "Unless a
man is born from above, he cannot see the Kingdom of God." This predisposition about the salvific character of their own human origins and
thus their own flesh is the converse of the refusal to believe in Jesus'
heavenly origins. Only the flesh informed by the spirit is salvific. The flesh
alone profits nothing. To see Jesus in the flesh alone is to be blind. To see
salvation in the flesh alone is to refuse the spirit.

The scene that introduces the second part of the gospel narrative
functions as a transition from the Book of Signs to the Book of Glory. It
articulates the ascending/descending theme and comments on its implications. John introduces the passage with the notation, "Jesus knew that
he had come from God and was returning to him." What follows is the
parabolic enactment of that movement.

[Jesus] . . . rose from supper, laid aside his garments, and girded
himself with a towel. Then he poured water into a basin, and be-

gan to wash the disciples' feet, and to wipe them with the towel
with which he was girded.

When he had washed their feet, and taken his garments, and re-
sumed his place, he said to them, "Do you know what I have done
to you?" (13:2-16)

The question is, as always, in John's Gospel, "Do you understand the
place I have left, the world to which I have come, the table to which I return?" The passage describes graphically the meaning of Jesus' life, his
origins, his works, his destiny. To respond affirmatively to the question,
"Do you know what I have done to you?"—which is addressed immediately to the disciples, and beyond the text to the reader—is to acknowledge belief in Jesus as the one sent by the Father, the one who seeks out
his own, the one who suffers, dies, and returns to the Father. From this
moment in the narrative, Jesus begins his ascent. The emphasis is not on
his origins but on his destiny, his homecoming. And the question of the
hearers is not, "How did you get here?" but "Where are you going?"
(13:36; 14:5; 16:18). From now on, the seekers are not seekers of wisdom
but of death. The moment of crisis has passed. In John 18:5, Jesus asks
again, "Whom do you seek?" They answered, "Jesus the Nazarene." After
the arrest and during the trial, Pilate inquires of Jesus' origins: "Where
do you come from?" But now Jesus does not answer. The ascent to the
Father has already begun. As with the imperative to seek, there is a moment that can be too late.

The arrest of Jesus alerts us to the contrast between classical and
Christian concepts of hero and god. Odysseus disguised himself until he
had gathered support and could overwhelm his enemies. His triumph was
due to what has been called his mastery of the delayed response. The gods
in Ovidian, and to some extent in Yahwistic narrative, do a competent job
of destroying sooner or later those who cannot recognize divinity. The
response to hostility within Christian narrative is quite different. Jesus
releases anyone who cannot withstand the consequences of being his fol-
lower, and he allows his enemies to exercise whatever power they have.
Most of the passion narrative is a study in the use of power. Brutality,
political compromise, misuse of authority—all flow from the blindness of
the secondary characters to possibility. The paradox of the hero in the
Fourth Gospel lies in the control of his power until his enemies had ex-
hausted all the possibilities of hatred and fear and seemed to be totally
victorious. One does not usually argue much with death, especially death
by public execution. Jesus' victory was delayed beyond the limits of human strategizing and human vengeance (a less-than-divine impulse too

often projected upon divinity). The whole problem of the Gospels is to comprehend the nature of that victory.

• The Word and the World •

To recognize Jesus is to be known by him. Four characters experience this *being known* in such a way as to respond in faith to him. Peter is identified and renamed as soon as he is brought into the presence of Jesus: "You are Simon, son of John. You are to be called Cephas" (John 1:42). Nathanael saw his objections to the possibility of Jesus' being the one whom Moses and the prophets wrote about swept aside by Jesus' declaration: "Before Philip called you, when you were under the fig tree, I saw you" (1:49). To the Samaritan woman, Jesus observes, "You are right to say you have no husband, for you have had five husbands, and he whom you now have is not your husband" (4:18). When she in turn testifies to Jesus, her appeal is based on the declaration, "*Come see* a man who told me all that I ever did. Can this be the Christ?" (4:29). And, as we noted previously, Mary Magdalene does not recognize Jesus at the tomb until he calls her by name.

The image that controls this theme of mutual recognition is that of the shepherd of the flock: "The sheep hear his voice, and he calls his own sheep by name and leads them out. When he has brought out all his own, he goes before them, and the sheep follow him for they know his voice" (10:3-5). "I am the good shepherd; I know my own and my own know me" (10:11).

What does this knowledge of Jesus imply, or the initiative we see in him as he seeks out, for example, the man whom he had cured of blindness. ("Jesus heard that they had cast him out, and having *found* him, he said, 'Do you believe?' " [9:35]) When Jesus calls by name, he reaches to the hidden recesses of the personality. He recognizes, accepts, summons. Such recognition is a calling forth, an invitation to presence, to belief, to commitment. In Hebrew usage, especially, to be called by name is to be vulnerable. Jesus compares his knowledge of his own with his Father's knowledge of him. Such mutual knowledge implies that belief in Jesus is not simply assent to testimony but a relationship to which the believer is invited on the initiative of Jesus. Because Jesus knows his own, he knows also those who do not, or will not, identify him truly. "Jesus knew them all," writes the Evangelist, "and did not trust himself to them; he could tell what a man had in him" (2:24-25).

Pilate, the Gentile equivalent of the unbelieving Jewish leaders, is with them an exemplar of "the world," which could not recognize what was not completely its own. His particular blindness models the response of the sec-

ular world to Jesus. Lacking the language and religious expectation of believers, he falls back upon philosophical and political debate, equivalent in
its own way to the sterile theological debate of the religious authorities. The
dialogue with Pilate is Jesus' most important encounter with the Roman
world. To Pilate, Jesus declares, "All who are of the truth hear my voice"
(18:37). It is a direct appeal to Pilate to make a decision, to hear and to recognize. But Pilate cannot hear or see because he does not believe in the existence of what Jesus declares: "What is truth?" (18:38). Here we see a
fundamental attitude of mind to which truth, when present, is opaque. Jesus'
silence when Pilate finally asks him "Where do you come from?" (19:9) is
wisdom's response to Pilate's indifference to its existence. Every action of
Pilate in the ensuing moments reveals his indifference not only to truth, but
to the demands of a world beyond the world he knew.[14] His actions indicate
that compromise for the sake of self-protection was the principle upon which
his life was based. Moreover, whatever commitment he had made, he had
made to Rome and thus to "this world." Mystery had to yield to political
facts and their demands.

The scene in the Praetorium is a striking paradigm of the Gospel. Jesus
testifies before a judge of this world, and his testimony is not understood. He bears witness to a truth that the world could not receive because it did not know him. The spatial arrangement of the scene is
particularly effective. Jesus and the Roman are within; the Jewish leaders, because of their fear of ritual impurity, are outside. Unlike Jesus, they
could not leave their own world. Pilate was required to move back and
forth between the Jews and Jesus to accommodate Jewish understanding
of law.[15] The Jews were required to present Jesus to Pilate to accommodate Roman law. The dialectic among the Jews, Pilate, and Jesus concerned kingship and thus power. Neither Pilate nor the Jews admitted to
a king, and thus to power, other than Caesar's. We are exposed to John's
cosmic dualism that mirrors, or is continuous with, human dualism.

In the midst of the Jewish and Roman worlds, between power and powerlessness, Jesus stands as testimony to power not of this world, to power
held back, a kingdom invisible. Both Pilate and the Jewish leaders are types

---

[14]See David Rensberger, "The Politics of John: The Trial of Jesus in the Fourth
Gospel," *Journal of Biblical Literature* 103:4 (September 1984): 395-411; Rudolf
Schnackenburg, *The Gospel according to St. John* (New York: Crossroad, 1982) 3.241ff.

[15]Raymond Brown observes that "Pilate's constant passing from one setting
to the other gives external expression to the struggle taking place within his soul."
The Gospel according to John 13-21, Anchor Bible 29A (New York: Doubleday, 1970)
858.

of unbelief because their allegiances are to visible power and thus to salvation from the flesh alone. Their inner dynamic is limited to obeying the powers of this world and destroying, or allowing to be destroyed, whatever threatens that private kingdom. "You are no friend of Caesar. . . . We have no king but Caesar" (19:12, 15). The extensive discussion of law, of charges, of testimony, of judgment, of punishment is an ironic commentary on the blindness of unbelievers to the testimony of the witness in their midst, and the preoccupations that obscure self-understanding and the vision of reality.

We can say that unbelief in John is both a rejection of Jesus as well as a rejection of the self that the presence of Jesus discloses. Unbelief for the author of this gospel involves the deliberate and unrelenting choice of an illusion about one's own identity and how it is to be saved. For John, there is no such thing as a "vital lie," as we see in Eugene O'Neill, for example, or Chekhov, or even Don Quixote. Illusions about the self are not vital but deadly. Blindness can never save. "How can you believe?" he describes Jesus as saying, "since you look to one another for approval?" (5:44).

Later, Jesus states, "The truth will make you free," to which his listeners respond with an astonishing assertion, given their history and their circumstances. "We are descendants of Abraham and we have never been the slaves of anyone" (8:33). Not admitting to their bondage—either spiritual, religious, or political—they are scarcely in a position to choose freedom. Subsequently some of the Pharisees are described as saying, "Are we also blind?" (9:40). The illusion, however, to which they had committed themselves impedes any possibility of *metanoia,* of altering their understanding of reality.

"Blind? If you were blind, you would have no guilt; but now that you say, 'We see,' your guilt remains" (9:41). Recognition of Jesus implies for all of these reasons a recognition of a character's deepest needs, a recognition that one can, in fact, need. Unbelievers in John's Gospel never admit to needing anything. A court official in Galilee is brought to (deeper) belief because of his need and because he manifested the kind of directness and guilelessness Jesus had admired so much in Nathanael. Having requested that Jesus come and cure his son, he waited while Jesus probed his faith.

"So you will not believe unless you see signs and portents!" The court official was too deeply aware of his need to engage in a theological debate.

"Sir, come down before my child dies."

"Go home," said Jesus, "your son will live" (4:49-50). We are told that the man believed what Jesus had said, that the cure was effected, and that subsequently he and all his household *believed.* The second stage of belief was belief in Jesus, not only in his words. The sign that Jesus offered was his response to human affliction and to a man's admission of powerlessness, a man who had no illusions about his own capacity to save.

• Text and Time •

On the threshold of textual and extratextual recognition and functioning as a mirror to the reader of the Gospel are three scenes that describe characters coming to awareness of the meaning of Jesus in their historical experience. In the first of these scenes (3:13-25), Jesus enters Jerusalem and upon seeing commercial activity in the Temple precincts, he drives the money changers and the sellers away. "Take these things away; you shall not make my Father's house a house of trade" (2:16). The Evangelist describes the response of the disciples to this scene: "They remembered the words of Scripture: 'Zeal for your house will consume me' " (2:18). In the ensuing dialogue the Jews ask, "What sign have you to show us for doing this?" (2:18). In response, Jesus rejects the possibility of offering a portent.

"Destroy this temple and in three days I will raise it up" (2:19). The Evangelist notes the ambiguity of the word *temple* and adds that only after Jesus rose from the dead did the disciples understand the meaning of his words. They "remembered" that he had said this, and they believed the Scriptures.

The sequence of coming to belief is gradual: first, the historical experience, which was ambiguous and puzzling; then Resurrection and their memory of him, followed by a deeper comprehension of the relationship between Scripture and Jesus. Scripture—in this instance, Hebrew Scripture—and Jesus illuminate each other. Full understanding of the historical experience is offered only in the light of Jesus' rising from the dead; and their memory of him is revived by the testimony of Scripture.

In a parallel scene (12:12-19), Jesus enters Jerusalem seated upon "an ass's colt." The Evangelist cites Scripture to explain the event: "Do not be afraid, daughter of Zion; see, your king is coming, sitting on an ass's colt" (Zec. 9:9). He adds that the disciples did not understand their historical experience until after the glorification of Jesus, but that then they remembered that this had been written about him. In chapter 20, we see the parallel post-Resurrection dialectic. Here Scripture is understood in the light of historical experience. Peter and "the other disciple" run to the tomb of Jesus. Discovering the linen cloths that had been used to wrap the body, "the other disciple" believes. "For as yet," writes the Evangelist, "they did not know the Scripture, that he must rise from the dead" (20:9). Clearly the testimony of Scripture in these scenes is ambiguous without some kind of experience of Jesus, especially the post-Resurrection Jesus. This experience illumines the meaning of the words he speaks and the testimony of Scripture about him. The historical experience of Jesus is in turn illumined by the words of Scripture. The writer attempts in his own use of testimony to draw his reader to belief by this same pattern. At the death of Jesus, when blood and water flow from the pierced side, he interrupts his story to stress the reality of the historical experience on which it is based:

> He who saw it has borne witness—his testimony is true, and he knows that he tells the truth—that you also may believe. For these things took place that the scripture might be fulfilled, "Not a bone of him shall be broken." And again another scripture says, "They shall look on him whom they have pierced." (19:35-37)

The writer intends that the scene be illumined by his recalling Scripture. But at the same time, he intends *his own text* to be a commentary on the experience of Jesus, a reliable testimony to him, so that the reader experiences two levels of time, which he or she must then correlate with the present: blood and water flow *now* from the side of Jesus into the life of the believer. As the Hebrew Scripture explained the experience of the characters in John's Gospel, the Evangelist's text is to assist readers and hearers of *his* narrative to understand their own experience.[16]

What was John saying over and over again if not that the glory of God was something the disciples saw and heard and touched in time and place: in Cana of Galilee, in Capernaum, in Bethany, on the Sea of Tiberias, in Jerusalem? Can the glory and the presence of God be yet discerned? What are we to see and hear and touch in this place and time, now that Jesus has returned to his Father?

---

[16]A recent persuasive study of the relationship of *text* to revelation is Gail R. O'Day, *Revelation in the Fourth Gospel: Narrative Mode and Theological Claim* (Philadelphia: Fortress, 1986). See also the same writer's article, "Narrative Mode and Theological Claim: A Study in the Fourth Gospel," *Journal of Biblical Literature* 105:4 (December 1986): 657-68. Especially pertinent to my own thesis is her comment:

> Further analysis of the "how" of the Johannine revelatory process will show that it is not the word alone, but words, language as creation and expression, which bring the reader to the experience of Jesus through imaginative participation in the text. . . . Through the dynamics of the Johannine revelatory narrative, the fourth evangelist is able to recreate the revelation experience for the reader, engaging the reader in the text in the same way that Jesus engaged those whom he encountered. (668)

John answers this question climactically throughout the text of the discourse at the Last Supper. First, the presence of Jesus will be transposed to the disciples. If Jesus were sent by the Father, they are to be sent by Jesus. "He who receives anyone whom I send receives me; and he who receives me receives him who sent me" (13:20). The disciples are to love one another. This is the normative effect of believing in Jesus. This is how they are to be recognized. Second, the presence of the historical Jesus will be succeeded by the presence of the Spirit of Truth, the Counselor-Paraclete, the Advocate, who will dwell with believers and be in them. The Paraclete will remind believers of all that Jesus said, will teach them. Believers will be united to Jesus as branches to a vine. Because of their identity with Jesus, they will suffer as he did; they will be hated by the world. But the Paraclete, as well as the disciples, will bear witness.

The final directive on faith is offered by the Johannine post-Resurrection Jesus. "Have you believed because you have seen me? Blessed are those who have not seen and yet believe" (20:29). Some degree of invisibility then is to be expected after Jesus returns to the Father. Nevertheless, according to John, recognition of Jesus can occur through the testimony of the disciples and by means of the Spirit sent by Jesus to console believers in his absence. The Spirit will remind believers of him.

But the idea of reminding is not a simple recall of the past. When the Spirit reminds, she recalls to life, she makes present. The signs that believers are to see now are related to John's concept of realized eschatology: "The hour is coming and now is when true worshippers will worship the Father in Spirit and in truth" (4:23). "The hour is coming and now is when the dead will hear the voice of the Son of God, and those who hear will live" (5:25). The signs offered to contemporary believers are the reminder of the Spirit that death is transformed into life eternal, that the blind can be brought to vision, that there is reason to rejoice now because the wine will never run out. Flesh, time, space—even death itself—none of these need be obstacles to belief. If John's theology is consistent, these realities are, even now, the means to belief. The manifestation of God's presence will occur within and through these very realities: the children of God are Christ to one another; their love for one another is the love of Christ; their forgiveness of one another is the forgiveness of Christ; their service to one another is the ministry of Christ. Those who perceive in one another the ministering and needing Christ are those to whom the signs of his presence are visible. For John, Christ is never out of touch with flesh, nor with the believers in whom he abides. Nor is there any place to find him except in the particular and the concrete, the historical, and the human— in what we see and touch and feel. This is the way he first came among us and the way in which he is still to be found. God, in other words, is human for all eternity.

To enter into belief requires, therefore, the same openness to reality or attitude of listening and searching that characterized the first disciples; the same trust in human testimony, when fulfilled by personal experience; the same dialogue with Scripture for the sake of understanding personal experience; the same willingness to believe that flesh can translate the Word of Life.

The crisis, in other words, is still very much with the readers of the Gospel. Andrew and Nathanael, Philip, Peter, Thomas, Pilate, the court official, the Pharisees, the crowds at the Feast—all ask the same questions, and they are the questions of every generation: "Where do you live?" "How did you come here?" "Can anything good come out of this place?"

If religious experience is rooted in history, even as Jesus is born of woman, is flesh, then good comes out of this place, this history. John gives us the crossroads of recognition: the subjective being-toward-life (and light) and the phenomenon: the light within, the hidden made visible by Sign, disclosed in flesh, in time, in human word. The Christian concept of subjective revelation, like the Hebrew understanding of wisdom, is a question of relationship. One hears about, searches for, sees, changes, follows, abides. "The hour will come," says John, "in fact it is here already." Time, as with Sophocles, discloses, but only when it is accepted, met, believed in as the environment of an unhidden god.

• C O N C L U S I O N •

THE LOCUS OF RECOGNITION:
AUDIENCE RESPONSE
AND THE GOSPEL NARRATIVE

When Penelope recognized that the disguised beggar in her house was really Odysseus, her own identity was once again complete. Rediscovering Odysseus in her presence, she was no longer widow, but wife and lover. At that point her life, interrupted by loss, oppression, and disorder, was renewed. The audience to the famous scene of the positioning of the marriage bed experiences recognition in a different mode from Penelope's. Knowing that the man who announces himself is indeed Penelope's husband, the reader waits only for *Penelope* to know, to prove beyond a doubt that she can trust this adventurer. We wait to see *how* she will discover and know, and the author does not leave us in doubt as to what she eventually learns. And so with Electra. And Oedipus. *We* know. How will these *characters* know? We wait, realizing that error will invoke further catastrophe. Greek writers were aware that truth could be withheld, but at the end of their narratives they were not about to imitate the gods. The audience would *know*. The mystery of identity would be resolved. Tragedy consisted in not knowing, or at least not knowing in time.

Given the influence of the Greek mind in Western thought, it is not surprising that as Christianity moved westward, borne by the language of the Greeks—whose culture had touched every corner of the Mediterranean world—it absorbed the Greek appetency for exact information and exact language. The divinity must be named. Creed and dogma emerged from both longing and necessity: the longing for some clear distillation of the mystery—some explanation of the inarticulate hope, and the necessity of knowing what was not a way into the mystery. The community of Christian believers had to understand which beliefs could divide and fragment them and which would keep them united. Christianity was a kerygmatic religious movement, calling believers to the task of inviting others to *metanoia* and to the responsibility of instructing new adherents. Such instruction called for specificity.

Perceval's story in *Li Contes del Graal* describes not only the kind of radical transformation of character possible within the Judeo-Christian worldview, but the dilemma of a writer in tension between mystery and logos. Perceval's change began with his psychological division and consequent self-doubt. It was made explicit by repentance and consent to creed. Perceval, engulfed by mystery and dissolved by his loss of memory, rediscovered himself through word: a credal resumé of Christ's death and Resurrection, the briefest of Christian narratives. His repentance and rediscovery of identity is so rapidly summarized in the narrative that the audience at that point is denied the experience of duration, as well as any access to Perceval's interior. A twelfth-century writer had neither the linguistic nor the psychological strategies to probe historical time or changing self-awareness. Revelation in such a culture was ahistorical in its expression and public in its claims—made visible by sacrament and ritual, and formulated by declarative statement.

Chrétien de Troyes, nevertheless, could bring his audience to a recognition that mystery can engulf a character, destroy his gods, and change his quest. In a larger sense, the audience of *Li Contes del Graal* was brought to awareness of the values Perceval had to choose between. Arthur's court is surely the portrait of a society corrupted by violence and displays of power, glittering in its initial appeal and ultimately destructive of human values and the memory of human origins. Surrender to its code led to oblivion, unless one was shocked into awareness by a different reality. The Grail Castle, somewhere between reality and dream, was Perceval's salvation.

With Don Quixote, we are grounded in reality. The dream is rejected and the incorporeal mocked. Word and flesh are reunited and truth is measured by individual and community consent. When *Don Quixote of la Mancha* was written, Europe was well into the great postmedieval theological conflicts about the force and meaning of language. Cervantes's audience knew that only a fool would assert a truth against the claims of body, time, space, and community witnesses. That realization opened theology also to the claims of history and interpretive communities, although some of those claims would require centuries to acknowledge.

Neither Emma nor Dorothea Brooke was allowed by their authors to live in sovereign isolation, like Oedipus and Electra, soaring above their immediate societies, bound only by the cosmos and the gods. The more earthbound eighteenth- and nineteenth-century audiences believed that societies have claims and norms, that no truth was discoverable apart from those norms or apart from the individual rootedness in historical experience that shaped belief. Only mystics and reformers could pit themselves against that societal force. If Dorothea Brooke had declared to Celia at the end, "You would have to feel with me, else you would never know," it was because her author conceived her as a (very) obscure Teresa of Avila, not as Don Quixote. An artistically acceptable Teresa of Avila in nineteenth-century England would have to be obscure indeed.

Only in the modern, post-Freudian, capitalistic world does the exclusively private fictive psyche find an audience and lose touch with history and place as well as the gods. The malaise of Walker Percy and the no-man's land of Harold Pinter are very recent dilemmas. But to say that we recognize ourselves in these universes is not mere cold comfort, for as Percy argues: "There is a great deal of difference between an alienated commuter riding a train and this same commuter reading a book about an alienated commuter riding a train." Insisting on the transforming power of language, Percy writes: "The non-reading commuter exists in true alienation, which is unspeakable; the reading commuter rejoices in the speakability of his alienation and in the new triple alliance between himself, the alienated character, and the author."[1]

• From Narrative to Community •

It is that transformation we refer to when we speak of the recognition experience of the audience. There is no one theory of audience-response to a text. Critics will focus on whatever theory enables them to account for what Aristotle sees as "the final cause": the effect of a text on a competent reader. In fact, even the expression *competent* implies a theory of reading. My focus has been on the experience of re-cognition and how that experience is a subjective apprehension of revelation, initiating change or conversion. For that reason, the audience-response theory invoked here is not based on the assumption that the reader or hearer dom-

---

[1]Walker Percy, "The Man on the Train," in *The Message in the Bottle* (1954; rpt., New York: Farrar, Straus, Giroux, 1982) 83.

inates the text[2] any more than Johannine characters dominated the Word before them. Some of those characters could be described as reading the Word before them incorrectly. The critical assumption here is that a text communicates something new but not alien, that it "calls" to the reader and invites participation. The reader and the text— like the Johannine characters, who themselves were "recognized"—interact to create a text's meaning. The text stimulates the experience of recognition, re-forms the reader/hearer, but is itself completed by its readers, by the *community* that is formed by it. Of the many theories of audience response, mine corresponds most closely to that of Wolfgang Iser[3] and especially to the proposal of Alcorn and Bracher cited earlier.[4] These theories suggest that any encounter with literature involves a variation of the reader's identity and thus a possible restructuring of the self. A text does not merely "name" experience—although it does that—nor does it offer an absolutely *new* experience. (It is, after all, always mimesis.[5]) Literature can "pressure the self."

I would argue that the Gospel as literature can "alter" the self, and here I agree with Alcorn and Bracher, whose arguments rest on the analogy of literature to psychoanalysis. But by *alter* I mean, in religious terms, death and resurrection: the death of a false self and the birth of a self defined or recognized by Another. The secondary characters in the Gospel are asked to become the hero, not merely to "look on at a distance." The readers of the Gospel are enabled to become the hero ("to put on Christ,"

---

[2]See Norman Holland, *5 Readers Reading* (New Haven: Yale University Press, 1975), and David Bleich, *Readers and Feelings: An Introduction to Subjective Criticism* (Urbana IL: National Council of Teachers of English, 1975). An especially clear discussion of reader-response theories is presented by James L. Resseguie, "Reader Response Criticism and the Synoptic Gospels," *Journal of the American Academy of Religion* 52 (June 1984): 307-24.

[3]Wolfgang Iser, *The Implied Reader: Patterns of Communication from Bunyan to Beckett* (Baltimore: Johns Hopkins University Press, 1974).

[4]Marshall W. Alcorn, Jr. and Mark Bracher, "Literature, Psychoanalysis, and the Re-formation of the Self: A New Direction for Reader-Response Theory," *Publications of the Modern Language Association of America* 100 (May 1985): 342-54.

[5]*Mimesis* here is best understood in Paul Ricoeur's sense of "creative redescription." Redescription corresponds to one's response to a work of art. In both cases, reality is "seen again." See Paul Ricoeur, *The Role of Metaphor* (Toronto: University of Toronto Press, 1977) 37-43, and David Tracy's reference in *The Analogical Imagination* to Paul Ricoeur's unpublished "From Picture to Fiction" and "The Bible and the Imagination" (149 n. 96).

in Pauline terms) by examining the responses of the secondary characters, experiencing their dilemma, and recognizing it as their own. At the same time, it is the *reader* who is present at the Crucifixion, who is enabled to see that death as a consequence of nonrecognition. The audience is thus suspended between the crucified hero himself and those who fled the scene, between vision and "spectacle." The reader is present to what unfaithful secondary characters do not see.

In any story, the experience of the reader is never the same as the experience of the characters, no matter how much self-projection that reader engages in or what the perspectival strategy of the writer. But the experience of a literary character can affect profoundly what kind of experience is made possible for the audience. At the end of *Oedipus at Colonus*, as at the end of the Gospel narrative, the audience can be transformed by their awareness of the tragic effects of moral blindness.

• The Genre of the Gospels •

To consider the Gospels as literature is to raise the question of genre, for the genre of a text shapes the questions we bring to it, our expectations, and how it can affect us.

To assume that the Gospel narratives open a window to first-century historical occurrences and simply transmit those occurrences, unselected and unretouched, for our information and reflection is to misunderstand both the historiographical enterprise and the function of narrative, sacred or otherwise. Events that are inscribed in the writing of history are done so on the basis of what Paul Ricoeur calls "narrative emplotment."[6] They are not events anymore in the same sense in which they occurred, because they are accessible to us now only as narrated events. The Gospel narratives constitute a unique genre, emerging as they do from history, but constituted from the faith experience of those events. Twenty and thirty years after the death of the central character of each of the four Gospels, the interpreted experience of that person was being recorded for distinct audiences in distinctly historical situations. As in most historiographical writing, itself an interpretation, the account of that faith experience generally assumed narrative form.

In the early part of this century, form critics were unenthusiastic and suspicious of biblical narrative. Dibelius was scarcely appreciative:

---

[6]Paul Ricoeur, *Time and Narrative*, vol. 1, trans. Kathleen McLaughlin and David Pellauer (Chicago: University of Chicago Press, 1984) 208.

The fortune of primitive Christianity is reflected in the history of the Gospel Form. The first beginnings of its shaping hardly deserve to be called literary. What Form was present was determined by ecclesiastical requirements arising in the course of missionary labor and preaching. The Passion story, the most significant piece of tradition for Christian faith, was told relatively early as a connected story. Moreover, isolated events from the life of Jesus suitable for sermons were told in short stories, and sayings and parables were used especially for a practical purpose. But pleasure in the narrative for its own sake arose and seized upon literary devices.[7]

Rudolf Bultmann was equally reluctant to concede that Gospel narratives had any artistic shape: "The first thing we observe is that the narratives do not give us long unified accounts, but rather single small pictures, individual scenes, narrated with the utmost simplicity."[8] Only in recent literary-critical analysis have scholars consistently acknowledged the correspondence between narrative as form and revelation as event. The concept of narrative is more than decorative embellishment emerging from the pleasure of storytelling, as Dibelius thought, and the Gospel accounts are indeed unified, as Bultmann suggested they are not. Narrative has its own declaration to make.

The selection of the narrative form at one stage in the history of the Gospel proclamation was theologically crucial. For a story with a beginning, middle, and end (as distinguished from chronicle) means linear time, purpose, destiny; and a story set in Galilee and Judaea at the time of the Roman occupation is quite different from a story taking place on Mt. Olympus or even Eden. As a genre, the Gospel is an announcement that the Christ-event took place in time, in human history. Nothing more fundamental to the Christian message could be said. The Christ that was proclaimed as Lord lived among a particular people in a specific place. What was important as the kerygma assumed an increasingly narrative shape after 70 C.E. was not the factual (or nonfactual) data that were offered, but the way the sequence of events was ordered. The arrangement of incidents, the seemingly unimportant details that were included in the story, the sensitivity to audience that the writers evidenced, the re-creation of time—all of these fictive devices declared that this language was not chronicle or chronology, but like all literature, the reordering of the world.

---

[7]Martin Dibelius, *From Tradition to Gospel,* rev. ed., trans. Bertram Lee Woolf (New York: Charles Scribner's Sons, 1934) 287.

[8]Rudolf Bultmann, *Form Criticism: Two Essays on New Testament Research,* ed. Frederick C. Grant (New York: Willett, Clark and Co., 1934) 32.

Bultmann urged that the central form of the Gospel was address and confrontation, not narrative. However, as William A. Beardslee has argued, "In theological terms the confrontational role of the proverb and parable are interpreted by the model of 'justification by faith,' while the story embodies other elements that cannot easily be fitted into this model."[9] While Beardslee does not opt for narrative as the fundamental Christian form, he does comment that it is important for theology to bring to expression the group of motifs expressed in the various forms. He discusses the implications of narrative for theological interpretation: "The affinity between these brief synoptic forms [parable and apothegm] and the existentialist theology is clear, for this theology concentrates on the moment of freedom and decision. . . . [The narrative] . . . functions to show the reader who he is by setting him in a larger dynamic framework. The story tells him where he has come from and where he is going."[10]

The confrontational approach to revelation assumes a God who breaks into history from outside. Theology that is more processive than existential assumes that the self-disclosure of God occurs within and through the history of men and women, that it depends to a great extent on that history, both personal and collective. The existential approach is dramatic, discontinuous. Berdyaev, for example, asserts that evolution has no role to play in the spiritual life:

> Revelation of the divine bears the character of a breakthrough of the other world into this world. There is something catastrophic about it, something of an upheaval. The light may be poured out in a flash; but the outpouring of the divine light is limited by the condition of man and of the peoples by the limits of human consciousness, by historical time and place.[11]

In contrast to Berdyaev's concept of revelation as a kind of shock therapy, it is more useful to reflect that God's revelation is conditioned by the limits of human consciousness. It can be assumed that the Creator is aware of the nature of the creature. Congar writes, for example:

> Saving faith is received by minds which must consider it not merely as something absolute, but as a deposit given once and for all by

---

[9]William A. Beardslee, *Literary Criticism of the New Testament* (Philadelphia: Fortress Press, 1970) 81. For Bultmann's comments, see his *Theology of the New Testament*, vol. 2, trans. Kendrick Grobel (New York: Charles Scribner's Sons, 1951) 239-41.

[10]Beardslee, *Literary Criticism*, 83.

[11]Nicolas Berdyaev, *Truth and Revelation* (London: Geoffrey Bles, 1953) 54.

the apostles. . . . But, at the same time, these minds must "receive" faith in an active way, in a manner which befits their nature. They are human minds, discursive intellects which perceive successively and only partially; hence, also, minds fulfilling themselves only when in contact with other minds; lastly *minds living in a cosmic biological and temporal continuum. Historicity is an essential characteristic of the human mind.*[12]

"Ongoingness" characterizes our lives. We neither live from existential crisis to existential crisis, nor see in our lives at every moment the patterns that make narrative so attractive. This is not to say that our lives have neither meaning nor pattern, but rather to recall that, because of our "unseeing" and "unhearing," we are in need.

• The Hearer of the Word •

No one hears the Word of Scripture apart from his or her own experience, apart from a specific moment in history. To assume that the hearer must somehow comprehend and accept the Gospel "out there" is to contradict our present understanding of human consciousness, as well as to violate that freedom without which no faith response is possible. This is true whether we interpret revelation as given to the human community or as accessible to an individual within community. If the hearer of the Gospel experiences a movement of conversion upon discovery of the Word, that movement is either initiatory, in the sense of being the first of other possible movements, or succeeds previous responses to God's self-offering. Thus, the faith response to Scripture can be an entrance into the world of faith or deeper conversion to the God who is revealed. The thunder clap of response is not only rare; it is impossible. When we study such events as the religious conversion of Paul Claudel, Edith Stein, or even Augustine, we discover soon enough that their "sudden" illuminations came after years of seeking. The power of the Gospel is not the power of intellectual argument, or of aesthetic attractiveness, or of catastrophic upheaval, but a power that works within and through the whole personality and history of the hearer. If that power works conversion in some measure, it is because the hearer has brought to the Gospel his or her own experience, and questions and needs, and can meet and recognize the Word within a particular history to which the Gospel responds and which it questions. The reader or listener of the Gospel text brings to it a personal world in time that can be merged with the story of Christ.

---

[12]Yves M.-J. Congar, *Tradition and Traditions* (New York: Macmillan and Co., 1967) 256. Italics mine.

Within that personal world, a thousand choices have already been made, multitudes of opportunities have been offered for transcendence of self. What is brought to the revelatory word is openness or opacity, recognition of need or hubris, questions, or complacency and indifference. In "secular" literature, truth grasps the hero(ine) only when self-definitions have been shattered. To *hear* the Gospel text is to have heard the Gospel in one's own history, to have read one's own text, and thus to recognize in the Gospel one's own story named anew. The Gospel brings to awareness the significance of our choices and it deepens self-understanding. "Till this moment they had failed to understand the teaching of Scripture, that he must rise from the dead" (John 20:8). The disciples' "this moment" was their own experience of the Christ-event, an experience that they had to live out before they could understand how Scripture testified to it. We see the dialectic between Scripture and human experience, a dialectic that, as it intensifies, reveals the meaning imbedded in both.

The narrative of the Christ-event experienced by one generation cannot be a substitute for the Christ-event experienced by subsequent generations. It can evoke that event, however, because it is not the Scripture word exclusively that leads to faith. The Gospel (and liturgy, the Christ-event in symbolic action) presumes "the emergence of religious experiences within human experiences";[13] that is, it presumes the possible religiousness of the previous experience of those to whom it is directed. In doing so, the Gospel as text creates an environment for recognition. When the listener or reader "recognizes" in the Gospel, he or she knows *again.* That *re-knowing* is dynamic, vitalizing.

Part of the saving power of the Gospel derives from its epiphanic character, its bringing to consciousness *meaning* in a pattern of events—that is, meaning to history, meaning to one's personal story. It is indeed an announcement that events in life are not disconnected from a larger pattern, that Being is gracious, that death is swallowed up in victory. The "sinner" and the "righteous" can be equally illumined by such meaning: the sinner by the dimension and significance of alienation, and the righteous by the ultimate incapacity of sheer righteousness to save. Awareness is always potentially life-giving. It can move us to a new world and reorganize our personality. It is characterized by what William E. Hocking has called "dawning novelty," and in such an experience,

---

[13]Edward Schillebeeckx, "Erfahrung und Glaube," *Christlicher Glaube in moderner Gesellschaft,* 25 (Freiburg/Basel/Vienna: Herder, 1980) 73-116; cited in *The Schillebeeckx Reader,* ed. and trans. Robert J. Schreiter (New York: Crossroad Publishing Co., 1984) 82.

we may observe the same sharpened consciousness of the old or usual idea, the idea with reference to which the new is defined as new and different. The old idea is *freshly realized;* which means freshly connected with reality, especially the reality which the thinker is conscious of in himself. . . . And this old idea, in being realized is at the same time repudiated, repudiated not with any pure and blank negation, but in favor of some positive thing which in time will make itself known. In this realizing and repudiating, the new thing is already asserting itself, and doing conscious work.[14]

"Realizing and repudiating" is very close to the idea of *metanoia* to which the Gospel calls its audience. "Awareness" is the beginning of the revelatory event, the initiation of the experient into transformation. "Faith in Christ," writes Joseph Fitzmyer in his commentary on Galatians, "does not substitute a new norm or goal of action; rather it reshapes [persons] anew internally, supplying [them] with a new principle of activity on the ontological level of [their] very being."[15]

"I am the Resurrection. . . . Do you believe this?" (John 11:25, 26). The refusal or the incapacity to believe does not mean that Christ is not the Resurrection, even for the unbeliever. Rather, it means that Resurrection within life is not experienced. It is not quite enough to be saved, if we believe that we are perishing. For that assumption constricts life, diminishes freedom, weakens the power that alone can vitalize, blinds one to presence. Believing the Gospel does not simply give a new motivation for living; it gives the power to live because it frees the believer to act without fear.

Such freedom is especially important when the experience brought to the Gospel text is the experience of suffering or oppression, or what Edward Schillebeeckx calls "contrast experience." Such experience asks for a *future.* It has "a critical epistemological power which appeals to a praxis which opens up the future."[16] Recognizing the "contrast experience" of Jesus himself in his passion and death does not (or should not) reduce the

---

[14]William Ernest Hocking, *The Meaning of God in Human Experience* (New Haven: Yale University Press, 1912) 481-82.

[15]Joseph Fitzmyer, "The Letter to the Galatians," *Jerome Biblical Commentary,* ed. Raymond E. Brown, Joseph Fitzmyer, and Roland Murphy (Englewood Cliffs NJ: Prentice-Hall, 1968) 241.

[16]Edward Schillebeeckx, "Naar een 'definitieve toekomst': belofte en menselijke bemiddeling," *Toekomst van de religie—Religie van de toekomst?* (Brugge/Utrecht: Desclée de Brouwer, 1972) 37-55. Cited in Schreiter, *Schillebeeckx Reader,* 56.

hearer to passive identification. Instead, it prompts struggle against oppression because recognition of one's own or humanity's suffering in Jesus' death discloses not only humanity's beauty, but the depth of horror to which we sink when human power is misused. There is no religious awareness that does not confront eventually the vast, unmerited, overwhelming suffering that marks the history of the human race and that calls for response, resistance. Suffering is "mystical" only to the extent that one struggles to relieve it in others.

Just as the Gospel as text is an effort to objectify the Christ-event, so it can in a given moment objectify the moral and spiritual life of the man or woman who is called to vision and to compassion. It can articulate the questions, the desires, the hope, the love of one who listens and hears. But more, it asks new questions. The Gospel in this sense *grasps* the audience. It can surprise the reader/hearer into recognition, bring to consciousness what has been forgotten, evoke the vision of a possible future, heal what has been broken or fragmented, restore the dead to life, and create new life. The Gospel text thematizes the faith of the believer and draws him or her to deeper faith.

To the unbeliever, it can articulate the hope and love that one has already chosen to live out, or identify the sense of loss that sin has occasioned. Even more, it can parabolically subvert the illusions of the myth one has chosen to live by, or that society and culture have imposed; and the subversion of illusion can begin the re-formation of the self, as the literature we have examined indicates.

To hear the Word is to enter the narrative that began at creation and to know that the stone of the prison-house of time has been rolled back. "He has gone before you into Galilee. There you will see him" (Mark 16:7). But dialectically, only if one has already seen him in a world threatened by destruction can one know who it is that approaches from the East, what "interminable adventurer comes constantly so near." The marriage bed of Penelope and Odysseus, their mutual recognition, is the beginning of new life, as is the empty tomb in the Gospel narratives. Vision in the darkness of a waiting world is always a question of knowing again, of recognizing the One who returns.

•INDEX OF PRINCIPAL NAMES•